CAMBRIDGE LIBRARY COLLECTION

Books of enduring scholarly value

Philosophy

This series contains both philosophical texts and critical essays about philosophy, concentrating especially on works originally published in the eighteenth and nineteenth centuries. It covers a broad range of topics including ethics, logic, metaphysics, aesthetics, utilitarianism, positivism, scientific method and political thought. It also includes biographies and accounts of the history of philosophy, as well as collections of papers by leading figures. In addition to this series, primary texts by ancient philosophers, and works with particular relevance to philosophy of science, politics or theology, may be found elsewhere in the Cambridge Library Collection.

Studies in the Hegelian Dialectic

What is the nature of dialectic according to Hegel? And what is achieved by its means? These are the main questions that John McTaggart (1866–1925) seeks to answer in this work, first published in 1896. At the beginning of the twentieth century, the Cambridge-educated philosopher and fellow of Trinity College enjoyed a prominent position within the circle of idealist philosophers, and was regarded as one of England's leading Hegel scholars. Although a proponent of the German philosopher's dialectical thinking in general, McTaggart was not uncritical of Hegel's philosophy and objected to his application of abstract thought. In this work, McTaggart not only gives the reader a thorough introduction to Hegel's understanding of the dialectic method but also exposes a number of points on which he considers Hegel's teaching to be inaccurate: one of these is Hegel's insistence that evil is merely a delusion.

T0372672

Cambridge University Press has long been a pioneer in the reissuing of out-of-print titles from its own backlist, producing digital reprints of books that are still sought after by scholars and students but could not be reprinted economically using traditional technology. The Cambridge Library Collection extends this activity to a wider range of books which are still of importance to researchers and professionals, either for the source material they contain, or as landmarks in the history of their academic discipline.

Drawing from the world-renowned collections in the Cambridge University Library, and guided by the advice of experts in each subject area, Cambridge University Press is using state-of-the-art scanning machines in its own Printing House to capture the content of each book selected for inclusion. The files are processed to give a consistently clear, crisp image, and the books finished to the high quality standard for which the Press is recognised around the world. The latest print-on-demand technology ensures that the books will remain available indefinitely, and that orders for single or multiple copies can quickly be supplied.

The Cambridge Library Collection brings back to life books of enduring scholarly value (including out-of-copyright works originally issued by other publishers) across a wide range of disciplines in the humanities and social sciences and in science and technology.

Studies in the Hegelian Dialectic

JOHN McTAGGART ELLIS McTAGGART

CAMBRIDGE
UNIVERSITY PRESS

CAMBRIDGE UNIVERSITY PRESS

Cambridge, New York, Melbourne, Madrid, Cape Town,
Singapore, São Paolo, Delhi, Tokyo, Mexico City

Published in the United States of America by Cambridge University Press, New York

www.cambridge.org
Information on this title: www.cambridge.org/9781108040334

© in this compilation Cambridge University Press 2012

This edition first published 1896
This digitally printed version 2012

ISBN 978-1-108-04033-4 Paperback

STUDIES

IN THE

HEGELIAN DIALECTIC.

London: C. J. CLAY AND SONS,
CAMBRIDGE UNIVERSITY PRESS WAREHOUSE,
AVE MARIA LANE.
Glasgow: 263, ARGYLE STREET.

Leipzig: F. A. BROCKHAUS.
New York: MACMILLAN AND CO.
Bombay: GEORGE BELL AND SONS.

STUDIES

IN THE

HEGELIAN DIALECTIC

BY

JOHN McTAGGART ELLIS McTAGGART, M.A.

FELLOW OF TRINITY COLLEGE IN CAMBRIDGE.

CAMBRIDGE:

AT THE UNIVERSITY PRESS.

1896

𝕮𝖆𝖒𝖇𝖗𝖎𝖉𝖌𝖊:
PRINTED BY J. AND C. F. CLAY,
AT THE UNIVERSITY PRESS.

TO

MISS FRANCES POWER COBBE

WITH MUCH GRATITUDE.

PREFACE.

THE first four chapters of this book are based on a dissertation submitted at the Fellowship Examination of Trinity College, Cambridge, in 1891. The fourth and fifth chapters, nearly in their present form, were published in *Mind* (New Series, Nos. 1, 2, 8, and 10). A part of the second chapter appeared in the *Revue de Métaphysique et de Morale* for November 1893.

In quoting from the Smaller Logic and the Philosophy of Spirit, I have generally availed myself of Professor Wallace's valuable translations.

I am most deeply indebted to Professor J. S. Mackenzie, of University College, Cardiff, for his kindness in reading the proof-sheets of these Studies, and in assisting me with many most helpful suggestions and corrections.

TABLE OF CONTENTS.

CHAPTER I.

THE GENERAL NATURE OF THE DIALECTIC.

CHAPTER III.

THE VALIDITY OF THE DIALECTIC.

CHAPTER IV.

THE DEVELOPMENT OF THE METHOD

CHAPTER V.

THE RELATION OF THE DIALECTIC TO TIME.

A.

B.

CHAPTER VI.

THE FINAL RESULT OF THE DIALECTIC.

A.

CHAPTER VII.

THE APPLICATION OF THE DIALECTIC.

CHAPTER I.

1. HEGEL's primary object in his dialectic is to establish the existence of a logical connection between the various categories which are involved in the constitution of experience. He teaches that this connection is of such a kind that any category, if scrutinised with sufficient care and attention, is found to lead on to another, and to involve it, in such a manner that an attempt to use the first of any subject while we refuse to use the second of the same subject results in a contradiction. The category thus reached leads on in a similar way to a third, and the process continues until at last we reach the goal of the dialectic in a category which betrays no instability.

If we examine the process in more detail, we shall find that it advances, not directly, but by moving from side to side, like a ship tacking against an unfavourable wind. The simplest and best known form of this advance, as it is to be found in the earlier transitions of the logic, is as follows. The examination of a certain category leads us to the conclusion that, if we predicate it of any subject, we are compelled by consistency to predicate of the same subject the logical contrary of that category. This brings us to an absurdity, since the predication of two contrary attributes of the same thing at the same time violates the law of contradiction. On examining the two contrary predicates further, they are seen to be capable of reconciliation in a higher category, which combines the contents of both of them, not merely placed side by side, but absorbed into a wider idea, as moments or aspects of which they can exist without contradiction.

This idea of the synthesis of opposites is perhaps the most characteristic in the whole of Hegel's system. It is certainly one of the most difficult to explain. Indeed the only way of grasping what Hegel meant by it is to observe in detail how he uses it, and in what manner the lower categories are partly altered and partly preserved in the higher one, so that, while their opposition vanishes, the significance of both is nevertheless to be found in the unity which follows.

Since in this way, and in this way only so far as we can see, two contrary categories can be simultaneously true of a subject, and since we must hold these two to be simultaneously true, we arrive at the conclusion that whenever we use the first category we shall be forced on to use the third, since by it alone can the contradictions be removed, in which we should otherwise be involved. This third category, however, when it in its turn is viewed as a single unity, similarly discloses that its predication involves that of its contrary, and the Thesis and Antithesis thus opposed have again to be resolved in a Synthesis. Nor can we rest anywhere in this alternate production and removal of contradictions until we reach the end of the ladder of categories. It begins with the category of Pure Being, the simplest idea of the human mind. It ends with the category which Hegel declares to be the highest—the Idea which recognises itself in all things.

2. It must be remarked that the type of transition, which we have just sketched, is one which is modified as the dialectic advances. It is only natural, in a system in which matter and form are so closely connected, that the gradual changes of the matter, which forms the content of the system, should react on the nature of the movement by which the changes take place. Even when we deal with physical action and reaction we find this true. All tools are affected, each time they are used, so as to change, more or less, their manner of working in the future. It is not surprising, therefore, that so delicate a tool as that which is used by thought should not remain unchanged among changing materials.

"The abstract form of the continuation or advance" says Hegel "is, in Being, an other (or antithesis) and transition into another; in the Essence, showing or reflection in its

opposite; in the Notion, the distinction of the individual
from the universality, which continues itself as such into, and
is as an identity with, what is distinguished from it[1]." This
indicates a gradual increase in the directness of the advance,
and a diminished importance of the movement from contrary
to contrary. But this point, which Hegel leaves undeveloped,
will require further consideration[2].

3. The ground of the necessity which the dialectic process
claims cannot, it is evident, lie merely in the category from
which we start. For in that case the conclusion of the process
could, if it were valid, have no greater content than was
contained in the starting point. All that can be done with
a single premise is to analyse it, and the mere analysis of
an idea could never lead us necessarily onwards to any other
idea incompatible with it, and therefore could never lead us
to its contrary. But the dialectic claims to proceed from the
lower to the higher, and it claims to add to our knowledge, and
not merely to expound it. At the same time it asserts that
no premise other than the validity of the lower category is
requisite to enable us to affirm the validity of the higher.

The solution of this difficulty, which has been the ground of
many attacks on Hegel, lies in the fact that the dialectic must
be looked on as a process, not of construction but of reconstruction. If the lower categories lead on to the higher, and
these to the highest, the reason is that the lower categories
have no independent existence, but are only abstractions from
the highest. It is this alone which is independent and real.
In it all one-sidedness has been destroyed by the successive
reconciliation of opposites. It is thus the completely concrete,
and for Hegel the real is always the concrete. Moreover,
according to Hegel, the real is always the completely rational.
("The consummation of the infinite aim...consists merely in
removing the illusion which makes it seem as yet unaccomplished[3].") Now no category except the highest can be
completely rational, since every lower one involves its contrary.
The Absolute Idea is present to us in all reality, in all the
phenomena of experience, and in our own selves. Everywhere

[1] *Encyclopaedia*, Section 240.   [2] Chap. IV.
[3] *Enc.* Section 212, lecture note.

it is the soul of all reality. But although it is always present to us, it is not always explicitly present. In the content of consciousness it is present implicitly. But we do not always attempt to unravel that content, nor are our attempts always successful. Very often all that is explicitly before our minds is some finite and incomplete category. When this is so, the dialectic process can begin, and indeed must begin, if we are sufficiently acute and attentive,—because the ideal which is latent in the nature of all experience, and of the mind itself, forbids us to rest content with the inadequate category. The incomplete reality before the mind is inevitably measured against the complete reality of the mind itself, and it is in this process that it betrays its incompleteness, and demands its contrary to supplement its one-sidedness. " Before the mind there is a single conception, but the whole mind itself, which does not appear, engages in the process, operates on the datum, and produces the result[1]."

4. The dialectic process is not a mere addition to the conception before us of one casually selected moment after another, but obeys a definite law. The reason of this is that at any point the finite category explicitly before us stands in a definite relation to the complete and absolute idea which is implicit in our consciousness. Any category, except the most abstract of all, can be analysed, according to Hegel, into two others, which in the unity of the higher truth were reconciled, but which, when separated, stand in opposition to each other as contraries. If abstraction consists in this separation, then, when we are using the most abstract of the categories, we fall short of the truth, because one side of the completely concrete truth has been taken in abstraction, and from that relatively concrete truth again one side has been abstracted, and so on, until the greatest abstraction possible has been reached. It must there-fore cause unrest in the mind which implicitly contains the concrete whole from which it was abstracted. And through this unrest the imperfection will be removed in the manner described above, that is, by affirming, in the first place, that contrary category, the removal of which had been the last stage

[1] Bradley's *Logic*, Book III. Part I. Chap. 2, Section 20.

of the abstraction, then by restoring the whole in which those two opposites had been reconciled, and so on.

Thus the first and deepest cause of the dialectic movement is the instability of all finite categories, due to their imperfect nature. The immediate result of this instability is the production of contradictions. For, as we have already seen, since the imperfect category endeavours to return to the more concrete unity of which it is one side, it is found to involve the other side of that unity, which is its own contrary. And, again, to the existence of the contradiction we owe the advance of the dialectic. For it is the contradiction involved in the impossibility of predicating a category without predicating its opposite which causes us to abandon that category as inadequate. We are driven on first to its antithesis. And when we find that this involves the predication of the thesis, as much as this latter had involved the predication of the antithesis, the impossibility of escaping from contradictions in either extreme drives us to remove them by combining both extremes in a synthesis which transcends them.

5. It has been asserted that Hegel sometimes declares the contradictions to be the cause of the dialectic movement, and sometimes to be the effect of that movement. This is maintained by Hartmann[1]. No doubt the contradictions are considered as the immediate cause of the movement. But the only evidence which Hartmann gives for supposing that they are also held to be the effect, is a quotation from the second volume of the *Logic*. In this, speaking of that finite activity of thought which he calls Vorstellung, Hegel says that it has the contradictions as part of its content, but is not conscious of this, because it does not contain " das Uebergehen, welches das Wesentliche ist, und den Widerspruch enthält[2]." Now all that this implies seems to be that the contradictions first become manifest in the movement, which is not at all identical with the assertion that they are caused by it, and is quite compatible with the counter-assertion that it is caused by them.

Moreover, Hartmann also gives the same account of the origin of the contradictions which I have suggested above. He says " Der (im Hegel'schen Geiste) tiefer liegende Grund der

---

[1] *Ueber die dialektische Methode*, B. II. 3.　　[2] *Logic*, Vol. II. p. 71.

Erscheinung ist aber die Flüssigkeit des Begriffes selbst[1]."
Flüssigkeit is certainly not equivalent to movement, and may
fairly be translated instability. There is then no inconsistency.
It is quite possible that the instability of the notion may be
the cause of the contradictions, and that the contradictions
again may be the cause of the actual motion. Hartmann does
not, apparently, see that there is any change in his position
when he gives first instability and then motion as the cause of
the contradictions, and it is this confusion on his own part
which causes him to accuse Hegel of inconsistency.

He endeavours to account for Hegel's supposed error by
saying that the contradictions were given as the cause of the
dialectic movement when Hegel desired to show the subjective
action of the individual mind, while the dialectic movement
was given as the cause of the contradictions when he wished to
represent the process as objective. If, as I have endeavoured
to show, there is no reason for supposing that Hegel ever did
hold the dialectic movement to be the cause of the contradictions, there will be no further necessity for this theory.
But it may be well to remark that it involves a false conception
of the meaning in which it is possible to apply the term
objective to the dialectic at all.

6. There is a sense of the word objective in which it may
be correctly said that the dependence of the contradictions
on the instability of the notion is more objective than the
dependence of the dialectic movement on the contradictions.
For the former is present in all thought, which is not the case
with the latter. A contradiction can be said to be present in
thought, when it is implied in it, even though it is not clearly
seen. But it can only cause the dialectic movement, when it *is*
clearly seen. Whenever a finite category is used it is abstract,
and consequently unstable, and, implicitly at least, involves its
contrary, though this may not be perceived, and, indeed, in
ordinary thought is not perceived. On the other hand, the
actual dialectic movement does not take place whenever a
category is used, for in that case finite thought would not exist
at all. It is only when the contradictions are perceived, when
they are recognised as incompatible, in their unreconciled form

---

[1] *Op. cit.* B. II. 3.

with truth, and when the synthesis which can reconcile them has been discovered, that the dialectic process is before us.

The contradiction has therefore more objectivity, in one sense of the word, because it is more inevitable and less dependent on particular and contingent circumstances. But we are not entitled to draw the sort of distinction between them which Hartmann makes, and to say that while the one is only an action of the thinking subject, the other is based on the nature of things independently of the subject who thinks them. Both relations are objective in the sense that they are universal, and have validity as a description of the nature of reality. Neither is objective in the sense that it takes place otherwise than in thought. We shall have to consider this point in detail later[1]: at present we can only say that, though the dialectic process is a valid description of reality, reality itself is not, in its truest nature, a process but a stable and timeless state. Hegel says indeed that reason is to be found in actual existence, but it is reason in its complete and concrete shape, under the highest and absolute form of the notion, and not travelling up from category to category. Till the highest is reached, all the results are expressly termed abstract, and do not, therefore, come up to the level of reality. Moreover they contain unsynthesised contradictions, and that which is contradictory, though it may have a certain relative truth, can never exist independently, as would be the case if it existed in the world of fact. The dialectic movement is indeed a guide to that world, since the highest category, under which alone reality can be construed, contains all the lower categories as moments, but the gradual passage from one stage of the notion to another, during which the highest yet reached is for the moment regarded as independent and substantial, is an inadequate expression of the truth.

7. This is not incompatible with the admission that various isolated phenomena, considered as phenomena and as isolated, are imperfect, for in considering them in this way we do not consider them as they really are. Hegel speaks of the untruth of an external object as consisting in the disagreement between the objective notion, and the object[2]. From this it might be inferred that even in the world of real objects there existed

---

[1] Chap. v.　　　　　[2] *Enc.* Section 24, lecture note.

imperfections and contradictions. But, on looking more closely, we see that the imperfection and contradiction are really, according to Hegel, due only to our manner of contemplating the object. A particular thing may or may not correspond to the notion. But the universe is not merely an aggregation of particular things, but a system in which they are connected, and a thing which in itself is imperfect and irrational may be a part of a perfect and rational universe. Its imperfection was artificial, caused by our regarding it, in an artificial and unreal abstraction, as if it could exist apart from other things.

A diseased body, for example, is in an untrue state, if we merely regard it by itself, since it is obviously failing to fulfil the ideal of a body. But if we look at it in connection with the intellectual and spiritual life of its occupant, the bodily imperfection might in some cases be seen, without going further, to be a part in a rational whole. And, taking the universe as a whole, Hegel declares "God alone exhibits a real agreement of the notion and the reality. All finite things involve an untruth." God, however, is held by Hegel to be the reality which underlies all finite things. It is therefore only when looked at as finite that they involve an untruth. Looked at *sub specie Dei* they are true. The untruth is therefore in our manner of apprehending them only. It would indeed, as Hartmann remarks, be senseless tautology for Hegel to talk of the objective truth of the world. But this Hegel does not do. It is in the nature of the world as a whole that it must be objectively true[1]. But isolated fragments of the world, just because they are isolated, cannot fully agree with the notion, and may or may not agree with a particular aspect of it. According as they do or do not do this Hegel calls them true or false.

Hegel's theory that the world as a whole must be objectively true, so rational, and therefore, as he would continue, perfect, comes no doubt in rather rude contact with some of the facts of life. The consideration of this must for the present be deferred[2].

8. We have seen that the motive power of the dialectic lies in the relation of the abstract idea explicitly before the mind to

---

[1] Cp. *Enc.* Section 212, quoted on p. 3 above.   [2] Chap. v.

the concrete idea implicitly before it in all experience and all consciousness. This will enable us to determine the relation in which the ideas of contradiction and negation stand to the dialectic.

It is sometimes supposed that the Hegelian logic rests on a defiance of the law of contradiction. That law says that whatever is A can never at the same time be not-A. But the dialectic asserts that, when A is any category, except the Absolute Idea, whatever is A may be, and indeed must be, not-A also. Now if the law of contradiction is rejected, argument becomes impossible. It is impossible to refute any proposition without the help of this law. The refutation can only take place by the establishment of another proposition incompatible with the first. But if we are to regard the simultaneous assertion of two contradictories, not as a mark of error, but as an indication of truth, we shall find it impossible to disprove any proposition at all. Nothing, however, can ever claim to be considered as true, which could never be refuted, even if it were false. And indeed it is impossible, as Hegel himself has pointed out to us, even to assert anything without involving the law of contradiction, for every positive assertion has meaning only in so far as it is defined, and therefore negative. If the statement All men are mortal, for example, did not exclude the statement Some men are immortal, it would be meaningless. And it only excludes it by virtue of the law of contradiction. If then the dialectic rejected the law of contradiction, it would reduce itself to an absurdity, by rendering all argument, and even all assertion, unmeaning.

The dialectic, however, does not reject that law. An unresolved contradiction is, for Hegel as for every one else, a sign of error. The relation of the thesis and antithesis derives its whole meaning from the synthesis, which follows them, and in which the contradiction ceases to exist as such. "Contradiction is not the end of the matter, but cancels itself[1]." An unreconciled predication of two contrary categories, for instance Being and not-Being, of the same thing, would lead in the dialectic, as it would lead elsewhere, to scepticism, if it was not for the reconciliation in Becoming. The synthesis alone has

---

[1] *Enc.* Section 119, lecture note.

reality, and its elements derive such importance as they have from being, in so far as their truth goes, members of a unity in which their opposition is overcome.

In fact, so far is the dialectic from denying the law of contradiction, that it is especially based on it. The contradictions are the cause of the dialectic process. But they can only be this if they are received as marks of error. We are obliged to say that we find the truth of Being and not-Being in Becoming, and in Becoming only, because, if we endeavour to take them in their independence, and not as synthesised, we find an unreconciled contradiction. But why should we not find an unreconciled contradiction and acquiesce in it without going further, except for the law that two contradictory propositions about the same subject are a sign of error? Truth consists, not of contradictions, but of moments which, if separated, would be contradictions, but which in their synthesis are reconciled and consistent.

9. It follows also from this view of the paramount importance of the synthesis in the dialectic process that the place of negation in that process is only secondary. The really fundamental aspect of the dialectic is not the tendency of the finite category to negate itself but to complete itself. Since the various relatively perfect and concrete categories are, according to Hegel, made up each of two moments or aspects which stand to one another in the relation of contrary ideas, it follows that one characteristic of the process will be the passage from an idea to its contrary. But this is not due, as has occasionally been supposed, to an inherent tendency in all finite categories to affirm their own negation as such. It is due to their inherent tendency to affirm their own complement. It is indeed, according to Hegel, no empirical and contingent fact, but an absolute and necessary law, that their complement is in some degree their negation. But the one category passes into the other, because the second completes the meaning of the first, not because it denies it.

This, however, is one of the points at which the difficulty, always great, of distinguishing what Hegel did say from that which he ought in consistency to have said becomes almost insuperable. It may safely be asserted that the motive force of the dialectic was clearly held by him to rest in the implicit presence in us of its goal. This is admitted by his opponents as well as his supporters. That he did to some extent recognise the consequence of this—the subordinate importance which it assigned to the idea of negation—seems also probable, especially when we consider the passage quoted above[1], in which the element of negation appears to enter into the dialectic process with very different degrees of prominence in the three stages of which that process consists. On the other hand, the absence of any detailed exposition of a principle so fundamental as that of the gradually decreasing share taken by negation in the dialectic, and the failure to follow out all its consequences, seem to indicate that he had either not clearly realised it, or had not perceived its full importance. But to this point it will be necessary to return.

10. What relation, we must now enquire, exists between thought as engaged in the dialectic process, and thought as engaged in the ordinary affairs of life? In these latter we continually employ the more abstract categories, which, according to Hegel, are the more imperfect, as if they were satisfactory and ultimate determinations of thought. So far as we do this we must contrive to arrest for the time the dialectic movement. While a category is undergoing the changes and transformations in which that movement consists, it is as unfit to be used as an instrument of thought, as an expanding rod would be for a yard measure. We may observe, and even argue about, the growth of the idea, as we may observe the expansion of a rod under heat, but the argument must be conducted with stable ideas, as the observation must be made with measures of unaltering size. For if, for example, a notion, when employed as a middle term, is capable of changing its meaning between the major and the minor premises, it renders the whole syllogism invalid. And all reasoning depends on the assumption that a term can be trusted to retain the same meaning on different occasions. Otherwise, any inference would be impossible, since all connection between propositions would be destroyed.

There are two ways in which we may treat the categories. The first is, in the language of Hegel, the function of the

[1] *Enc.* Section 240, quoted on p. 2 above.

Reason—to perform, namely, the dialectic process, and when that culminates in the highest category, which alone is without contradiction, to construe the world by its means. As this category has no contradictions in it, it is stable and can be used without any fear of its transforming itself under our hands. The second function is that of the Understanding, whose characteristic it is to treat abstractions as if they were independent realities. They are thus forced into an artificial stability and permanence, and can be used for the work of ordinary thought. Of course the attempt to use an imperfect and unbalanced category as if it were perfect and self-subsistent leads to errors and contradictions—it is just these errors and contradictions which are the proof that the category is imperfect. But for many purposes the limit of error is so small, that the work of the Understanding possesses practical use and validity. If we take an arc three feet long of the circumference of a circle a mile in diameter, it will be curved, and will show itself to be so, if examined with sufficient accuracy. But in practice it would often produce no inconvenience to treat it as a straight line. So, if an attempt is made to explain experience exclusively by the category, for example, of causality, it will be found, if the matter is considered with enough care, that any explanation, in which no higher category is employed, involves a contradiction[1]. Nevertheless, for many of the everyday occurrences on which we exercise our thoughts, an explanation by the Understanding, by means of the category of causality only, will be found to rationalise the event sufficiently for the needs of the moment.

11. To this explanation an objection has been raised by Hartmann[2]. He "emphatically denies" our power to arrest the progress of the Notion in this manner. It might, he admits, be possible to do so, if the Notion were changed by us, but it is represented as changing itself. The human thinker is thus only "the fifth wheel to the cart," and quite unable to arrest a process which is entirely independent of him.

Now in one sense of the words it is perfectly true, that, if the Notion changes at all, the change is caused by its own nature, and not by us. If the arguments of the dialectic are

[1] *Enc.* Sections 153, 154.   [2] *Op. cit.* B. II. 6.

true, they must appeal with irresistible force to every one who looks into the question with sufficient ability and attention, and thus the process may be said to be due to the Notion, and not to the thinker. But this is no more than may be said of every argument. If it is valid, it is not in the power of any man who has examined it, to deny its validity. But when there is no logical alternative there may be a psychological one. No intelligent man, who carefully examines the proofs, can doubt that the earth goes round the sun. But any person who will not examine them, or cannot understand them, may remain convinced all his life that the sun goes round the earth. And any one, however clearly he understands the truth, can, by diverting his attention from comparatively remote astronomical arguments, and fixing it on the familiar and daily appearances, speak of and picture the movement as that of the sun, as most men, I suppose, generally do.

So with the dialectic. The arguments are, if Hegel is right, such as to leave the man who examines them no option. But for those who have no time, inclination, or ability to examine them, the categories will continue to be quite separate and independent, while the contradictions which this view will produce in experience will either be treated as ultimate, or, more probably, will not be noticed at all. And even for the student of philosophy, the arguments remain so comparatively abstruse and unfamiliar that he finds no difficulty, when practical life requires it, in assuming for a time the point of view of the Understanding, and regarding each category as unchanging and self-supporting. This he does merely by diverting his attention from the arguments by which their instability is proved.

Although therefore the change in the Notion is due to its nature, it does not follow that it cannot be stopped by peculiarities in the nature of the thinker, or by his arbitrary choice. The positive element in the change lies wholly in the Notion, but that it should take place at all in any particular case requires certain conditions in the individual mind in question, and by changing these conditions we can at will arrest the process of the categories, and use any one of them as fixed and unchanging.

Any other view of the dialectic process would require us to suppose that the movement of the categories became obvious to us, not as the result of much hard thinking, but spontaneously and involuntarily. It can scarcely be asserted that Hegel held such a theory, which would lead to the conclusion that everyone who ever used the category of Being—that is everyone who ever thought at all, whether he reflected on thought or not,—had gone through all the stages of the Hegelian logic, and arrived at all its conclusions.

12.   Another difficulty which Hartmann brings forward in this connection arises from a misapprehension of Hegel's meaning. He affirms[1] that, so far from stopping the dialectic process, we could not even perceive it when it took place. For we can only become aware of the change by comparing stage A with stage B, and how is it possible that we should do this, if A turns into B, beyond our control, whenever it appears?

In the first place, we may answer, it is possible, as we have seen, to arrest the dialectic movement, in any given case, at will, so that the development of the categories is not beyond our control. In the second place the thesis is not held by Hegel to turn into the antithesis in the simple and complete way which this objection supposes. The one category leads up to and postulates the other but does not become completely the same as its successor. The thesis and antithesis are said no doubt to be the same, but the same with a difference. If we predicate A, we are forced to predicate B, but there remains nevertheless a distinction between A and B. It is just the coexistence of this distinction with the necessary implication of the one category in the other, which renders the synthesis necessary as a reconciliation. If the thesis and antithesis were not different, the simultaneous predication of both of them would involve no difficulty.

13.   Such is the general nature of the dialectic as conceived by Hegel. How does he attempt to prove its truth and necessity? The proof must be based on something already understood and granted by those to whom it is addressed. And since the proof should be one which must be accepted by all men, we must base it on that which all men allow to be

[1] *Op. cit.* B. ii. 6.

justifiable—the ordinary procedure, that is, of thought in common sense and science, which Hegel calls the Understanding as opposed to the Reason. We must show that if we grant, as we cannot help granting, the validity of the ordinary exercise of our thought, we must also grant the validity of the dialectic.

This necessity Hegel recognises. He says, it is true, that, since only the Reason possesses the complete truth, up to which the merely partial truth of the Understanding leads, the real explanation must be of the Understanding by the Reason[1]. But this is not inconsistent with a recognition of the necessity of justifying the Reason to the Understanding. The course of real explanation must always run from ground to consequent, and, according to Hegel, from concrete to abstract. On the other hand, the order of proof must run from whatever is known to whatever is unknown. When, as we have seen is the case with the dialectic, we start from explicit knowledge of the abstract only, and proceed to knowledge of the concrete, which alone gives reality to that abstract, the order of explanation and the order of proof must clearly be exactly opposite to one another.

The justification of the Reason at the bar of the Understanding, depends upon two facts. The one is the search for the Absolute which is involved in the Understanding, the other is the existence in the Understanding of contradictions which render it impossible that it should succeed in the search. The Understanding demands an answer to every question it can ask. But every question which it succeeds in answering suggests fresh questions. Any explanation requires some reference to surrounding phenomena, and these in their turn must be explained by reference to others, and nothing can therefore be fully explained unless everything else which is in direct or indirect connection with it, unless, that is, the whole universe, be fully explained also. And the explanation of a phenomenon requires, besides this, the knowledge of its causes and effects, while these again require a knowledge of their causes and effects, so that not only the whole present universe, but the whole of the past and future must be known before any single

[1] *Logic*, Vol. I. p. 198.

fact can be really understood. Again, since the knowledge of a phenomenon involves the knowledge of its parts, and all phenomena, occurring as they do in space and time, are infinitely divisible, our knowledge must not only be infinitely extended over space and time, but also infinitely minute. The connection of the phenomenal universe by the law of reciprocity has a double effect on knowledge. It is true, as Tennyson tells us, that we could not know a single flower completely without also knowing God and man. But it is also true that, till we know everything about God and man, we cannot answer satisfactorily a single question about the flower. In asking any question whatever, the Understanding implicitly asks for a complete account of the whole Universe, throughout all space and all time. It demands a solution which shall really solve the question without raising fresh ones—a complete and symmetrical system of knowledge.

This ideal it cannot, as Hegel maintains, reach by its own exertions, because it is the nature of the Understanding to treat the various finite categories as self-subsistent unities, and this attempt leads it into the various contradictions pointed out throughout the dialectic, owing to the inevitable connection of every finite category with its contrary. Since, then, it postulates in all its actions an ideal which cannot be reached by itself, it is obliged, unless it would deny its own validity, to admit the validity of the Reason, since by the Reason alone can the contradictions be removed, and the ideal be realised. And, when it has done this, it loses the false independence which made it suppose itself to be something different from the Reason.

14. One of the most difficult and important points in determining the nature of the Hegelian logic is to find its exact relation to experience. Whatever theory we may adopt has to fall within certain limits. On the one hand it is asserted by Hegel's critics, and generally admitted by his followers, that, rightly or wrongly, there is some indispensable reference to experience in the dialectic—so that, without the aid of experience it would be impossible for the cogency of the dialectic process to display itself. On the other hand it is impossible to deny that, in some sense, Hegel believed that by the dialectic process takes place in pure thought, that, however incomplete the Logic might be without the Philosophy of Nature, and the Philosophy of Spirit, however much the existence of Nature and Spirit might be involved in the existence of pure thought, yet nevertheless within the sphere of logic we had arrived at pure thought, unconditioned in respect of its development as thought.

And both these characteristics of the dialectic are, independently of Hegel's assertion, clearly necessary for the validity of any possible dialectic. The consideration of pure thought, without any reference to experience, would be absolutely sterile, or rather impossible. For we are as unable to employ "empty" pure thought (to borrow Kant's phrase) as to employ "blind" intuition. Thought is a process of mediation and relation, and implies something immediate to be related, which cannot be found in thought. Even if a stage of thought could be conceived as existing, in which it was self-subsistent, and in which it had no reference to any *data*—and it is impossible to imagine such a state, or to give any reason for supposing thought thus to change its essential nature—at any rate this is not the ordinary thought of common life. And as the dialectic process professes to start from a basis common to everyone, so as to enable it to claim universal validity for its conclusions, it is certain that it will be necessary for thought, in the dialectic process, to have some relation to data given immediately, and independent of that thought itself. Even if the dialectic should finally transcend this condition it would have at starting to take thought as we use it in every-day life—as merely mediating, and not self-subsistent. And I shall try to show later on that it never does transcend, or try to transcend that limitation [1].

On the other hand it is no less true that any argument would be incapable of leading us to general conclusions relating to pure thought, which was based on the nature of any particular piece of experience in its particularity, and that, whatever reference to experience Hegel may or may not have admitted into his system, his language is conclusive against the possibility that he has admitted any empirical or contingent basis to the dialectic.

15. The two conditions can, however, be reconciled. There

[1] Chap. II.

is a sense in which conclusions relating to pure thought may
properly be based on an observation of experience, and in this
sense, as I believe, we must take the Logic in order to arrive at
Hegel's true meaning. According to this view, what is observed
is the spontaneous and unconditioned movement of the pure
notion, which does not in any way depend on the matter of
intuition for its validity, which, on the contrary, is derived from
the character of the pure reason itself. But the process,
although independent of the matter of intuition, can only be
perceived when the pure notion is taken in conjunction with
matter of intuition—that is to say when it is taken in experience—because it is impossible for us to grasp thought in
absolute purity, or except as applied to an immediate *datum*.
Since we cannot observe pure thought at all, except in experience, it is clear that it is only in experience that we can
observe the change from the less to the more adequate form
which thought undergoes in the dialectic process. But this
change of form is due to the nature of thought alone, and not
to the other element in experience—the matter of intuition[1].

The presence of this other element in experience is thus a
condition of our perceiving the dialectical movement of pure
thought. We may go further. It does not follow, from the
fact that the movement is due to the nature of pure thought
alone, that pure thought can ever exist, or ever be imagined
to exist by itself. We may regard pure thought as a mere
abstraction of one side of experience, which is the only concrete
reality, while the matter of intuition is an abstraction of the
other side of the same reality—each, when considered by itself,
being false and misleading. This, as we shall see, is the
position which Hegel does take up. Even so, it will still
remain true that, in experience, the dialectic process was due

---

[1] Since I am here dealing only with the question of epistemology, it will be
allowable, I think, to assume that there *is* a matter of intuition, distinct from
thought, and not reducible to it, (though incapable of existing apart from it,)
since this is the position taken up within Hegel's Logic. Whether the dialectic
process has any relation to it or not, its existence is, in the Logic, admitted,
at least provisionally. If Hegel did make any attempt to reduce the whole
universe to a manifestation of pure thought, without any other element, he
certainly did not do so till the transition to the world of Nature at the end of
the Logic. Even there I believe no such attempt is to be found.

exclusively to that element of experience which we call pure thought, the other element—that of intuition—being indeed an indispensable condition of the dialectic movement, but one which remains passive throughout, and one by which the movement is not determined. It is only necessary to the movement of the idea because it is necessary to its existence. It is not itself a principle of change, which may as fairly be said to be independent, as the changes in the pictures of a magic lantern may be ascribed exclusively to the camera, and not at all to the canvas on which they are reflected, although, without the canvas, the pictures themselves, and therefore the transition from one to another of them would be impossible.

16. If this is the relation of the dialectic process to the medium in which it works, what postulate does it require to start from? We must distinguish its postulate from its basis. Its basis is the reality which it requires to have presented to itself, in order that it may develop itself. Its postulate is the proposition which it requires to have admitted, in order that from this premise it may demonstrate its own logical validity as a consequence. The basis of the dialectic is to be found in the nature of pure thought itself, since the reason of the process being what it is, is due, as we have seen, to the nature of the highest and most concrete form of the notion, implicit in all experience. Since pure thought, as we have seen, even if it could exist at all in any other manner, could only become evident to us in experience, the basis which the dialectic method will require to work on, may be called the nature of experience in general.

It is only the general nature of experience—those characteristics which are common to all of it—which forms the basis of the process. For it is not the only object of the dialectic to prove that the lower and subordinate categories are unable to explain all parts of experience without resorting to the higher categories, and finally to the Absolute Idea. It undertakes also to show that the lower categories are inadequate, when considered with sufficient intelligence and persistence, to explain *any* part of the world. What is required, therefore, is not so much the collection of a large mass of experience to work on, but the close and careful scrutiny of some part, however small. The whole chain of categories is implied in any and every phenomenon. Particular fragments of experience may no doubt place the inadequacy of some finite category in a specially clear light, or may render the transition to the next stage of the idea particularly obvious and easy, but it is only greater convenience which is thus gained; with sufficient power any part, however unpromising, would yield the same result.

17. The basis of the dialectic process, then, is the nature of experience, in so far as the nature of pure thought is contained in it. If the other element in experience has really a primary and essential nature of its own, it will not concern us here, for, as it takes no part in the development of the idea, its existence, and not its particular qualities, is the only thing with which we are at present concerned. The nature of experience however, though it is the basis of the dialectic, is not its logical postulate. For it is not assumed but ascertained by the dialectic, whose whole object is the gradual discovery and demonstration of the Absolute Idea, which is the fundamental principle which makes the nature of experience. The general laws governing experience are the *causa essendi* of the logic, but not its *causa cognoscendi*.

The only logical postulate which the dialectic requires is the admission that experience really exists. The dialectic is derived from the nature of experience, and therefore if it is to have any validity of real existence, if it is to have, that is to say, any importance at all, we must be assured of the existence of some experience—in other words, that something *is*.

The object of the dialectic is to discover the forms and laws of all possible thought. For this purpose it starts from the idea of Being, in which all others are shown to be involved. The application of the results of the dialectic to experience thus depends on the application to experience of the idea of Being, and the logical postulate of the dialectic is no more than that something *is*, and that the category of Being is therefore valid.

It will be noticed that the basis and the postulate of the dialectic correspond to the two aspects of the idea which we mentioned above as the fundamental cause of the process. The basis—the nature of pure thought—is the complete and concrete idea which is present in our minds, though only implicitly, and which renders it impossible that we should stop short of it by permanently acquiescing in any finite category. The postulate—the abstract idea in its highest state of abstraction, which is admitted to be valid—is that which is explicitly before the mind, and from which the start is made.

18. We are justified in assuming this postulate because it is involved in every action and every thought, and its denial is therefore suicidal. All that is required is the assertion that there is such a thing as reality—that something is. Now the very denial of this involves the reality of the denial, and so contradicts itself and affirms our postulate. And the denial also implies the reality of the person who makes the denial. The same dilemma meets us if we try to take refuge from dogmatic denial in mere doubt. If we really doubt, then the doubt is real, and there is something of whose reality we do not doubt; if on the other hand we do not really doubt the proposition that there is something real, we admit its truth. And doubt, as well as denial, places beyond doubt the existence of the doubter. This is, of course, the Cartesian argument, which is never stated by Hegel precisely in this form, but on which the justification of his use of the category of Being, as valid of reality, appears to depend.

19. The dialectical process thus gains its validity and importance by means of a transcendental argument. The higher categories are connected with the lower in such a manner that the latter inevitably lead on to the former as the only means by which they can be rescued from the contradictions involved in their abstractness. If the lower categories be admitted, and, ultimately, if the lowest of all, the category of Being, be admitted, the rest follows. But we cannot by the most extreme scepticism deny that something is, and we are therefore enabled to conclude that the dialectic process does apply to something. And as whatever the category of Being did not apply to would not exist, we are also able to conclude that there is nothing to which the dialectic process does not apply.

It will be seen that this argument is strictly of a transcendental nature. A proposition denied by the adversary—in this case the validity of the higher categories—is shown to be involved in the truth of some other proposition, which he is not prepared to attack—in this case the validity of the category of Being. But the cogency of ordinary transcendental arguments is limited, and they apply only to people who are prepared to yield the proposition which forms the foundation of the argument, so that they could be outflanked by a deeper scepticism. Now this is not the case with the dialectic. For the proposition on which it is based is so fundamental, that it could be doubted only at the expense of self-contradiction, and the necessity of considering that proposition true is therefore universal, and not only valid in a specially limited argument, or against a special opponent. It is doubtful indeed whether a condition so essential as this is correctly termed a postulate, which seems to denote more properly a proposition which it would be at least possible for an adversary to challenge. At any rate the very peculiar nature of the assumption should be carefully remembered, as it affords a clue for interpreting various expressions of Hegel's, which might otherwise cause serious difficulties [1].

20. Having thus endeavoured to explain the nature of the dialectic, we must ask ourselves at what results we are entitled to arrive by means of that process. These results will be, to begin with, epistemological. For the conditions of the dialectic are, first, the concrete notion, which we are able to examine because it is implicit in all our consciousness, and, second, the category of Being, which we are entitled to postulate, because it is impossible to avoid employing it in judging experience. Our conclusions will therefore relate primarily to the general laws of experience, and will so far be, like those of Kant's Aesthetic and Analytic, concerned with the general conditions of human knowledge. And the result arrived at will be that no category will satisfactorily explain the universe except the Absolute Idea. Any attempt to employ for that purpose a lower category must either accept a gradual transformation of the idea employed until the Absolute Idea is reached, or acquiesce in unreconciled contradictions—which involves the rejection of a fundamental law of reason.

21. This position has two results. In the first place it

---

[1] Cp. Chap. ii. Section 46.

disproves the efforts which are made from time to time to explain the whole universe by means of the lower categories only. Such an attempt lay at the bottom of Hume's scepticism, when he endeavoured to treat the notion of causality as derived from that of sequence, and to consider all that was added as false and illusive. For absolute scepticism is impossible, and his treatment of the higher category as an unwarranted inference from the lower involves the assertion of the validity of the latter. Such an attempt, again, has been made by Mr Spencer, as well as by the large number of writers who adopt the provisional assumptions of physical science as an ultimate position. They endeavour to explain all phenomena in terms of matter and motion, and to treat all special laws by which they may be governed as merely particular cases of fundamental principles taken from physical science.

But if we agree with Hegel in thinking that the category of Being is inadequate to explain the world which we know without the successive introduction of the categories, among others, of Cause, Life, and Self-Consciousness, and that each category inevitably requires its successor, all such attempts must inevitably fail. Any attempt, for example, to reduce causation to an unjustifiable inference from succession, to explain life merely in terms of matter and motion, or knowledge merely in terms of life, would involve a fatal confusion. For it would be an attempt at explanation by that which is, in itself, incomplete, unreal, and contradictory, and which can only be made rational by being viewed as an aspect of those very higher categories, which were asserted to have been explained away by its means.

22. Even if this were all, the result of the dialectic would be of great importance. It would have refuted all attempts to establish a complete and consistent materialism, and would have demonstrated the claims of the categories of spirit to a place in construing part at least of the universe. But it has done more than this. For it does not content itself with showing that the lower categories lead necessarily to the higher, when the question relates to those portions of experience in which the higher categories are naturally applied by the uncritical consciousness. It also demonstrates that the lower categories, in themselves, and to whatever matter of intuition they may be applied, involve

the higher categories also. Not only is Being inadequate to explain, without the aid of Becoming, those phenomena which we all recognise in ordinary life as phenomena of change, but it is also unable to explain those others which are commonly considered as merely cases of unchanging existence. Not only is the idea of Substance inadequate to deal with ordinary cases of scientific causation, but without the idea of Cause it becomes involved in contradictions, even when keeping to the province which the uncritical consciousness assigns to it. Not only is it impossible to explain the phenomena of vegetable and animal life by the idea of mechanism, but that idea is inadequate even to explain the phenomena of physics. Not only can consciousness not be expressed merely in terms of life, but life is an inadequate category even for biological phenomena. With such a system we are able to admit, without any danger either to its consistency or to its practical corollaries, all that science can possibly claim as to the interrelation of all the phenomena of the universe, and as to the constant determination of mind by purely physical causes. For not only have we justified the categories of spirit, but we have subjected the whole world of experience to their rule. We are entitled to assert, not only that spirit cannot be reduced to matter, but also that matter must be reduced to spirit. It is of no philosophical importance, therefore, though all things should, from the scientific standpoint be determined by material causes. For all material determination is now known to be only spiritual determination in disguise.

23. The conclusion thus reached is one which deals with pure thought, since the argument has rested throughout on the nature of pure thought, and on that only, and the conclusion itself is a statement as to the only form of pure thought which we can use with complete correctness. But we have not found anything which would enable us to discard sensation from its position as an element of experience as necessary and fundamental as pure thought itself, and if Hegel did draw such a consequence from it, we must hold that he has taken an unjustifiable step forwards. All the thought which we know is in its essential nature mediate, and requires something immediate to act on, if it is to act at all. And this immediate element can be found—so far as our present knowledge is concerned—only in sensation, the necessary background and accompaniment of the dialectic process, which is equally essential at its end as at its beginning. For an attempt to eliminate it would require that Hegel should, in the first place, explain how we could ever conceive unmediated or self-mediated thought, and that he should, in the second place, show that the existence of this self-subsistent thought was implied in the existence of the mediating and independent thought of every-day life. For since it is only the validity of our every-day thought which we find it impossible to deny, it is only that thought which we can take as the basis of the dialectic process. Even if, in the goal of the dialectic, thought became self-subsistent in any intelligible sense, it would be necessary to show that this self-subsistence issued naturally from the finite categories, in which thought is unquestionably recognised as mediate only.

I shall endeavour to prove later on[1] that Hegel made no attempt to take up this position. The conclusion of the Logic is simply the assertion that the one category by which experience can be judged with complete correctness is the Absolute Idea. It makes no attempt to transcend the law which we find in all experience by which the categories cannot be used of reality, nor indeed apprehended at all, without the presence of immediate data to serve as materials for them.

24. To sum up, the general outline of the Hegelian Logic, from an epistemological point of view, does not differ greatly, I believe, from that of Kant. Both philosophers justify the application of certain categories to the matter of experience, by proving that the validity of those categories is implied in the validity of other ideas which the sceptical opponent cannot or does not challenge. The systems differ largely in many points, particularly in the extent to which they push their principles. And Hegel has secured a firmer foundation for his theory than Kant did, by pushing back his deduction till it rests on a category—the category of Being,—the validity of which with regard to experience not only never had been denied, but could not be denied without contradiction. It is true also that Kant's work was clearly analytic, while Hegel's had also a synthetic side, and may even be said to have brought

---

[1] Chap. II. Section 48.

that side into undue, or at any rate misleading, prominence.
But the general principle of the two systems was the same, and
the critic who finds no fundamental fallacy in Kant's criticism
of knowledge, should have no difficulty in admitting that the
Hegelian Logic, if it keeps itself free from errors of detail, forms
a valid theory of epistemology.

25. But the Logic claims to be more than this, and we
must now proceed to examine what has been generally held to be
at once the most characteristic and the weakest part of Hegel's
philosophy. How far does he apply the results of his analysis
of knowledge to actual reality, and how far is he justified in
doing so?

It is beyond doubt that Hegel regarded his Logic as
possessing, in some manner, ontological significance. But this
may mean one of two very different things. It may mean
only that the system rejects the Kantian thing-in-itself, and
denies the existence of any reality except that which enters into
experience, so that the results of a criticism of knowledge are
valid of reality also. But it may mean that it endeavours to
dispense with or transcend all *data* except the nature of thought
itself, and to deduce from that nature the whole existing
universe. The difference between these two positions is considerable. The first maintains that nothing is real but the
reasonable, the second that reality is nothing but rationality.
The first maintains that we can explain the world of sense, the
second that we can explain it away. The first merely confirms
and carries further the process of rationalisation, of which all
science and all finite knowledge consist; the second differs
entirely from science and finite knowledge, substituting a
self-sufficient and absolute thought for thought which is
relative and complementary to the *data* of sense.

It is, I maintain, in the first of these senses, and the first
only, that Hegel claims ontological validity for the results of
the Logic, and that he should do as much as this is inevitable.
For to distinguish between conclusions epistemologically valid
and those which extend to ontology implies a belief in the
existence of something which does not enter into the field of
actual or possible knowledge. Such a belief is totally unwarranted. The thing-in-itself as conceived by Kant, behind

and apart from the phenomena which alone enter into experience, is a contradiction. We cannot, we are told, know what it is, but only that it is. But this is itself an important piece of knowledge relating to the thing. It involves a judgment, and a judgment involves categories, and we are thus forced to surrender the idea that we can be aware of the existence of anything which is not subject to the laws governing experience. Moreover, the only reason which can be given for our belief in things-in-themselves is that they are the ground or substratum of our sensuous intuitions. But this is a relation, and a relation involves a category. Indeed every statement which can be made about the thing-in-itself contradicts its alleged isolation.

26. It cannot be denied, however, that Hegel does more than is involved in the rejection of a thing-in-itself outside the laws of experience. Not only are his epistemological conclusions declared to have also ontological validity, but he certainly goes further and holds that, from the consideration of the existence of pure thought, we are able to deduce the existence of the worlds of Nature and Spirit. Is this equivalent to an admission that the worlds of Nature and Spirit can be reduced to, or explained away by, pure thought?

We shall see that this is not the case when we reflect that the dialectic process is no less analytic of a given material than it is synthetic from a given premise, and owes its impulse as much to the perfect and concrete idea which is implicit in experience, as to the imperfect and abstract idea which is explicitly before the student. For if the idea is, when met with in reality, always perfect and concrete, it is no less true that it is, when met with in reality, invariably, and of necessity, found in connection with sensuous intuition, without which even the relatively concrete idea which ends the Logic is itself an illegitimate abstraction. This being the case it follows that, as each stage of the Logic insists on going forward to the next stage, so the completed logical idea insists on going forward and asserting the coexistence with itself of sensuous perception. It does not postulate any particular sensuous perception, for the idea is equally implicit in all experience, and one fragment is as good as another in which to perceive it. We are thus unable to deduce any of the particulars of the world of sense from the

Logic. But we are able to deduce that there must be such a world, for without it the idea would be still an abstraction and therefore still contradictory. We are able to predicate of that world whatever is necessary to make it the complement of the world of pure thought. It must be immediate, that thought may have something to mediate, individual and isolated piece from piece that thought may have something to relate. It must be, in short, the abstract individual, which, together with the abstract universal of thought, forms the concrete reality, alike individual and universal, which alone is consistent and self-sustained.

27. If this is so, it follows that there is nothing mysterious or intricate about the deduction of the world of Nature from the Logic, and of the world of Spirit from the world of Nature. It is simply the final step in the self-recovery of the spirit from the illegitimate abstractions of the understanding—the recovery which we have seen to be the source of all movement in the dialectic. Once granted a single category of the Logic, and all the others follow, since in the world of reality each lower category only exists as a moment of the Absolute Idea, and can therefore never by itself satisfy the demands of the mind. And, in like manner, the world of pure thought only exists as an abstraction from concrete reality, so that, granted pure thought, we are compelled by the necessity of the dialectic to grant the existence of some sensuous intuition also. It is perhaps conceivable that, in some future state of knowledge, the completion of the dialectic process might be seen to involve, not only the mere existence of Nature and Spirit, but their existence with particular characteristics, and that this might be carried so far that it amounted to a complete determination, in one way or another, of every question which could be asked concerning them. If this should be the case, we should be able to deduce *à priori* from the character of pure thought the whole contents of science and history. Even then, however, we should not have taken up the position that the immediate element in Nature and Spirit could be reduced to pure thought. For we should not be endeavouring to deduce the immediate merely from the mediate, but from the mediate compared with the concrete reality of which they are both moments. The true force of the proof would lie in the existence of this synthesis. At present, however, the world of sense appears to us to contain a large number of particulars which are quite indifferent to pure thought, so that it might be as well embodied in one arrangement of them as in another. This may possibly be an inevitable law of knowledge. It certainly expresses the state of our knowledge at present. It follows that the Philosophy of Nature and Spirit will consist only in observing the progress of the pure idea as it appears in the midst of phenomena to a large extent contingent to it, and cannot hope to account for all the particulars of experience. But this is all that Hegel attempts to do. He endeavours to find the idea in everything, but not to reduce everything to a manifestation of the idea. Thus he remarks in the Philosophy of Spirit, "This development of reality or objectivity brings forward a row of forms which must certainly be given empirically, but from an empirical point of view should not be placed side by side and outside each other, but must be known as the expression which corresponds to a necessary series of definite notions, and only in so far as they express such a series of notions have interest for philosophic thought[1]."

28. If this explanation be correct, it will follow that Hegel never endeavoured to claim ontological validity for his Logic in the second sense mentioned above—by attempting, that is, to deduce all the contents of experience from the nature of pure thought only. The deduction which does take place is not dependent merely on the premise from which it starts, which is certainly to be found in the nature of pure thought, but also on the whole to which it is working up, and which is implicit in our thought. If we can proceed in this way from Logic to Nature and Spirit, it proves that Logic without the additional elements which occur in Nature and Spirit is a mere abstraction. And an abstraction cannot possibly be the cause of the reality from which it is an abstraction. There can be no place here, therefore, for the attempt to construct the world out of abstract thought, of which Hegel's philosophy is sometimes supposed to have consisted.

---

[1] *Enc.* Section 387, lecture note, p. 42.

The importance of the ontological significance of the dialectic, even in this limited extent, is, however, very great. We are now enabled to assert, not only that, within our experience, actual or possible, everything can be explained by the Absolute Idea, but also that all reality, in any sense in which we can attach any intelligible meaning to the word, can also be explained by that idea. I cannot have the least reason to believe in, or even to imagine possible, anything which does not in the long run turn out to contain and be constituted by the highest category. And since that category, as was pointed out above, expresses the deepest nature of the human mind, we are entitled to believe that the universe as a whole is in fundamental agreement with our own nature, and that whatever can rightly be called rational may be safely declared to be also real.

29. From this account of the Hegelian system it will appear that its main result is the completion of the work which had been carried on by German philosophy since the publication of the Critique of Pure Reason—the establishment, by means of the transcendental method, of the rationality of the Universe. There was much left for Hegel to do. For the Critique of Pure Reason was a dualism, and had all the qualities of a dualism. Man's aspirations after complete rationality and complete justice in life were checked by the consideration of the phenomenal side of his own nature, which delivered him over to the mercy of a world in one of whose elements—the irrational manifold— he saw only what was alien to himself. And the defect of the Critique of Pure Reason in this respect was not completely remedied by the Critique of Practical Reason. The reconciliation was only external: the alien element was not to be absorbed or transcended but conquered. It was declared the weaker, but it kept its existence. And the whole of this argument had a slighter basis than the earlier one, since it rested, not on the validity of knowledge, but on the validity of the moral sense— the denial of which is not as clearly a contradiction of itself. Moreover, it is not by any means universally admitted that the obligation to seek the good is dependent on the possibility of realising it in full. And if it is not so dependent then the validity of the moral sense does not necessarily imply the validity of the Ideas of Reason. Even in the Critique of

Judgment the reconciliation of the two sides was still external and incomplete.

Nor had spirit a much stronger position with Kant's immediate successors. Fichte, indeed, reduced the Non-Ego to a shadow, but just for that reason, as Dr Caird remarks, rendered it impossible to completely destroy it. And the Absolute of Schelling, standing as it did midway between matter and spirit, could be but slight comfort to spirit, whose most characteristic features and most important interests had little chance of preservation in a merely neutral basis.

Hegel on the other hand asserted the absolute supremacy of reason. For him it is the key to the interpretation of the whole universe; it finds nothing alien to itself wherever it goes. And the reason for which he thus claimed unrestricted power was demonstrated to contain every category up to the Absolute Idea. It is this demonstration—quite as much as the rejection of the possibility that anything in the universe should be alien to reason—which gives his philosophy its practical interest. For from the practical point of view it is of little consequence that the world should be proved to be the embodiment of reason, if we are to see in reason nothing higher than reciprocity, and are compelled to regard the higher categories as mere subjective delusions. Such a maimed reason as this is one in which we can have scarcely more pleasure or acquiescence than in chaos. If the rational can be identified with the good, it can only be in respect of the later categories, such as End, Life, and Cognition.

CHAPTER II.

30. In the last chapter I have explained the view of Hegel's philosophy which seems to me the most probable. It is now necessary to examine some objections which have been raised to the possibility of interpreting Hegel in this manner. With regard to three points in particular various commentators have taken a different view of Hegel's meaning. It has been held that the dialectic process has no reference whatever to experience, but takes place in pure thought considered apart from anything else. It has been held that, whether this be so or not, yet at the end of the dialectic we reach, in the Absolute Idea, a form of thought which exists in and by itself, and does not merely mediate *data* immediately given to the mind by some other source. And, lastly, it has been held that the deduction of Nature and Spirit from Logic is to be taken as an attempt to degrade them into mere forms of the latter, and to declare that all things are reducible to thought alone.

31. The first of these points has been discussed by Trendelenburg in his *Logische Untersuchungen*. According to him, Hegel attempted what was impossible, and achieved what was useless. He attempted, by observation of the pure notion in its most abstract stage, and apart from everything but itself, to evoke all the other stages of the pure notion, and so reach a result of general validity *à priori*. But since we can extract from an idea, taken by itself, nothing more than is already in it, and since an idea, independent of the *data* which it connects and mediates, is unthinkable, any such dialectical evolution as Hegel desired was impossible. In point of fact, all appearance of advance from one category to another is due, according to Trendelenburg, to surreptitious appeals to experience. In this way the sterility of pure thought was conquered, but with it the cogency of this dialectic process also disappeared, and it became merely empirical and contingent, without a claim to be called philosophy.

On the question as to the actual results of the dialectic we shall consider Trendelenburg's views further on. As to Hegel's intention, he says " Although the Wissenschaftslehre of Fichte extracted the Non-Ego from the Ego, yet he does not go on to real notions. The dialectic has appropriated his methods; it takes the same course in position, opposition, and reconciliation. It does not make so much difference that it begins with the notion of Being, for it is the empty image of Being. If it nevertheless comes to the notions of reality and to concrete forms, we do not perceive whence it gets to them. For pure thought will not accept them, and then permeate them, but endeavours to make them. Thought, expressed in this way, is born blind and has no eyes towards the outside [1]."

32. In answer to this we may quote Mr F. H. Bradley. "An idea prevails that the Dialectic Method is a sort of experiment with conceptions *in vacuo*. We are supposed to have nothing but one single isolated abstract idea, and this solitary monad then proceeds to multiply by gemmation from or by fission of its private substance, or by fetching matter from the impalpable void. But this is a mere caricature, and it comes from confusion between that which the mind has got before it and that which it has within itself. Before the mind there is a single conception, but the mind itself, which does not appear, engages in the process, operates on the *datum*, and produces the result. The opposition between the real, in the fragmentary character in which the mind possesses it, and the true reality felt within the mind, is the moving cause of that unrest which sets up the dialectical process [2]."

The fact seems to be that Trendelenburg's interpretation of

---

[1] *Logische Untersuchungen*, Vol. I. p. 92. My references to this work are to the edition of 1862.

[2] *Logic*, Book III. Part I. Chap. 2. Section 20.

Hegel's attempt to construct a dialectic of pure thought, is inadequate in two ways. He supposes, first, that the incomplete thought from which we start is conceived to exist only in its incompleteness, and is *intended* to have as yet no actual relation to the concrete reality to which it is afterwards to attain. In fact, he says, the process *does* depend on a reference to concrete reality, but, in so far as this is so, the original attempt, which was to construct an objectively valid dialectic by means of pure thought, has broken down. I shall try, however, to show that such a relation to reality was in Hegel's mind throughout, and that it leads to conclusions of objective validity. If pure thought meant anything inconsistent with this, it would certainly be sterile. But there is nothing in this which is inconsistent with pure thought, for the notion, as contained implicitly in reality and experience, is precisely of the same nature as the isolated piece which we begin by consciously observing, though it is more complete.

And, secondly, Trendelenburg appears to think that thought, to be pure, must be perceived by itself, and not in concrete experience, which always contains, along with pure thought, the complementary moment of sensation. If this was the case, it would most certainly be sterile, or rather impossible. So far from one category being able to transform itself, by the dialectic process, into another, no category could exist at all. For all thought, as we have seen[1], requires something immediate on which to act. But this need not prevent the dialectic process from being one of pure thought. As was explained above[2] the only part of experience from which the dialectic process derives its cogency, and the only part which changes in it, is the element of pure thought, although the dialectic process, like all other acts of reasoning, can only take place when the thought is joined with sensation.

Whether the reference to experience in Hegel's Logic destroys its claims to absolute and *à priori* validity will be discussed in the next chapter. At present we have to ask whether the appeal to experience is inconsistent with the original intention of the dialectic, as Trendelenburg asserts, and whether it was only used by Hegel because the absurdity

[1] Chap. I. Section 27.   [2] Chap. I. Section 15.

of his original purpose drove him, more or less unconsciously, to make such an appeal, or whether, on the other hand, it was all along an essential part of the system that it should have such a relation to experience.

33. At the beginning of Section 6 of the Encyclopaedia Hegel says that "at first we become aware of these contents" of philosophical knowledge "in what we call experience....As it is only in form that philosophy is distinguished from other modes of obtaining an acquaintance with this same sum of being, it must necessarily be in harmony with actuality and experience." This passage supports the view that Hegel was conscious of the manner in which his dialectic rested on experience. For, even if it were possible for philosophy to observe pure thought independently of experience, it is certain that "other means of obtaining an acquaintance with this same sum of being"—science, namely, and common sense—have no field for their action except experience. It is no doubt the case that, as Hegel mentions in Section 8, philosophy has "another circle of objects, which" empirical knowledge "does not embrace. These are Freedom, Mind, and God." But, although philosophy deals with these conceptions, it does so, according to Hegel, only by starting from empirical knowledge. It is, for example, only by the contemplation of the finite objects perceived by the senses that we arrive at the knowledge of God [1]. And, as we are now considering the basis, and not the extent, of philosophy, the fact that we can rise to knowledge of that which is never represented in sensuous intuition is not to the point.

34. Again, in Section 9, he points out that "the method of empirical science exhibits two defects. The first is that the Universal, or general principle contained in it, the genus or kind, &c., is of its own nature indeterminate and vague, and therefore not on its own account connected with the Particular or the details. Either is external and accidental to the other, and it is the same with the particular facts which are brought into union: each is external and accidental to the others. The second defect is that the beginnings are in every case data and postulates, neither accounted for nor deduced. In both these

---

[1] *Enc.* Section 12, quoted on p. 37 below.

points the form of necessity fails to get its due.   Hence reflection, whenever it sets itself to remedy these defects, becomes speculative thinking, the thinking proper to philosophy."   Further on in the same section he says that "the relation of speculative science to the other sciences may be stated in the following terms.   It does not in the least neglect the empirical facts contained in the other sciences but recognises and adopts them: it appreciates and applies towards its own structure the universal element in these sciences, their laws and classifications; but besides all this, into the categories of science, it introduces, and gives currency to, other categories. The difference looked at in this way is only a change of categories."

The method of philosophy then is separated by no difference of kind from the method of science, and must therefore also deal with experience.   It takes the materials of science, and carries further the process of arrangement and analysis which science began.   Whether, in doing so, it actually goes so far as to destroy the basis from which it started, is a question which will be considered later[1].   The changes which it produces are in any case very extensive.   Fresh categories are introduced, and not merely as additions, but as altering materially the meaning of the categories of science which now turn out to be abstract and of imperfect validity.   The process must not be confounded with one which should simply carry scientific generalisations up to the highest point, using only the categories of science, and making the ordinary scientific presuppositions.   The result may in one sense be said to differ from the result of science in kind and not only in degree.   But the method only differs in degree.   The special categories of philosophy are not introduced "out of a pistol" but are the necessary consequence of reflection on the categories of science and the contradictions they display.   And, if there is this continuity between science and philosophy, we are placed in the dilemma of either supposing that Hegel imagined science to be possible without experience, or admitting that for him the dialectic method, the method of philosophy, also required experience as its presupposition.

[1] Sections 47–49.

35. The whole of Section 12 has a very important bearing on this question. The following extracts are especially significant. Philosophy "takes its departure from experience; including under that name both our immediate consciousness and the inductions from it. Awakened, as it were, by this stimulus, thought is vitally characterised by raising itself above the natural state of mind, above the senses and inferences from the senses into its own unadulterated element, and by assuming, accordingly, at first a stand-aloof and negative attitude towards the point from which it draws its origin." And further on "On the relation between immediacy and mediation in consciousness...here it may be sufficient to premise that, although the two 'moments' or factors present themselves as distinct, still neither of them can be absent, nor can one exist apart from the other. Thus the knowledge of God" (compare Section 1—"Truth, in that supreme sense in which God and God only is the Truth") "as of every supersensible reality, is in its true character an exaltation above sensations or perceptions: it consequently involves a negative attitude to the initial data of sense, and to that extent implies mediation. For to mediate is to take something as a beginning, and to go onward to a second thing; so that the existence of this second thing depends on our having reached it from something else contradistinguished from it. In spite of this the knowledge of God is independent (selbstständig) and not a mere consequence of the empirical phase of consciousness; in fact, its independence is essentially secured through this negation and exaltation. No doubt, if we attach an unfair prominence to the fact of mediation, and represent it as implying a state of conditionedness (Bedingtheit), it may be said—not that the remark would mean much—that philosophy is the child of experience, and owes its rise to an à posteriori fact. (As a matter of fact, thinking is always the negation of what we have immediately before us.) With as much truth however we may be said to owe eating to the means of nourishment, so long as we can have no eating without them. If we take this view, eating is certainly represented as ungrateful; it devours that to which it owes itself. Thinking, upon this view of its action, is equally ungrateful." And again, "In relation to the first abstract universality of thought there is a correct and well-grounded sense in which we may say, that we may thank experience for the development of philosophy. For, firstly, the empirical sciences do not stop short at the perception of the individual features of a phenomenon. By the aid of thought, they come forward to meet philosophy with materials for it, in the shape of general uniformities, i.e. laws and classifications of the phenomena. When this is done, the particular facts which they contain are ready to be received into philosophy. This, secondly, implies a certain compulsion on thought itself to proceed to these concrete specific truths. The reception into philosophy of these scientific materials, now that thought has removed its immediacy, and made it cease to be mere data forms at the same time a development of thought out of itself. Philosophy then owes its development to the empirical sciences. In return it gives their contents what is so vital to them, the freedom of thought—gives them, in short, an *à priori* character. These contents are now warranted necessary, and no longer depend on the evidence of facts merely, that they were so found and so experienced. The fact of experience thus becomes an illustration and image of the original and completely self-supporting activity of thought."

36. The peculiar importance of this section lies in the emphasis laid simultaneously on both the elements of the dialectic process. On the one hand the start is definitely asserted, as in the quotation from Section 9, to be made from experience. On the other hand we are told that the result relates itself negatively towards the point from which it draws its origin. This precludes on the one side the theory that Hegel endeavoured to produce the dialectic process by mere reflection on the nature of pure thought in abstraction, and, on the other side, denies that a reference to experience involves a merely empirical argument. The reception into philosophy of the material furnished by science is declared to be identical with the development of thought out of itself. We are enabled also to understand correctly, by means of this Section, certain expressions with regard to the dialectic process which are occasionally interpreted by critics as meaning that the medium of the Logic is abstract pure thought. For example, here as in

other places, Hegel repudiates the idea that "philosophy is a child of experience, and owes its existence to an *à posteriori* element." Such an idea, we are told, is "unfair." Such expressions might lead us to reject the theory of the dialectic offered above, if it was not for the explanation which here follows them. It is only unfair to say this, Hegel continues, in the same sense in which it would be unfair to say that we owe eating to the means of nourishment. Now it is unquestionable that, without something to eat, eating is impossible, and if eating does not depend on the existence of something to eat, it follows that the existence of experience may be indispensable to the existence of philosophy, although philosophy has been declared not to depend on experience. Mediation, as Hegel uses the word, is not equivalent to dependence, and it is possible for thought to require a mediation by sense, and therefore to be helpless without it, while it is nevertheless, in Hegelian terminology, not in a state of dependence (Bedingtheit) on it. Without the *data* which are supplied to us by sense, the dialectic could not exist. It is not, however, caused by those *data*, but is necessarily combined with them in a higher unity. It is no more dependent on them than any other abstraction from a whole is on its fellow abstractions from the same whole. Each step which it takes depends, as we have seen, on the relation which the previous step bears to the goal of the process. The whole process may thus fairly be said not to be dependent at all.

The independence of the idea of God is declared to rest on its negation and exaltation above the empirical side of consciousness. This independence cannot possibly mean, therefore, the absence of all connection between the two, for to be related to a thing even negatively, is, as Hegel himself points out on occasion (as in his treatment of the ideas of finitude and infinity, Section 95), itself a condition, and in this sense a dependence. The independence here can only consist in the fact that, although the beginning is in experience, which contains an empirical side, yet in the result the idea of God is separated from the particular empirical facts with which the process started, and is free from all likeness to them, although they form its demonstration and justification. Whether this is possible or not, it appears to be this which Hegel means in asserting his dialectic to be independent of all experience, and this is quite compatible with an experiential basis.

It may be objected that in this Section Hegel is not speaking of his own system, but of the origin of philosophy in general. It is, no doubt, true that the origin of philosophy from a historical standpoint is one of the points discussed here. But if we look at Section 14, we shall find that the two questions are considered by Hegel as identical. "The same evolution of thought," he says, "which is exhibited in the history of philosophy is presented in the System of Philosophy itself." It is clear, therefore, that he regards the process traced in Section 12 as one which is not only historically accurate but also philosophically valid, and that he holds the relation of experience to the dialectic, which is there defined, as that which really exists.

37. We find similar statements in his criticism of the Intuitionist School. In explaining their position, he says (Section 70), "What this theory asserts is that truth lies neither in the Idea as a merely subjective thought, nor in mere being on its own account; that mere being *per se*, a being that is not of the Idea, is the sensible and finite being of the world. Now all this only affirms, without demonstration, that the Idea has truth only by means of being, and being has truth only by means of the Idea. The maxim of immediate knowledge rejects an indefinite empty immediacy (and such is abstract being, or pure unity taken by itself) and affirms in its stead the unity of the Idea with being. And it acts rightly in so doing. But it is stupid not to see that the unity of distinct terms or modes is not merely a purely immediate unity, i.e. unity empty and indeterminate, but that it involves the principle that one term has truth only as mediated through the other, or, if the phrase be preferred, that either term is only mediated with truth through the other."

On the one hand then he asserts that truth does not lie in the idea as separated from the sensible and finite being of the world. But the idea in its unity with the sensible and finite being of the world is experience. This unity, however, is only mediate—that is to say, it is not, as the Intuitionists supposed it to be, perceived immediately, nor evident from the nature of thought itself. It lies rather in the mediation of each with truth only by means of the other, which supports the view asserted above—that Hegel makes no attempt to use pure thought in abstraction from the data of sense, but holds truth to lie only in the whole from which these two elements are abstracted.

Hegel here denies one immediacy and admits another, both of which are called by the same name in English. He denies the validity of intuition, if by intuition is meant Jacobi's unmittelbares Wissen, which perceives immediately the unity of thought and being. But he admits that intuition, if we mean by it the Kantian Anschauung, is essential to knowledge, for without "the sensible and finite being of the world" the idea has no truth.

38. Bearing this in mind we are able to see that there is nothing in Section 75 inconsistent with the position I have attributed to Hegel. He there says, "It has been shown to be untrue in fact to say that there is an immediate knowledge, a knowledge without mediation either by means of something else or in itself. It has also been explained to be false in fact to say that thought advances through finite and conditioned categories only, which are always mediated by something else, and to forget that in the very act of mediation the mediation itself vanishes."

The first of these statements will present no difficulties, for it is quite consistent to deny the existence of immediate knowledge, while admitting the existence of an immediate element in knowledge. Indeed, the assertion that all knowledge consists in the mediation of the immediate at once affirms that there is an immediate, and denies that it is knowledge.

Hegel's reminder that in the act of mediation the mediation itself vanishes does not concern us here. For we are now considering the basis on which the dialectic process rests, and not the end which it reaches. The latter must be considered further on. The fact that the dialectic process consists in mediating the immediate is enough to show that it must have some relation to experience, since only in experience can the immediate be found.

39. Passing on to the Doctrine of the Notion, we have (Section 166, lecture note): "The notion does not, as understanding supposes, stand still in its own immobility. It is rather an infinite form, of boundless activity, as it were the *punctum saliens* of all vitality, and thereby self-differentiating (sich von sich selbst unterscheidend). This disruption of the notion into the difference of its constituent functions,—a disruption imposed by the native act of the notion, is the judgment. A judgment therefore, means the particularising of the notion. No doubt the notion is implicitly the particular. But in the notion as notion, the particular is not yet explicit, and still remains in transparent unity with the universal. Thus for example, as we remarked before (Section 160, lecture note), the germ of a plant contains its particular, such as root, branches, leaves, &c., but these details are at first present only potentially, and are not realised till the germ uncloses. This unclosing is, as it were, the judgment of the plant. The illustration may also serve to show how neither the notion nor the judgment is merely found in our head, or merely framed by us. The notion is the very heart of things, and makes them what they are. To form a notion of an object means therefore to become aware of its notion; and when we proceed to a criticism or judgment of the object, we are not performing a subjective act, and merely ascribing this or that predicate to the object. We are, on the contrary, observing the object in the specific character imposed by its notion."

This analogy may illustrate the view which we have been considering. In the growth of a tree the positive element is in the seed only. The air, earth, and water, although they are necessary to the development of the tree, do not play a positive part in its growth. It is the nature of the seed alone which determines that a plant shall be produced, and what sort of plant it shall be. But the surrounding conditions, of suitable soil and so on, are conditions without which the seed cannot realise the end of its nature. In this analogy, the seed will correspond to the category of Being, the completely mature plant to the Absolute Idea, and the air, earth, and water, to the matter of intuition. If we look more closely, the resemblance to actual plant life is not perfect, since different amounts of light, heat, and manure will change the size and colour, though not the species of the flower, which gives to these surroundings a more active part than Hegel allows to the matter of intuition. But since Hegel says, without restriction, that the germ of the plant contains its particulars, he must be supposed to ignore the amount of quantitative change which depends on the circumstances in which the plant is placed, and in this case the analogy is exact.

The point of the comparison, if the above explanation is correct, lies in the fact that the growth of the plant has certain conditions which do not determine the nature of the development, though without their presence the development could not exist at all. That this is the point which Hegel wished to make is rendered probable by his having taken as his example a case of organic life. For in organic life we are able to distinguish between the cause of growth and the essential conditions of it in a way that would be impossible if we were considering an event governed only by mechanical laws. In the latter case we can only say that the cause is the sum of all the necessary conditions, and we are unable to consider any one of them as more fundamental than the others. But with organic life we have introduced the idea of a final cause, and we are thus enabled to distinguish between the positive cause and the conditions which are necessary but not positive. Hegel's declaration that the growth of the notion must be judged by the principles of organic growth, enables us to make this distinction, without which we should be unable to understand that the relation held by the data of sense to the dialectic process should be indispensable, and yet negative.

40. Again (Section 232, lecture note) he says, "The necessity which cognition (Erkennen) reaches by means of demonstration is the reverse of what formed its starting-point. In its starting-point cognition had a given and a contingent content; but now, at the close of its movement, it knows its content to be necessary. This necessity is reached by means of subjective activity. Similarly, subjectivity at starting was quite abstract, a bare *tabula rasa*. It now shows itself as a modifying and determining principle. In this way we pass from the idea of cognition to that of will. The passage, as will be

apparent on a closer examination, means that the universal, to
be truly apprehended, must be apprehended as subjectivity, as
a notion self-moving, active, and form-imposing." Hegel is
speaking here of finite cognition at the point at which it
passes over into volition. But he is speaking of it before the
change has yet been made, for the "it", which knows its
content to be necessary, can only be taken as meaning
cognition. The process here described starts with finite
cognition, which is not philosophy, but the ordinary thought
of every-day life. By this process the passage is made to
volition. The advance lies in the fact that, while knowledge
started from the given and contingent, it now knows its content to be necessary. But when this change has taken place
in the content, cognition has become philosophy. (Compare
Section 9, quoted on p. 35 above. "The second defect is that
the beginnings are in every case data and postulates, neither
accounted for nor deduced. In both these points the form of
necessity fails to get its due. Hence, reflection whenever it
sets itself to remedy these defects, becomes speculative thinking,
the thinking proper to philosophy.") And the universal, under
the form of subjectivity, has been apprehended as a self-
moving notion, which also shows that by this point knowledge
has become philosophy. And the process by which it has
advanced begins with the given and the contingent, which can
only be found in sense. The advance of the dialectic towards
the Absolute Idea has therefore a basis in experience.

41. In Section 238, Hegel, in considering the organic
elements of the speculative method, states that its beginning
is being or immediacy. "When it means immediate being the
beginning is taken from intuition (Anschauung) and perception
—the initial stage in the analytical method of finite cognition.
When it means universality, it is the beginning of the synthetic
method. But since the Logical Idea (das Logische) is as much
a universal as it is in being, since it is as much presupposed by
the notion as the notion itself immediately *is*, its beginning is
a synthetical as well as an analytical beginning.

(Lecture note.) "Philosophical method is analytical as well
as synthetical, not indeed in the sense of a bare juxtaposition
or mere alternating employment of these two methods of finite

cognition, but rather in such a way that it holds them merged in itself. In every one of its movements, therefore, it displays an attitude at once analytical and synthetical. Philosophic thought proceeds analytically, in so far as it only accepts its object, the Idea, and while allowing it its own way is only, as it were, an onlooker at its movement and development. To this extent philosophising is wholly passive. Philosophic thought, however, is equally synthetic, and evinces itself to be the action of the notion itself. To that end, however, there is required an effort to keep back the incessant impertinence of our own fancies and private opinions."

Continuing the same subject, he says in Section 239, "The advance renders explicit the *judgment* implicit in the Idea. The immediate universal, as the notion implicit, is the dialectical force, which on its own part deposes its immediacy and universality to the level of a mere stage or 'moment.' Thus is produced the negative of the beginning, the original *datum* is made determinate : it exists for something, as related to those things which are distinguished from it—the stage of Reflection.

Seeing that the immanent dialectic only states explicitly what was involved in the immediate notion, this advance is analytical, but seeing that in this notion this distinction was not yet stated, it is equally synthetical.

(Lecture note.) " In the advance of the idea the beginning exhibits itself as what it implicitly is. It is seen to be mediated and derivative, and neither to have proper being nor proper immediacy. It is only for the consciousness which is itself immediate, that Nature forms the commencement or immediacy, and that Spirit appears as what is mediated by Nature. The truth is that Nature is due to the statuting of Spirit, (das durch den Geist Gesetzte,) and it is Spirit itself which gives itself a presupposition in Nature."

42. In this passage the double foundation of the dialectic is clearly admitted, and its connection with the double aspect of the process is made clear. We must have, in the first place, pure thought given to us as a fact—we cannot know the nature of thought unless thinking has taken place. From one point of view, then, the dialectic process is the observation of a

subject matter already before us. In this aspect philosophy "allows the idea its own way" and "is only, as it were, an onlooker at its movement and development." And in so far as this is so we have the unequivocal declaration that "the beginning is taken from sensation or perception"—since pure thought is never found except as an element in the whole of experience. But at the same time the process is not merely one of empirical selection of first one character and then another from the concrete whole. When once the first and simplest judgment has been made about experience—the judgment which is involved in the application of the category of Being—the various steps of the dialectic process will grow by an inner necessity out of that judgment. This judgment will be the beginning as universality, as the other aspect was the beginning as immediate being; and, in so far as the beginning is universal, the process is synthetic and "evinces itself to be the action of the notion itself."

The explanation of the union of the two processes lies in the fact that the reality present to our minds in experience is always the full and concrete notion. This is the logical *prius* of the movement, although the unanalysed mass and the abstract notion of Being may be the temporal *prius* in that stage of finite reflection which precedes philosophy. "In the onward movement of the idea the beginning exhibits itself as what it is implicitly. It is seen to be mediated and derivative, and neither to have proper being nor proper immediacy." And again, in Section 242, the notion "is the idea, which, as absolutely first (in the method) regards this terminus as merely the annihilation of the show or semblance, which made the beginning appear immediate, and made itself seem a result. It is the knowledge that the idea is one systematic whole." All less complete ideas are illegitimate abstractions from this whole, and naturally tend therefore to approximate to it. And such a process may be viewed from two sides. It may be regarded from the point of view of the whole—in which case the dialectic process will be viewed as gradually retracing the steps of abstraction which had led to the idea of pure Being, and rebuilding the concrete object till it again coincided with reality. Or it may be regarded from the point of view of the incomplete and growing notion, when the advance will seem to be purely out of the notion itself. "Seeing that the immanent dialectic only states explicitly what was involved in the immediate notion, this advance is analytical, but seeing that in this notion this distinction was not yet stated, it is equally synthetical."

And these two aspects—the analytic from the stand-point of the concrete and perfect notion, and the synthetic from the stand-point of the yet imperfect notion,—correspond respectively to aspects for which the beginning is taken from sensation or perception, and from the action of the notion itself. In so far as we look on the motive force of the dialectic process as residing in the completeness of the concrete notion, the process depends on the contemplation of reality and therefore of sensation and perception. For the sensation, although contributing no positive element to the process, is the necessary condition of our becoming conscious of the nature of thought. But in so far as we look on the motive force of the process as supplied by the incompleteness of the growing notion, we shall bring into prominence the fact that the process is after all one of pure thought. And we only get a true view of the whole when we combine the two and see that the stimulus is in the relation of the abstract and explicit idea to the complete and implicit idea, that the process is one of pure thought perceived in a medium of sensation and therefore synthetic and analytic at once.

43. To this we may add the following extract from the Philosophy of Spirit (Encyclopædia, Section 447, lecture note), "In sensation there is present the whole Reason—the collected material of Spirit. All our images, thoughts, and ideas, of external nature, of justice, of ethics, and of the content of religion, develop themselves from our intelligence as used in sensation; as they themselves, on the other hand, when they have received their complete explanation are again concentrated in the simple form of sensation....This development of Spirit out of sensation, however, has commonly been understood as if the intelligence was originally completely empty, and therefore received all content from outside as something quite strange to it. This is a mistake. For that which the intelligence appears to take in from outside is in reality nothing else than the reasonable, which is therefore identical with spirit, and immanent in it. The activity of spirit has therefore no other goal, except, by the removal of the apparent externality to self of the implicitly reasonable object, to remove also the apparent externality of the object to spirit."

Here we learn that the reasonable, with which the Logic deals, is first given to us in sensation, and as apparently external to self, and that it is by starting from that which is given in sensation that we learn the nature of spirit. To act in this way is a fundamental characteristic of spirit— "the activity of spirit has no other goal"—and therefore it must be in this way that our minds act when they are engaged on the dialectic process.

44. I have endeavoured to show, by the consideration of these passages from Hegel's writings, that his method possesses two characteristics. These are, first, that it is a process of pure thought, but only possible in the presence of matter of intuition; second, that the motive force of the whole process is involved in the relation between the incomplete form of the notion, which at any moment may be explicitly before us, and the complete form which is present implicitly in all our thought as in all other reality.

We must now pass to another question. The validity of each stage of the dialectic, as we have seen, depended on the one before, and all of them ultimately on the first stage—the category of Being. The validity of this again we found to depend on the fact that its denial would be suicidal[1].

Now it must be admitted that this is a mere inference, and not explicitly stated by Hegel. Such a statement would be most natural at the beginning of the whole dialectic process, but it is neither there nor elsewhere. No justification whatever is given of the idea of Being. It is merely assumed and all the consequences that follow from it, however cogent in themselves, are left, so to speak, suspended in the air with no explicit argument anywhere to attach them to reality. The explanation of this strange peculiarity is, I think, largely to be found in the state of philosophy at the time when Hegel wrote.

[1] Chap. I. Section 18.

45. The argument of the dialectic could, if the theory in the previous chapter is correct, have been so arranged as to be obviously transcendental. The basis of the whole would be the existence of the world of experience, which no sceptic can wholly deny, since denial itself always implies the existence of something. The barest admission that could be made, however, with regard to this world of experience, would involve that it should be brought under the category of Being whose validity would be therefore granted. But as, in the process of the dialectic, the category of Being developed contradictions which led up to fresh categories, and so on, the validity of these categories also, as applied to reality, must be granted, since they follow from the validity of the category of Being.

Kant, who had to establish his system in the face of sceptical criticism, naturally emphasised the transcendental character of the argument, and the cogency with which his conclusions could be applied to the world of reality, involved as they were in propositions which his adversaries were not prepared to dispute. But Hegel's position was different. He lived in an age of Idealism, when the pure scepticism of Hume had ceased to be a living force, and when it was a generally accepted view that the mind was adequate to the knowledge of reality. Under such circumstances Hegel would naturally lay stress on the conclusions of his system, in which he more or less differed from his contemporaries, rather than on the original premises, in which he chiefly agreed with them, and would point out how far the end was from the beginning, rather than how clearly it might be derived from it. To this must be added Hegel's marked preference for a constructive, rather than a polemical treatment, which appears so strongly in all his works. Transcendental arguments, as Mr Balfour remarks in the Defence of Philosophic Doubt, convince by threats, and are not the form into which an exposition addressed, as Hegel's was, to a friendly audience, would naturally fall. But this has exposed his system to severe disadvantages in the reaction against all Idealism which has taken place since his death. For the transcendental form becomes necessary when the attacks of scepticism have to be met, and its absence, though due chiefly to the special character of the audience to whom the philosophy was first

addressed, has led to the reproaches which have been so freely
directed against Absolute Idealism, as a mere fairy tale, or
as a theory with internal consistency, but without any relation
to facts.

The same causes may perhaps account for the prominence
of the synthetic over the analytic aspect of the dialectic,
which may be noticed occasionally throughout the Logic. The
criticism of idealists would naturally be devoted more to the
internal consistency of the system than to its right to exist at
all, on which point they would probably have no objection to
raise. To meet such criticisms it would be necessary to lay
emphasis on the synthetic side of the process, while to us, who
in most cases approach the whole question from a comparatively
negative stand-point, it would seem more natural to bring
forward the analytic side, and to show that the whole system
was involved in any admission of the existence of reality.

46. Hegel speaks of his logic as without any pre-supposition.
This is taken by Trendelenburg as equivalent to an assertion that
it has no basis in experience. But we have seen that the only
postulate which Hegel assumed was the validity of the category
of Being—that is, the existence of something. Now this, though
not directly proved, can scarcely be said to be assumed, if it is
involved in all other assertions. And a system which requires
no other postulate than this might fairly be said to have no
pre-supposition. The very fact that the argument exists
proves that it was entitled to its assumption, for if the
argument exists, then the category of Being has validity, at
any rate, of one thing—the argument itself. And this is
compatible with all the relation to experience which the
dialectic needs, or will admit.

A parallel case will be found in Hegel's criticism of Kant's
refutation of the ontological argument[1]. He then treats the
actual existence of God, who for him is equivalent to the
Absolute Reality, as a matter which can be passed over in
silence, since its denial—the denial of any reality in the
universe—is suicidal. It is really the same fact—the existence
of some reality—which, under another aspect, is assumed at
the beginning of the Logic. We may reasonably suppose that

[1] Cp. Sections 63, 64.

Hegel treated it in the same way, holding that a postulate which could not be denied without self-contradiction need not be considered as a pre-supposition at all. From all more particular pre-suppositions he doubtless claims that his logic is free. But this claim is not incompatible with the relation of the dialectic to experience, which was suggested in the last chapter.

It must also be noted that Hegel says of the proofs of the existence of God which are derived from the finite world " the process of exaltation might thus appear to be transition, and to involve a means, but it is not a whit less true that every trace of transition and means is absorbed, since the world, which might have seemed to be the means of reaching God, is explained to be a nullity[1]." And in section 12, in the passage quoted above, he tells us that philosophy is unfairly said to be the child of experience, since it " involves a negative attitude to the initial acts of the senses." Now in the Logic the result certainly stands in a negative relation to the beginning, for the inadequacy of the category of Being to express reality has been demonstrated in the course of the dialectic. The category of Being would then, in Hegel's language, have been absorbed, and it would be unfair to say that the dialectic depended on it. Under these circumstances it is only natural that he should not call its validity a pre-supposition.

47. There is, then, a constant relation to experience throughout the course of the dialectic. But, even if this is so, does that relation remain at the end of the process? It has been asserted that, although throughout the Logic Hegel may treat thought as mediate, and as only existing as an element in a whole of which the other element is an immediate datum, yet, when we reach the Absolute Idea, that Idea is held to be self-centred and capable of existing by itself in abstraction from everything else. It must be admitted that such a transition would be unjustifiable[2], but I am unable to see any reason to suppose that Hegel held any such belief.

We must discriminate between those characteristics of the immediate element of experience which are indispensable if experience is to be constituted at all, and those which are not

---

[1] *Enc.* Section 50. [2] Cp. Chap. III. Section 99.

indispensable. The essential characteristics may all be summed up in immediacy. All thought that we know, or that we can conceive, has its action only in mediation, and its existence without something immediate on which it may act would be a contradiction. On the other hand it is not essential that this immediate should be also contingent. "The contingent may be described as what has the ground of its being, not in itself, but in somewhat else.[1]" Now it is quite possible that, in a more advanced state of knowledge, we might be able to trace back all the data immediately given in experience till we had referred them to an individuality or organic whole from the nature of which they could all be deduced. Contingency would be here eliminated, for all experience would be referred to a single unity and determined by its notion. The only question which could then arise would be, "Why was the ultimate nature of reality thus and not otherwise?" The question would, no doubt, be one to which no answer could be given. This would not, however, render the nature of reality in any way contingent. For such a question would be meaningless. Enquiries as to the reasons of things have their place only within the universe, whose existence they presuppose. We have no right to make them with regard to the universe itself. Thus in the case we have supposed contingency would be entirely eliminated, yet immediacy would remain untouched. We should still know reality, not by thought alone, but because it was given to us.

48. It seems probable that Hegel did suppose that the Absolute Idea, when completely realised, involved the elimination of the contingent, which indeed he treats[2] as part of a lower category, which is, of course, transcended in the highest. It may certainly be doubted whether human knowledge could ever attain, as a matter of fact, to this height of perfection. In particular, it may be asked whether such a state of knowledge would not require other means than our present senses for the perception of reality outside ourselves. But whether the elimination of Contingency is or is not possible, the point which is important to us here is that, should it take place, it does not involve the elimination of the immediate, and

---

[1] *Enc.* Section 145, lecture note.   [2] *Enc.* Section 145.

therefore does not prove that Hegel had any intention of declaring thought to be self-sufficing, even when it reached the Absolute Idea.

In the stage immediately before the Absolute Idea—that of ordinary cognition and volition—it is evident that the idea is not self-sufficing, since it is certain that we can neither think nor resolve in every-day life without some immediate data. Now the point of transition between this category and the Absolute Idea is stated to be "the unity of the theoretical and practical idea, and thus at the same time the unity of the idea of life with that of cognition. In cognition we had the idea in the shape of differentiation. The process of cognition has issued in the overthrow of this differentiation, and the restoration of that unity which, as unity, and in its immediacy, is in the first instance the Idea of Life[1]." In this there is nothing which tends to the elimination of immediacy, or to the self-sufficiency of thought, but only the complete discovery in the outside world of the pure thought which is also in us.

Again, in the idea of Life, thought is certainly not self-sufficing, since one of the essential characteristics of this category is that the soul is in relation to a body, which involves, of course, sensation. Now the Absolute Idea is a synthesis of this category and the category of Cognition. Thought is mediate in both of these. How then can it be immediate in the synthesis? The correction of inadequacies in the Hegelian logic comes by the emphasis of one side in the thesis and of the other in the antithesis, the synthesis reconciling the two. The synthesis, throughout the entire dialectic, can only advance on the thesis and antithesis on points in which they disagree with one another. On points in which they agree it can make no change. And when, in Absolute Spirit, Hegel reaches that which he unquestionably believes to be self-mediated and self-sufficing, he only does so because it is a synthesis of the mediating logic and the element of immediacy or "givenness" which first occurs in nature. But within the logic there is no immediacy to balance the admitted mere mediacy of the finite categories, and the distinction of mediacy and immediacy cannot therefore, within the logic, be transcended.

---

[1] *Enc.* Section 236, lecture note.

49. We find no sign again of transcended mediation in the direct definition of the Absolute Idea. "Dieses aus der Differenz und Endlichkeit des Erkennens zu sich zurück-gekommene und durch die Thätigkeit des Begriffs mit ihm identisch gewordene Leben ist die speculative oder absolute Idee. Die Idee als Einheit der subjectiven und der objectiven Idee ist der Begriff der Idee, dem die Idee als solche der Gegenstand, dem das Objekt sie ist; ein Objekt, in welches alle Bestimmungen zusammen gegangen sind[1]."

The second sentence of the definition asserts that the idea is the "Gegenstand und Objekt" to the notion of the idea. This cannot, it appears to me, be taken as equivalent to a statement that thought here becomes self-subsistent and self-mediating. It seems rather to signify that that which is immediately given to thought to mediate, is now known to be itself thought, although still immediately given. In other words, the Absolute Idea is realised when the thinker sees in the whole world round him nothing but the realisation of the same idea which forms his own essential nature—is at once conscious of the existence of the other, and of its fundamental similarity to himself. The expression that the idea as such is the object to the notion of the idea seems rather to support this view by indicating that the idea as object is viewed in a different aspect from the idea as subject. If immediacy was here gained by thought, so that it required no object given from outside, it would have been more natural to say that the idea was its own object, or indeed that the distinction of subject and object had vanished altogether.

If this is the correct interpretation of this passage, then thought remains, for Hegel, in the Absolute Idea, what it has been in all the finite categories. Although the content of all experience contains, in such a case, nothing which is not a manifestation of the pure Absolute Idea, yet to every subject in whom that idea is realised, the idea is presented in the form of immediate *data*, which are mediated by the subject's own action. The fundamental nature of subject and object is the same, but the distinction between them remains in their relation to one another.

[1] *Enc.* Sections 235, 236.

No doubt Hegel regards as the highest ideal of the dialectic process something which shall be self-mediated, and in which mediation as an external process vanishes. But this he finds in Absolute Spirit, which is a synthesis of the Absolute Idea with the element of immediate presentation. The Absolute Idea is still an abstraction, as compared with the whole of Absolute Spirit, and is not self-mediated.

50. We have now to consider the third objection which has been raised to the theory of Hegel's meaning explained in the first chapter. This objection is that Hegel has ascribed ontological validity to his dialectic to a greater extent than this theory admits, and that he has attempted to account by pure thought, not only for the rationality, but also for the entire existence of the universe. This is maintained by Professor Seth, who objects to the system chiefly, it would seem, on this ground. He says, for example, " Hegel apparently says, on one occasion, that his own elaborate phraseology means no more than the ancient position that *νοῦς* rules the world, or the modern phrase, there is Reason in the world[1]. If the system is reducible to this very general proposition, our objections would certainly fall to the ground[2]."

Somewhat earlier he expresses the position, which he believes Hegel to hold, with great force and clearness. Hegel " apparently thinks it incumbent upon him to prove that spirit exists by a necessity of thought. The concrete *existence* of the categories (in Nature and Spirit) is to be deduced from their *essence* or thought-nature; it is to be shown that they cannot *not* be. When we have mounted to the Absolute Idea, it is contended, we cannot help going further. The *nisus* of thought itself projects thought out of the sphere of thought altogether into that of actual existence. In fact, strive against the idea as we may, it seems indubitable that there is here once more repeated in Hegel the extraordinary but apparently fascinating attempt to construct the world out of abstract thought or mere universals[3]."

51. The passages from which most information on this

---

[1] *Enc.* Section 24, lecture note.
[2] *Hegelianism and Personality,* pp. 124, 125.   [3] *op. cit.* pp. 110, 111.

point are to be expected will be those in the Greater and
Smaller Logics, in which the transition to the world of Nature
is described. These are quoted and abridged as follows by
Professor Seth. "'The Absolute Idea is still logical, still
confined to the element of pure thoughts...But inasmuch as
the pure idea of knowledge is thus, so far, shut up in a species
of subjectivity, it is impelled to remove this limitation; and
thus the pure truth, the last result of the logic, becomes also
the beginning of another sphere and science[1].' The Idea, he
recalls to us, has been defined as 'the absolute unity of the
pure notion and its reality'—'the pure notion which is related
only to itself;' but if this is so, the two sides of this relation
are one, and they collapse, as it were, 'into the immediacy of
Being.' 'The Idea as the totality in this form is *Nature*. This
determining of itself, however, is not a process of becoming, or
a transition' such as we have from stage to stage in the Logic.
'The passing over is rather to be understood thus—that the
Idea freely lets itself go, being absolutely sure of itself and at
rest in itself. On account of this freedom, the form of its
determination is likewise absolutely free—namely, the externality of space and time existing absolutely for itself without
subjectivity.' A few lines lower he speaks of the 'resolve
(Entschluss) of the pure Idea to determine itself as external
Idea.' Turning to the Encyclopædia we find, at the end of
the smaller Logic[2], a more concise but substantially similar
statement. 'The Idea which exists for itself, looked at from
the point of view of this unity with itself, is Perception; and
the Idea as it exists for perception is Nature...The absolute
freedom of the Idea consists in this, that in the absolute truth
of itself' (i.e., according to Hegel's usage, when it has attained
the full perfection of the form which belongs to it) 'it *resolves*
to let the element of its particularity—the immediate Idea as
its own reflection—go forth freely from itself as Nature.' And
in the lecture-note which follows we read, as in the larger
Logic, 'We have now returned to the notion of the Idea with
which we began. This return to the beginning is also an
advance. That with which we began was Being, abstract

---

[1] *Werke*, v. pp. 352, 353.   [2] *Enc.* Section 244.

Being, and now we have the *Idea* as Being; but this existent Idea is Nature[1].' "

52. It is certainly possible at first sight to take these passages as supporting Professor Seth's theory. But we must consider that, according to that theory, Hegel is made to occupy a position, not only paradoxical and untenable, but also inconsistent. If, as I have endeavoured to show above, and as is admitted by Professor Seth, Hegel fully recognises the fact that the whole dialectic movement of pure thought only takes place in that concrete whole in which sense *data* are a moment correlative with pure thought—because thought could not exist at all without immediate *data*—how can he suppose that the movement of pure thought produces the sensations which are the conditions of its own existence? Are we not bound to adopt any other explanation, rather than suppose him guilty of such a glaring contradiction?

Such an explanation was offered in the last Chapter[2], where it was pointed out that, as the comparison of the abstract idea with the concrete idea was the origin of the dialectic movement within the Logic, so the comparison of the concrete idea with the full whole of reality, compared with which the concrete notion itself was an abstraction, was the origin of the transition from Logic to Nature and Spirit—a transition in which there was no attempt to construct the world out of abstract thought, because the foundation of the argument was the presence, implicit in all experience, of the concrete reality whose necessity was being demonstrated.

Such a theory, at one time, Professor Seth was willing to accept as correct, and now considers as " the explanation which a conciliatory and soberminded Hegelian would give of Hegel's remarkable *tour de force.*" His account is substantially the same as that given above. " Here, again, then, as throughout the Logic, it might be said we are merely undoing the work of abstraction and retracing our steps towards concrete fact. This, as we have seen, implies the admission that it is our experiential knowledge of actual fact which is the real motive-force impelling us onward—impelling us here from the abstract determinations

---

[1] *Hegelianism and Personality*, pp. 105, 106.
[2] Section 26.

of the Logic to the *quasi*-reality of Nature, and thence to the full reality of spirit. It is because we ourselves are spirits that we cannot stop short of that consummation. In this sense we can understand the feeling of 'limitation' or incompleteness of which Hegel speaks at the end of the Logic. The pure form craves, as it were, for its concrete realisation[1]."

He subsequently, however, rejects this position, and indeed seems scarcely to see its full meaning. For his "soberminded Hegelian," who accepts this reading, will, he informs us, "lay as little stress as possible upon the so-called deduction. Further reflection," he continues, "has convinced me, however, that Hegel's contention here is of more fundamental import to his system than such a representation allows. Perhaps it may even be said, that, when we surrender this deduction, though we may retain much that is valuable in Hegel's thought, we surrender the system as a whole. For, however readily he may admit, when pressed, that in the *ordo ad individuum* experience is the quarry from which all the materials are derived, it must not be forgotten that he professes to offer us an *absolute* philosophy. And it is the characteristic of an absolute philosophy that everything must be deduced or constructed as a necessity of thought. Hegel's system, accordingly, is so framed as to elude the necessity of resting anywhere on mere fact. It is not enough for him to take self-conscious intelligence as an existent fact, by reflection on whose action in his own conscious experience and in the history of the race certain categories are disclosed, reducible by philosophic insight to a system of mutually connected notions, which may then be viewed as constituting the essence or formal structure of reason. He apparently thinks it incumbent on him to prove that spirit exists by a necessity of thought. The concrete *existence* of the categories (in Nature and Spirit) is to be deduced from their *essence* or thought-nature: it is to be shown they cannot *not* be[2]."

53. Now in this passage there are two separate charges made against Hegel, which Professor Seth apparently thinks are identical. The one is that "thought of its own abstract nature gives birth to the reality of things," that is, that, given

op. cit. pp. 108, 109.   [2] op. cit. pp. 109, 110.

thought, Nature and Spirit can be deduced. That they are deduced from thought in some way cannot be denied, but Professor Seth rejects the idea that the deduction is partly analytical, and declares that Hegel endeavoured to demonstrate the existence of the worlds of Nature and Spirit by pure synthesis from the world of Logic. But this is not all. Hegel is also accused of endeavouring to prove "the concrete *existence* of the categories from their *essence*." This is properly a second charge. But Professor Seth appears to identify it with the first, by speaking of the concrete existence as "in nature and spirit," and by making essence identical with the nature of thought. This identification is, I venture to think, unjustifiable.

In the first place every proposition about Nature and Spirit is not one which involves real existence. We might say, for example, "Dragons must occupy space," or "Angels must have some way of gaining immediate knowledge." Both propositions might be perfectly correct, even if neither dragons nor angels existed, because our propositions would deal only with essence. They might be put in a hypothetical form, such as, "If there were dragons, they would occupy space." (In this discussion I adopt Professor Seth's use of the word essence to signify the nature of a thing, which remains the same, whether the thing exists or not. It must not, of course, be confounded with Hegel's use of the same word to denote the second stage of the Logic, which merely describes one stage among others in what Professor Seth would call the essence of thought.)

On the other hand, as we have seen above, a proposition relating to pure thought may refer to real existence. "Being is synthesised in Becoming" is such a proposition, for the category of Being is applicable, we know, to real existence. And as the essences of Being and Becoming are united, and as the existence of Being has been proved, we are able to state the proposition concerning the relation of Being and Becoming as one of real existence.

The confusion of real existence with the worlds of Nature and Spirit is not inexplicable. For all real existence has its immediate side, and must therefore be presented by sense, outer or inner, while thought, again, is correlative to sense, and, so to speak opposed to it, both being complementary elements in experience. Thought consequently gets taken as if it was opposed to real existence. But the fact of the existence of thought can be presented to us by inner sense as something immediate, and we are then as sure of its real existence as we could be of anything in the world of Nature. The office of thought is to mediate; but it actually exists, or it could not mediate; and in virtue of its actual existence any instance of thought may be immediately known; in which case it is mediated by other thought. The existence of logic proves in itself that we can think about thought. Thought therefore can become a *datum*, and its real existence can be known. It is true that it is an abstraction, and that its real existence is only as an element of experience. But this is true also of the particulars of sense.

54. Since, then, propositions concerning Nature and Spirit may be really " essential and hypothetical" while propositions concerning pure thought may deal with real existence, it follows that the deduction of Nature and Spirit from Logic does not necessarily involve the fallacious attempt to argue from essence to existence. This is the case whether the deduction is both analytic and synthetic in its nature, as I have endeavoured to maintain, or is of a purely synthetic nature, as Professor Seth supposes.

In the first of these suppositions the argument might have been merely from the essence of thought to the essence of Nature. In that case the final conclusion would have run, thought cannot exist without Nature, or, if there is thought there is Nature. Hegel, however, was not satisfied with such a meagre result, and his argument is from existence to existence. The course of the Logic, in the first place, may be summed up thus—we have an immediate certainty that something exists, consequently the category of Being is valid of reality. But the Absolute Idea is involved in the category of Being. Therefore the Absolute Idea is applicable to that which really exists, and we can predicate reality of that Idea. After this follows the transition to the world of Nature, which is of a similar character. The Absolute Idea really exists. But it (since it is of the nature of thought) can only exist in combination with *data* of sense. Therefore *data* of sense really exist. Thus the conclusion certainly deals with real existence, but that character has been given to the argument, not by any juggling with pure thought, but by a premise at the beginning relating to real existence—namely, that *something* must exist. The evidence for this proposition is immediate, for it rests on the impossibility of denying it without asserting at the same time the reality at least of the denial and of the thinker. And this assertion depends on the immediately given, for the existence of the words or ideas which form the denial are perceived by sense, outer or inner, while the existence of the thinker is an inference from, or rather an implication in, the fact that he has sensations or thoughts, of the existence of which—thoughts as well as sensations—he has immediate knowledge.

The same would be the case if the deduction were purely synthetic, one which endeavoured to make the world of Nature and Spirit a mere consequence and result of the world of thought. The argument would be invalid for reasons which we shall presently notice, but not because it attempted to pass from essence to existence. For we have every right to believe that thought exists, and it is from this existent thought (the presence of which *within* the Logic passes unchallenged by Professor Seth), that Hegel passes on to Nature and Spirit.

The two charges then—of deducing Nature and Spirit merely from thought, and of deducing existence from essence— are by no means identical, and must be taken separately. It will perhaps be more convenient to begin with the first, which is the less sweeping of the two.

55. "Thought out of its own abstract nature gives birth to the reality of things" says Professor Seth in his criticism, and, if this is Hegel's meaning, we must certainly admit that he has gone too far. Thought is, in its essential nature, mediate. As Trendelenburg remarks[1] the immediacy of certain ideas in the dialectic is only comparative and equivalent to self-mediation. Real immediacy belongs to nothing but the *data* of intuition. And therefore thought cannot exist unless it has something immediately given which it may mediate. It is, of course, perfectly true that the immediate cannot remain unmediated. The only merely immediate thing is the pure

---

[1] *Logische Untersuchungen*, Vol. I. p. 68.

sensation, and the pure sensation taken by itself cannot become part of experience, and therefore, since it has certainly no existence out of experience, does not exist at all. But although immediacy, as such, is a mere abstraction, so is mediation, and, therefore, thought. Green's extraordinary suggestion that " the notion that an event in the way of sensation is something over and above its conditions may be a mistake of ours[1]," and again that "for the only kind of consciousness for which there is reality, the conceived conditions are the reality," ignores the fact that the ideal of knowledge would in this case be a mass of conditions which conditioned nothing, and of relations with nothing to relate. Such an elevation of an abstraction into an independent reality is not excelled in audacity by any of the parallel fallacies of materialism, against which Green was never weary of protesting.

But if thought is a mere element in the whole of reality, having no more independent existence than mere sense has, it is certainly impossible that thought should produce reality— that the substantial and individual should depend on an abstraction formed from itself. And this is what Hegel believed, if we are to accept Professor Seth's statement.

56. This theory is rendered the more remarkable by the admission that, within the Logic, the deduction has that analytic aspect which is required to make it valid. " The forward movement is in reality a movement backward : it is a retracing of our steps to the world as we know it in the fulness of its real determinations[2]." Can we believe that Hegel, after using one method of dialectic process to display the nature of pure thought, employs the same dialectic in an absolutely different sense when he wishes to pass from logic to nature? Logic, Nature, and Spirit are declared to be thesis, antithesis, and synthesis ; so are Being, Not-Being, and Becoming. In the case of the latter it is admitted that the true reality lies only in the synthesis, and that no attempt is made to construct it out of the thesis. What reason is there for supposing such an attempt in the case of the more comprehensive deduction which we are now discussing?

Professor Seth attempts to answer the question by drawing

---

[1] *Works*, Vol. II. p. 190.   [2] *Hegelianism and Personality*, p. 92.

a distinction between epistemology and ontology in this respect. As to the former, he says, it may be true that Hegel held that we only arrive at a knowledge of pure thought by abstraction from experience, while yet it may be true that he considered that the other element in experience was originally produced by, and is in the objective world dependent on, pure thought. It is perhaps worth remarking that this derives no countenance from Sections 238 and 239 of the Encyclopædia quoted above[1], where the union of analysis and synthesis is spoken of as "the philosophic method" and as belonging to "philosophic thought" without any suggestion that it only applies to one department of philosophy.

But the distinction is one which would only be tenable if the elements of which experience is composed were self-subsistent entities, capable of existing apart as well as together. Thus it might be said that, although in a certain experiment oxygen and hydrogen were produced out of water, yet from a scientific point of view we should rather consider them as the elements of which water was made up, they, and not the water, being the ultimate reality. But this analogy will not hold here. For the element of immediacy—the *datum* given through sense—is as necessary and essential to the existence of the idea, as the sides of a triangle are to its angles. The existence of the immediate element is essential to anything really concrete, and the idea is only an element in, and an abstraction from, the concrete. Now the existence of an abstraction apart from the concrete, or the dependence of the concrete on an abstraction from itself, is a contradiction. And that the idea is a mere abstraction from experience is not merely an accident of a particular way of discovering it, but its very essence. Its existence lies solely in mediation, and it cannot therefore, ever be self-sufficient. It is rather an aspect which we can perceive in experience, than an element which can be separated from it, even ideally, without leading us into error.

Its independent existence would thus be a very glaring contradiction. And for Hegel, as for other people, contradictions could not really exist. Each stage in the Logic is a contradiction, it is true, but then those stages have no independent

---

[1] p. 44.

existence. The self-consistent reality is always behind it. "The consummation of the infinite aim...consists merely in removing the illusion which makes it seem as yet unaccomplished[1]."

57.   And Hegel himself distinctly denies the asserted purely synthetical character of the transition. "It is clear," he says, "that the emergence of Spirit from Nature ought not to be expressed as if nature was the Absolute Immediate, the First, that which originally statutes, and Spirit on the other hand was only statuted (gesetzt) by it; rather is Nature statuted by Spirit, and the latter is the absolute First. Spirit, in and for itself, is not the simple result of Nature, but in truth its own result; it evolves itself out of the assumptions which it itself makes, out of the logical idea and external nature, and is the truth of the former as well as of the latter—that is to say the true form of the Spirit which is merely in itself, and of the Spirit which is merely outside itself. The appearance of the mediation of Spirit by another is transcended by Spirit itself, since this, so to say, has the consummate ingratitude to transcend that through which it seeks to be mediated, to mediatise it, to reduce it to something which only exists through spirit, and in this way to make itself completely independent[2]." Spirit, the final result of the process, is thus declared to be also its logical ground, and the process of the Idea to Nature and from Nature to Spirit has therefore an analytic, as well as a synthetic aspect, since the end of the process is only to come to explicit knowledge of its ground, which, as its ground, must have been present to it all along, though not yet in full and explicit consciousness. It may be remarked that Hegel uses exactly the same metaphor of ingratitude to describe the relation of Spirit to the apparent commencement of the process, as he used long before to express the connection between pure thought and the empirical details, from the consideration of which pure thought started[3]. This may serve as a slight additional reason for our belief in the theory that the force of the transition to Spirit lies in the implicit presence of Spirit all along, and not in a merely synthetic advance from pure thought through Nature.

---

[1] *Enc.* Section 212, lecture notes.

[2] *Enc.* Section 381, lecture note, p. 23.

[3] *Enc.* Section 12, p. 37 above.

For in the logic, as Professor Seth admits, the logical prius of the advance is to be found at the end, and not at the beginning, of the process. We may also compare Section 239 of the Encyclopaedia, lecture note—"the truth is that Nature is due to the statuting of Spirit, and it is Spirit itself which gives itself a presupposition in Nature." This view is incompatible with any attempt to represent Nature as statuted by Logic alone.

58. To deny the purely synthetic deduction of Nature from Logic, which we have just been considering, is not equivalent to denying that there is any deduction at all intended, which would be obviously incorrect. It is implied that these are the only two alternatives, when Professor Seth tells us that the "soberminded Hegelian," who denies the purely synthetic deduction, "will lay as little stress as possible upon the so-called deduction. Further reflection has convinced me, however," he continues, "that Hegel's contention here is of more fundamental importance to his system than such a representation allows. Perhaps it may even be said that, when we surrender this deduction, though we may retain much that is valuable in Hegel's thought, we surrender the system as a whole[1]." No doubt it is essential to the theory that there shall be a deduction, so that the whole system, from the category of Being to Absolute Spirit, shall be bound closely together. But this is not incompatible with the soberminded view of the dialectic, for, as we have seen, the deduction may be one which is analytic as well as synthetic, and may derive its cogency from the implicit presence, at its starting point, of its result.

59. The treatment of the problem of contingency in the dialectic presents a curious alternation between two incompatible points of view, by the first of which contingency is treated as a category, while by the second it is attributed to the incapacity of Nature to realise the Idea. It is not necessary to consider here the criticisms which might be made on either of these explanations. It is sufficient to point out that, while the former does not imply the theory which Professor

[1] *op. cit.* pp. 109, 110.

Seth adopts as to the general purpose of the Logic, the latter is quite incompatible with it.

As to the first, it is to be noticed that the attempt to convert contingency into a logical category is not necessarily identical with an attempt to ignore reality. " The contingent," says Hegel, " roughly speaking, is what has the ground of its being, not in itself, but in somewhat else. ... The contingent is only one side of the actual, the side namely of reflection into somewhat else[1]." It is thus by no means the same thing as the real, which includes, even if it does not consist exclusively of, the self-subsistent entity or entities which have their ground in themselves, or, if that expression be objected to, are primary and without any ground at all. The elimination of the contingent is thus quite compatible with the existence of factual reality. This is confirmed by Hegel's remark in the same section that " to overcome this contingency is, roughly speaking, the problem of science." For the object of ordinary science is certainly not to eliminate factual reality.

The same expression suggests that the elimination of contingency does not, for Hegel, involve the elimination of immediacy. For the object of ordinary science is not to eliminate the data of sense, but to arrange and classify them. And this is confirmed by the definition quoted above. Contingency consists in explanation from the outside. That which can be explained entirely from itself would not, it appears, be contingent to Hegel, even if part of the explanation was given in the form of a mere datum. No doubt at present all immediacy, involving as it does presentation in sense, outer or inner, requires explanation from outside, and is therefore contingent. But, as was pointed out above in a different connection[2], there is nothing in the nature of immediacy which prevents us from supposing a state of knowledge in which the immediate data, being traced back to some self-centred reality, should require no explanation from without, and consequently should lose their contingency, while they preserved their immediacy. The introduction, therefore, of contingency as a category which, like other categories, is transcended, does not

---

[1] *Enc.* Section 145, lecture note.   [2] Section 47.

fairly lead to the conclusion that Hegel believed in the possibility of mediating thought ever becoming self-sufficient.

On the other hand, the theory that contingency is caused by the inability of Nature to realise the idea[1], is clearly incompatible with an attempt to produce Nature out of pure thought. For, if the world of Nature, as such an attempt would require, is deduced by pure synthesis from the world of reason, and by the free passage of the latter, how can the impotence arise? The only possible explanation of such impotence must be in some independent element, which the idea cannot perfectly subdue, and this is inconsistent with the theory of pure synthesis. It may be doubted whether this view is compatible with the general theory of the dialectic at all. But it is certainly, as Professor Seth admits[2], quite incompatible with "an absolute philosophy" in his use of the phrase. If this was Hegel's view of contingency, it must be taken as a proof of the presence of an analytic element in the process. For then the failure of thought to embody itself completely in nature, whether consistent or not, would not be so glaringly inconsistent as in the other case. It might then possibly be a casual error. But it is difficult to suppose that Hegel could have slipped by mistake into the assertion that thought, while producing the whole universe, was met in it by an alien element.

60. We must now proceed to the second charge made against the transition from the Logic—that it involves an argument from essence to existence. Such an argument would doubtless be completely fallacious. Any proposition about existence must either be directly based on immediate experience of reality, or must be connected, by a chain of inferences, with a proposition that is so based. The difference between the real and the ideal worlds is one which mere thought can never bridge over, because, for mere thought, it does not exist. As Kant says, the difference between twenty real thalers and twenty thalers which are only imagined to be real, does not appear in the idea of them, which is the same whether they exist or not. The difference lies in the reference to reality, which makes no part of the idea. If, therefore, we confined ourselves to thought, we should be unable to discover whether

---

[1] *Enc.* Section 16.   [2] *op. cit.* p. 139.

our thalers were in truth real, or whether we had only imagined their reality. And even if, starting from the nature of thought taken in abstraction from sense, we could evolve the idea of the entire universe (and we have seen[1] that without sense we could perceive nothing of the nature of thought), it would remain purely ideal, and never be able to explain the fact that the world actually existed. For the difference between the real world, and a world, exactly like it, but only imagined to exist, is a difference which pure thought could not perceive, and therefore could not remove. It is impossible to argue that contradictions would drive it on, for the contradictions of thought, as we have seen, arise from its being abstract, and can do no more than restore the concrete whole from which a start was made. If reality was not given as a characteristic of that concrete whole, no abstraction from it will afford a basis from which the dialectic process can attain to reality.

61. Before, however, we decide that Hegel has been guilty of so great a confusion, we should require convincing evidence that his language must be interpreted to mean that existence in reality can be deduced from the essence of thought. And the evidence offered seems by no means sufficient.

In discussing the first charge made by Professor Seth, I have given reasons for supposing that the analytic aspect of the method, which Professor Seth admits to be present within the Logic, is also to be found in the transition from Logic to Nature and Spirit. Now we have seen above[2] that the absence of such an analytic element would not imply of necessity that the argument is from essence to existence. But, on the other hand, the presence of that element would render it certain that no attempt was made to proceed to existence from essence. For the presence of the analytic aspect in the transition means that we are working towards the development, in explicit consciousness, of the full value of the whole which was previously before us in implicit consciousness, and the existence of this whole is the motive force of the transition. If, therefore, the result reached by the dialectic has real existence, so also the *datum*, of which the dialectic process is an analysis,

---

[1] Section 14.   [2] Section 54.

must have real existence. The argument is thus from existence to existence. That a movement is in any way analytic implies that its result is given, at any rate implicitly, in its *data*. But an argument from essence to existence would most emphatically go beyond its *data*, producing something fresh. If, therefore, we have reason to reject the first charge of Professor Seth against the validity of the transition from the Logic to the rest of the system, the second charge falls to the ground with it.

62. In defence of his view Professor Seth, pointing out that Hegel calls his philosophy absolute, says that "it is the characteristic of an absolute philosophy that everything must be deduced or constructed as a necessity of thought[1]." No quotations, however, are given from Hegel in support of this interpretation. And the one definition which Hegel himself gives of the word in the Enyclopaedia turns on quite a different point. "According to Kant, the things that we know about are *to us* appearances only, and we can never know their essential nature, which belongs to another world, which we cannot approach.... The true statement of the case is rather as follows. The things of which we have direct consciousness are mere phenomena, not for us only, but in their own nature; and the true and proper case of these things, finite as they are, is to have their existence founded not in themselves but in the universal divine Idea. This view of things, it is true, is as idealist as Kant's, but in contradistinction to the subjective idealism of the Critical Philosophy should be termed absolute idealism[2]." The meaning of the epithet Absolute is here placed exclusively in the rejection of the Kantian theory that knowledge is only of phenomena. But the assertion that reality may in itself become the object of knowledge is not equivalent to the assertion that conclusions regarding reality can be reached by merely considering the nature of thought. If Absolute had this additional and remarkable meaning Hegel would surely have mentioned it explicitly.

63. Again, Hegel rejects Kant's well known criticism on the ontological proof of the existence of God, and, as this criticism turns on the impossibility of predicating reality

---

[1] *op. cit.* p. 110.   [2] *Enc.* Section 45, lecture note.

through any arguments based only on the definition of the subject, it has been supposed that Hegel did not see this impossibility. "It would be strange," Hegel says, "if the Notion, the very inmost of mind, if even the Ego, or above all the concrete totality we call God were not rich enough to include so poor a category as Being[1]." "Most assuredly" is Professor Seth's comment on this, "the Notion contains the *category* of Being; so does the Ego, that is to say, the Idea of the Ego, and the Idea of God, both of which are simply the Notion under another name. The category of Being is contained in the Ego and may be disengaged from it." But, he continues, "It is not the *category* 'Being' of which we are in quest, but that reality of which all categories are only descriptions, and which itself can only be experienced, immediately known, or lived. To such reality or factual existence, there is no logical bridge[2]."

But before we conclude that Hegel has asserted the existence of such a logical bridge, it will be well to bear in mind his warning in the section quoted above, that in God "we have an object of another kind than any hundred thalers, and unlike any one particular notion, representation, or whatever else it may be called." In what this peculiarity consists is not clearly explained here. But in the middle of the preceding section we find, "That upward spring of the mind signifies that the being which the world has is only a semblance, no real being, no absolute truth; it signifies that beyond and above that appearance, truth abides in God, so that true being is another name for God[3]."

Now, if God is identical with all true being, he certainly has "that reality of which all categories are only descriptions." For, if he has not, nothing has it, since there is no reality outside him, and the denial of all reality is as impossible as the denial of all truth,—to deny it is to assert it. For if the denial is true, it must be real, and so must the person who makes it. The only question then is whether the category of Being can be predicated of this real God, and in this case Professor Seth admits that Hegel was quite right in his judgment that the predication could be made, if it was worth while. It would

---

[1] *Enc.* Section 51.   [2] *op. cit.* p. 119.   [3] *Enc.* Section 50.

seem then that he is scarcely justified in charging Hegel with endeavouring to construct a logical bridge to real or factual existence. Hegel was speaking of something whose real existence could not be doubted except by a scepticism which extended to self-contradiction. Thus he considered himself entitled to assume in his exposition the actual existence of God, and only deliberated whether the predicate of Being could or could not be attached to this existence. To do this he pronounced to be perfectly legitimate, and perfectly useless— legitimate, because we can say of all reality that it is; useless, because the full depth of reality, in which all categories can be found, is expressed so inadequately by this, the simplest and most abstract of all the categories.

64. Kant's objections do not affect such an ontological argument as this. He shows, no doubt, that we have no right to conclude that anything really exists, on the ground that we have made real existence part of the conception of the thing. No possible attribute, which would belong to the thing if it existed, can give us any reason to suppose that it does exist. But this was not Hegel's argument. He did not try to prove God's existence simply from the divine attributes. He relied on two facts. The first was that the conception of God proved that all attributes predicated of anything must, in the last resort, be predicated of God. The second was that experience did exist, and consequently that attributes must be predicated of some existent subject, to account for experience. The important point in the conception of God, for Hegel's purpose here, was not that he was the most real of beings, nor that he contained all positive qualities, but that he was the *only* real being. For the existence of an *ens realissimum* or of an *omnitudo realitatis* can be denied. But the existence of all reality cannot be denied, for its denial would be contradictory. And, on Hegel's definition, to deny God's existence is equivalent to denying all reality, for " true being is another name for God."

" If, in an identical judgment," says Kant, " I reject the predicate and retain the subject, there arises a contradiction and hence I say that the former belongs to the latter necessarily. But if I reject the subject as well as the predicate there is no contradiction, because there is nothing left which can be contradicted.... The same applies to the concept of an absolutely necessary being. Remove its existence, and you remove the thing itself, with all its predicates, so that a contradiction becomes impossible[1]." But the Hegelian argument rests on the fact that you cannot remove "the thing itself" because the statement by which you do it, and yourself likewise, are actually existent, and must have some ultimate reality behind them, which ultimate reality, called by Hegel God, is the thing whose removal is in question. Thus there *is* a contradiction. You can only get rid of the Hegelian God by getting rid of the entire universe. And to do this is impossible.

It must be noticed, however, that this form of the ontological argument can only prove the existence of a God who is conceived as the sole reality in the universe. If we ourselves, or anything else, are conceived as existing, except as parts of him, then the denial of his existence does not involve the denial of *all* reality, and has therefore no contradiction contained in it. Kant's refutation will stand as against all attempts to prove, by the ontological argument, the existence of a God not conceived as immanent in all existence. It will also be conclusive against all attempts to demonstrate, by means of the ontological argument, any particular quality or attribute of God, unless that attribute can be shown to be essential to his all-inclusive reality, in which case, of course, we should, by denying it, deny the reality also. Kant was right in holding that the ontological argument could not establish the existence of a God, as conceived by his dogmatic predecessors, or as conceived by himself in the Critique of Practical Reason. Hegel was right in holding that it was valid of a God, defined in the Hegelian manner.

65. Professor Seth also relies on Hegel's treatment of the individual character of existence. "He adroitly contrives to insinuate that, because it is undefinable, the individual is therefore a valueless abstraction[2]." And he quotes from the Smaller Logic, " Sensible existence has been characterised by

---

[1] *Critique of Pure Reason*, Book ii. Chap. iii. Section 4.
[2] *op. cit.* p. 128.

the attributes of individuality, and a mutual exclusion of the members. It is well to remember that these very attributes are thoughts and general terms.... Language is the work of thought, and hence all that is expressed in language must be universal.... And what cannot be uttered, feeling or sensation, far from being the highest truth is the most unimportant and untrue[1]." Professor Seth calls this "Hegel's insinuated disparagement of the individual." But, if anything is disparaged, it is not the individual, but sensible existence. When we say that individuality is not a quality of sensible existence, but depends upon thought, this diminishes the fullness and reality of sensible existence, but not necessarily of individuality. And it is of vital importance which of these two it is which Hegel disparages. For "the individual is the real," and an attack on individuality, an attempt to make it a mere product of thought, would go far to prove that Hegel did cherish the idea of reducing the whole universe to a manifestation of pure thought. "The meanest thing that exists has a life of its own, absolutely unique and individual, which we can partly *understand* by terms borrowed from our own experience, but which is no more identical with, or in any way like, the description we give of it, than our own inner life is identical with the description we give of it in a book of philosophy[2]." But to deny the importance of the sensible element in experience, taken as independent, is justifiable.

It is no doubt perfectly true that we are only entitled to say that a thing is real, when we base that judgment on some *datum* immediately given to us, and also that those *data* can only be given us by sense,—inner or outer. But it does not at all follow that the sensible, taken by itself, is real. Thought also is essential to reality. In the first place it would be impossible for us to be self-conscious without thought, since mere unrelated sensation is incompatible with self-consciousness. Now without self-consciousness nothing would be real for us. Without self-consciousness sensations could not exist. For an unperceived sensation is a contradiction. Sensations exist only in being perceived; and perception is impossible without com-

---

[1] *Enc.* Section 20.   [2] *Hegelianism and Personality*, p. 125.

parison at the least, which involves thought, and so self-consciousness.

Mere sensation may surely then be called unimportant—even Kant called it blind—since it has no reality at all, except in a unity in which it is not *mere* sensation. It is as much an abstraction as mere thought is. The importance lies only in the concrete whole of which they are both parts, and this reality is not to be considered as if it was built up out of thought and sensation. In that case the mere sensation might be said to have some reality, though only in combination. But here the sensation, as a mere abstraction, must be held not to exist in the concrete reality, but merely to be capable of distinction in it, and thus to have of itself no reality whatever.

It is of course true that it is only the immediate contents of experience which need mediation by thought to give them reality, and not self-subsistent entities,—such as our own selves. But Hegel's charge of unimportance was made against sensations, which are not self-subsistent entities, but simply part of the content of experience.

In the Introductory Chapter, in which the passage quoted above is found, Hegel was merely trying to prove that thought was essential, not that it was all-sufficient. It will therefore quite agree with the context if we take this view of what it was to which he denied importance. It would certainly have made his position clearer, if he had, at the same time, asserted the abstractness and unimportance of thought without sense, as emphatically as he had asserted the abstractness and unimportance of sense without thought, but the former is implied in the passages[1] by which the dialectic is made to depend on experience, and explicitly affirmed in the passage from the Philosophy of Spirit[2] in which the logical idea is declared to be dependent on Spirit, and to be mediated by it. For in Spirit we have the union of the two sides which, when separated, present themselves to us as the mediating thought and the immediate *datum*.

66. We are told also that the tendency of the whole system is towards the undue exaltation of logic and essence, at the

---

[1] Sections 33–42 above.   [2] Section 43 above.

expense of nature and reality. In support of this it is said that, although Hegel "talks (and by the idiom of the language cannot avoid talking) of 'der absolute Geist' (the absolute spirit) that by no means implies, as the literal English translation does, that he is speaking of God as a Subjective Spirit, a singular intelligence....... The article goes with the noun in any case, according to German usage; and 'absolute spirit' has no more necessary reference to a Concrete Subject than the simple 'spirit' or intelligence which preceded it[1]." It may be the case that Hegel did not conceive Absolute Spirit as a single intelligence. Indeed it seems probable that he did not do so, but the point is too large to be discussed here. But even in that case, it does not follow that the Absolute Spirit cannot be concrete. If it is conceived as an organism or society of finite intelligences, it will still be a concrete subject, although it will possess no self-consciousness or personality of its own. If it is regarded as manifested in an unconnected agglomeration of finite intelligences, it may not be a subject, but will still be concrete, since it will consist of the finite intelligences, which are certainly concrete. No doubt, if a definition or description be asked for of Absolute Spirit, the answer, like all definitions or descriptions, will be in abstract terms, but a definition, though in abstract terms, may be the definition of a concrete thing. Even if the Absolute Spirit was a singular intelligence, any explanation of its nature would have to be made by ascribing to it predicates, which are necessarily abstract terms.

And against this asserted tendency on Hegel's part to take refuge in abstractions we may set his own explicit declarations. He continually uses abstract as a term of reproach and declares that the concrete alone is true. Now it cannot be denied that Nature is more concrete than the pure idea, or that Spirit is more concrete than Nature. This would lead us, apart from other considerations, to suppose that the logical prius of the universe was to be looked for in Spirit, which is the most concrete of all things[2], and not in the Idea, which is only imperfectly concrete, even in its highest form.

[1] *Hegelianism and Personality*, p. 151.
[2] *Philosophy of Spirit*, Section 377, p. 3.

CHAPTER III.

67. THE question now arises, whether the dialectic as sketched in the last two chapters, is a valid system of philosophy. The consideration of this question here must necessarily be extremely incomplete. Some seventy or eighty transitions from one category to another may be found in the Logic, and we should have to consider the correctness of each one of these, before we could pronounce the dialectic, in its present form at least, to be correct. For a chain is no stronger than its weakest link, and if a single transition is inconclusive, it must render all that comes beyond it uncertain. All we can do here is to consider whether the starting point and the general method of the dialectic are valid, without enquiring into its details.

We shall have in the first place to justify the dialectical procedure—so different from that which the understanding uses in the affairs of every-day life. To do this we must show, first, that the ordinary use of the Understanding implies a demand for the complete explanation of the universe, and then that such an explanation cannot be given by the Understanding, and can be given by the Reason in its dialectical use, so that the Understanding itself postulates in this way the validity of dialectic thought. In the second place we must prove that the point from which the dialectic starts is one which it may legitimately take for granted, and that the nature of the advance and its relation to experience are such as will render the dialectic a valid theory of knowledge. In this connection the relation of the idea of Movement to the dialectic process must also be considered. And finally the question will arise whether we are justified in applying this theory of knowledge as also a theory of being, and in deducing the worlds of Nature and Spirit from the world of Logic.

68. It is to be noticed that both the first and second arguments are of a transcendental nature. We start respectively from the common thought of the Understanding, and from the idea of Being, and we endeavour to prove the validity of the speculative method and of the Absolute Idea, because they are assumed in, and postulated by, the propositions from which we started. Before going further, therefore, we ought to consider some general objections which have been made against transcendental arguments as such.

They have been stated with great clearness by Mr Arthur Balfour in his Defence of Philosophic Doubt. " When a man," he says, " is convinced by a transcendental argument, it must be...because he perceives that a certain relation or principle is necessary to constitute his admitted experience. This is to him a fact, the truth of which he is obliged to recognise. But another fact, which he may also find it hard to dispute, is that he himself, and, as it would appear, the majority of mankind, have habitually had this experience without ever thinking it under this relation; and this second fact is one which it does not seem easy to interpret in a manner which shall harmonise with the general theory. The transcendentalist would, no doubt, say at once that the relation in question had always been thought implicitly, even if it had not always come into clear consciousness; and having enunciated this dictum he would trouble himself no further about a matter which belonged merely to the 'history of the individual.' But if an implicit thought means in this connection what it means everywhere else, it is simply a thought which is logically bound up in some other thought, and which for that reason may always be called into existence by it. Now from this very definition, it is plain that so long as a thought is implicit it does not exist. It is a mere possibility, which may indeed at any moment become an actuality, and which, when once an actuality, may be indestructible; but which so long as it is a possibility can be said to have existence only by a figure of speech.

"If, therefore, this meaning of the word 'implicit' be accepted, we find ourselves in a difficulty. *Either* an object can exist and be a reality to an intelligence which does not think of it under relations which, as I now see, are involved in it, *i.e.* without which I cannot now think of it as an object; *or else* I am in error, when I suppose myself and other people to have ignored these relations in past times[1]."

The second of these alternatives, as Mr Balfour points out, cannot be adopted. It is certain that a large part of mankind have never embraced the transcendental philosophy, and that even those who accept it did not do so from their earliest childhood. It follows, he continues, that we must accept the first alternative, in which case the whole transcendental system "vanishes in smoke."

69. The dilemma, however, as it seems to me, rests upon a confusion of the two different senses in which we may be said to be conscious of thought. We may be said, in the first place, to be conscious of it whenever we are conscious of a whole experience in which it is an element. In this sense we must be conscious of all thought which exists at all. We must agree with Mr Balfour that "if the consciousness vanishes, the thought must vanish too, since, except on some crude materialistic hypothesis, they are the same thing[2]." But in the second sense we are only conscious of a particular thought when we have singled it out from the mass of sensations and thoughts, into which experience may be analysed, when we have distinguished it from the other constituents of experience, and know it to be a thought, and know what thought it is. In this sense we may have thought without being conscious of it. And indeed we *must* always have it, before we can be conscious of it in this sense. For thought first comes before us as an element in the whole of experience, and it is not till we have analysed that whole, and separated thought from sensation, and one thought from another, that we know we have a particular thought. Till then we have the thought without being explicitly conscious that we have it.

Now I submit that Mr Balfour's argument depends on a

---

[1] *Defence of Philosophic Doubt*, p. 94.   [2] *op. cit.* p. 100.

paralogism. When he asserts that we must always be conscious of any relation which is necessary to constitute experience, he is using "to be conscious of" in the first sense. When he asserts that all people are not always conscious of all the ideas of the dialectic as necessary elements in experience, he is using "to be conscious of" in the second sense. And if we remove this ambiguity the difficulty vanishes.

We are only conscious of thought as an element in experience. Of thought outside experience we could not be conscious in any sense of the word, for thought except as relating and mediating *data* cannot even be conceived. But thought of which we are not conscious at all is, as Mr Balfour remarks, a non-entity. And no thought does exist outside experience. Both thought and the immediate *data* which it mediates exist only as combined in the whole of experience, which is what comes first into consciousness. In this lie the various threads of thought and sensation, of which we may be said to be conscious, in so far as we are conscious of the whole of which they are indispensable elements. But we do not know how many, nor of what nature, the threads are, until we have analysed the whole in which they are first presented to us, nor, till then, do we clearly see that the whole is made up of separate elements. Even to know this involves some thinking about thought. There is no contradiction between declaring that certain relations must enter into all conscious thought, and admitting that those relations are known *as such* only to those who have endeavoured to divide the whole of experience into its constituent parts, and have succeeded in the attempt.

The use of the word "implicit" to which Mr Balfour objects, can be explained in the same way. If it means only what he supposes, so that an implicit thought is nothing but one "which is logically bound up in some other thought, and which for that reason may always be called into existence by it"—then indeed to say that a thought is implicit is equivalent to saying that it does not exist. But if we use the word—and there seems no reason why we should not—in the sense suggested by its derivation, in which it means that which is wrapped up in something else, then it is clear that a thing may be implicit, and so not distinctly seen to be itself, while it nevertheless exists and is perceived as part of the whole in which it is involved.

70. In speaking of such an answer to his criticisms, Mr Balfour objects that it concedes more than transcendentalism can afford to allow. "If relations can exist otherwise than as they are thought, why should not sensations do the same? Why should not the 'perpetual flux' of unrelated objects—the metaphysical spectre which the modern transcendentalist labours so hard to lay—why, I say, should this not have a real existence? *We*, indeed, cannot in our reflective moments think of it except under relations which give it a kind of unity; but once allow that an object may exist, but in such a manner as to make it nothing for us as thinking beings, and this incapacity may be simply due to the fact that thought is powerless to grasp the reality of things[1]."

This, however, is not a fair statement of the position. The transcendentalist does not assert that an object can exist in such a manner as to be nothing for us as thinking beings, but only that it may exist, and be something for us as thinking beings, although we do not recognise the conditions on which its existence for us depends. Thus we are able to admit that thought exists even for those people who have never made the slightest reflection on its nature. And, in the same way, no doubt, we can be conscious of related sensations without seeing that they are related, for we may never have analysed experience as presented to us into its mutually dependent elements of sensation and thought. But it does not follow that sensations could exist unrelated. That would mean that something existed in consciousness (for sensations exist no-where else), which not only is not perceived to comply with the laws of consciousness, but which actually does not comply with them. And this is quite a different proposition, and an impossible one.

71. Passing now to the peculiarities of the dialectic method, their justification must be one which will commend itself to the Understanding—that is to thought, when, as happens in ordinary life, it acts according to the laws of formal logic, and treats the various categories as stable and independent

---

[1] *op. cit.* p. 101.

entities, which have no relation to one another, but that of exclusion. For if speculative thought, or Reason, cannot be justified before the Understanding, there will be an essential dualism in the nature of thought, incompatible with any satisfactory philosophy. And since mankind naturally, and until cause is shown to the contrary, takes up the position of the Understanding, it will be impossible that we can have any logical right to enter on the dialectic, unless we can justify it from that standpoint, from which we must set out when we first begin to investigate metaphysical questions.

The first step towards this proof is the recognition that the Understanding necessarily demands an absolute and complete explanation of the universe. In dealing with this point, Hartmann[1] identifies the longing for the Absolute, on which Hegel here relies, with the longing to "smuggle back" into our beliefs the God whom Kant had rejected from metaphysics. God, however, is an ideal whose reality may be demanded on the part either of theoretical or of practical reason. It is therefore not very easy to see whether Hartmann meant that the longing, as he calls it, after the Absolute, is indulged only in the interest of religion and ethics, or whether he admits that it is demanded, whether justifiably or not, by the nature of knowledge. The use of the term "longing," (Sehnsucht), however, and the expressions "mystisch-religiöses Bedürfuiss," and "unverständliche Gefühle," which he applies to it, seem rather to suggest the former alternative.

In this case grave injustice is done to the Hegelian position. The philosopher does not believe in the Absolute merely because he desires it should exist. The postulate is not only an emotional or ethical one, nor is the Absolute itself by any means primarily a religious ideal, whatever it may subsequently become. If, for example, we take the definition given in the Smaller Logic, "der Begriff der Idee, dem die Idee als solche der Gegenstand, dem das Objekt sie ist[2]," it is manifest that what is here chiefly regarded is not a need of religion, but of cognition. Indeed the whole course of the Logic shows us that it is the desire for complete knowledge, and the impatience of knowledge which is seen to be unsatisfactory, which act as the

---

[1] *Ueber die dialektische Methode*, B. II. 4.   [2] *Enc.* Section 236.

motive power of the system. It is possible, no doubt, that Hegel's object in devoting himself to philosophy at all was, as has often been the case with philosophers, mainly practical, and that his interest in the absolute was excited from the side of ethics and religion rather than of pure thought. But so long as he did not use this interest as an argument, it does not weaken his position. The ultimate aim which a philosopher has in his studies is irrelevant to our criticism of his results, if the latter are valid in themselves.

72. The need of the Absolute is thus a need of cognition. We must ask, then, whether the Understanding, in its attempts to solve particular problems, demands a complete explanation of the universe, and the attainment of the ideal of knowledge? This question must be answered in the affirmative. For although we start with particular problems, the answer to each of these will raise fresh questions, which must be solved before the original difficulty can be held to be really answered, and this process goes on indefinitely, till we find that the whole universe is involved in a complete answer to even the slightest question. As was pointed out above[1] any explanation of anything by means of the surrounding circumstances, of an antecedent cause, or of its constituent parts, must necessarily raise fresh questions as to the surroundings of those surroundings, the causes of those causes, or the parts of those parts, and such series of questions, if once started, cannot stop until they reach the knowledge of the whole surrounding universe, of the whole of past time, or of the ultimate atoms, which it is impossible to subdivide further.

In fact, to state the matter generally, any question which the Understanding puts to itself must be either, What is the meaning of the universe? or, What is the meaning of some part of the universe? The first is obviously only to be answered by attaining the absolute ideal of knowledge. The second again can only be answered by answering the first. For if a thing is part of a whole it must stand in some relation to the other parts. The other parts must therefore have some influence on it, and part of the explanation of its nature must lie in these other parts. From the mere fact that they are

[1] Section 13.

parts of the same universe, they must all be connected, directly
or indirectly.

73. The Understanding, then, demands the ideal of knowledge, and postulates it whenever it asks a question. Can it,
we must now enquire, attain, by its own exertions, to the ideal
which it postulates? It has before it the same categories as the
Reason, but it differs from the Reason in not seeing that the
higher categories are the inevitable result of the lower, and in
believing that the lower are stable and independent. "Thought,
as Understanding, sticks to fixity of characters, and their
distinctness from one another: every such limited abstract it
treats as having a subsistence and being of its own[1]." It can
use the higher categories, then, but it has no proof of their
validity, which can only be demonstrated, as was explained in
Chap. I., by showing that they are involved in the lower ones,
and finally in the simplest of all. Nor does it see that an
explanation by a higher category relieves us from the necessity
of finding a consistent explanation by a lower one. For it does
not know, as the Reason does, that the lower categories are
abstractions from the higher, and are unfit to be used for the
ultimate explanation of anything, except in so far as they are
moments in a higher unity.

It is this last defect which prevents the Understanding
from ever attaining a complete explanation of the universe.
There is, as we have said, nothing to prevent the Understanding
from using the highest category, that of the Absolute Idea.
It contains indeed a synthesis of contradictions, which the
Understanding is bound to regard as a mark of error, but so
does every category above Being and Not-Being, and the
Understanding nevertheless uses these categories, not perceiving that they violate the law of contradiction, as conceived
by formal logic. It might therefore use the Absolute Idea as
a means of explaining the universe, if it happened to come
across it (for the perception of the necessary development of
that idea from the lower categories belongs only to the Reason)
but it would not see that it summed up all other categories.

And this would prevent the explanation from being completely satisfactory. For the only way in which contradictions

---

[1] *Enc.* Section 80.

caused by the use of the lower categories can be removed by the employment of the Absolute Idea lies in the synthesis, by the Absolute Idea, of those lower categories. They must be seen to be abstractions from it, to have truth only in so far as they are moments in it, and to have no right to claim existence or validity as independent. This can only be known by means of the Reason. For the Understanding each category is independent and ultimate. And therefore any contradictions in which the Understanding may be involved through the use of the lower categories can have no solution for the Understanding itself. Till we can rise above the lower categories, by seeing that they express only inadequate and imperfect points of view, the contradictions into which they lead us must remain to deface our system of knowledge. And for this deliverance we must wait for the Reason.

74. If the lower categories do produce contradictions, then, we can only extricate ourselves from our difficulty by aid of the Reason. But are such contradictions produced, in fact, when we treat those categories as ultimate and endeavour to completely explain anything by them? This question would be most fitly answered by pointing out the actual contradictions in each case, which is what Hegel undertakes throughout the Logic. To examine the correctness of his argument in each separate case would be beyond the scope of this work. We may however point out that this doctrine did not originate with Hegel. In the early Greek philosophy we have demonstrations of the contradictions inherent in the idea of Motion, and traces of a dialectic process are found by Hegel in Plato. Kant, also, has shown in his Antinomies that the attempt to use the lower categories as complete explanations of existence leads with equal necessity to directly contradictory conclusions.

And we may say on general grounds that any category which involves an infinite regress must lead to contradictions. Such are, for example, the category of Force, which explains things as manifestations of a force, the nature of which must be determined by previous manifestations, and the category of Causality, which traces things to their causes, which causes again are effects and must have other causes found for them. Such an infinite regress can never be finished. And an unfinished regress, which we admit ought to be continued, explains nothing, while to impose an arbitrary limit on it is clearly unjustifiable.

Again, all categories having no ground of self-differentiation in themselves may be pronounced to be in the long run unsatisfactory. For thought demands an explanation which shall unify the data to be explained, and these data are in themselves various. If the explanation, therefore, is to be complete, and not to leave something unaccounted for, it must show that there is a necessary connection between the unity of the principle and the plurality of the manifestation.

Now many of the lower categories do involve an infinite regress, and are wanting in any principle of self-differentiation. They cannot, therefore, escape falling into contradictions, and as the Understanding cannot, as the Reason can, remove the difficulties by regarding these categories as sides of a higher truth in which the contradiction vanishes, the contradictions remain permanent, and prevent the Understanding from reaching that ideal of knowledge at which it aims.

75. On this subject Hartmann[1] reminds us that Hegel confesses that the Understanding cannot think a contradiction —in the sense of unifying it and explaining it. All, as he rightly points out, that the Understanding can do is to be conscious of the existence of contradictions. This, he contends, will not serve Hegel's purpose of justifying the Reason. For, since the recognition of the existence of contradictions can never change the incapacity of the Understanding to think them, the only result would be " a heterogeneity or inconsequence " of being, which presents these contradictions, and thought, which is unable to think them. This inconsequence might end, if Hegel's assertion be correct that contradictions are everywhere, in a total separation between thought and being, but could have no tendency to make thought dissatisfied with the procedure of the Understanding, and willing to embrace that of the Reason.

This, however, misrepresents Hegel's position. The contradictions are not in being, as opposed to thought. They are in all finite thought, whenever it attempts to work at all. The contradiction on which the dialectic relies is, that, if we use

[1] *op. cit.* B. II. 4.

one finite category of any subject-matter, we find ourselves compelled, if we examine what is implied in using, to use also, of the same subject-matter, its contrary. The Understanding recognises this contradiction, while at the same time it cannot think it,—cannot, that is, look at it from any point of view from which the contradiction should disappear. It cannot therefore take refuge in the theory that there is a heterogeneity between itself and being, for it is in its own working that it finds something wrong. If the law of contradiction holds, thought must be wrong when it is inevitably led to ascribe contrary predicates to the same subject, while if the law of contradiction did not hold, no thought would be possible at all. And if, as the dialectic maintains, such contradictions occur with every finite category—that is, whenever the Understanding is used, the Understanding must itself confess that there is always a contradiction in its operations, discoverable when they are scrutinised with sufficient keenness. Either, then, there is no valid thought at all—a supposition which contradicts itself, —or there must be some form of thought which can harmonise the contradictions which the Understanding can only recognise.

76. But if the Understanding is reduced to a confession of its own insufficiency, is the Reason any better off? Does the solution offered by the Reason supply that complete ideal of knowledge which all thought demands? The answer to this question will depend in part on the actual success which the Absolute Idea may have in explaining the problems before us so as to give satisfaction to our own minds. But the difference between the indication in general terms of the true explanation, and the working out of that explanation in detail is so enormous, that we shall find but little guidance here. It may be true that "the best proof that the universe is rational lies in rationalising it," but, if so, it is a proof which is practically unattainable[1].

The only general proof open to us is a negative one. The dialectic comes to the conclusion that each of the lower categories cannot be regarded as ultimate, because in each, on examination, it finds an inherent contradiction. In proportion as careful consideration and scrutiny fail to reveal any corre-

[1] Cf. Chap. VII.

sponding contradiction in the Absolute Idea, we may rely on the conclusion of the dialectic that it is the ultimate and only really adequate category.

It may, however, be worth while to point out that the Absolute Idea does comply with several requirements which we should be disposed to regard à *priori* as necessary for an idea which should prove itself adequate to the task of offering a complete explanation of the universe. The explanation afforded by the use of the Absolute Idea is that in all reality the idea, while it finds an independent Other given to it, finally learns that in that Other there is nothing alien to itself, so that it finds itself in everything. The key which is applied is thus the idea of the human mind itself, as engaged in activity, whether theoretical or practical. Such an explanation, if it can be proved to be true, must, it would seem, be satisfactory to us. For we can reach no standing point outside the human mind, from which we could pronounce that an explanation which showed the intelligibility of the whole universe, and its fundamental similarity to that mind, was unsatisfactory. Our object, in pursuit of which we rejected the limitations of the Understanding and took to the use of the Reason, was to explain, that is, to rationalise the universe. And it would be impossible to rationalise it more than this category does, which regards it as the manifestation and incarnation of reason.

77.   What then should be the attitude of the Understanding towards the Reason ? We have shown that the Understanding at once postulates, and cannot attain, a complete and harmonious ideal of knowledge. Supposing that the Reason can, as it asserts, attain this ideal, is the Understanding therefore bound to admit its validity ?

It is no doubt perfectly true, as Hartmann points out [1], that our power of seeking for anything, or even the necessity we may be under of seeking it, is not in itself the least proof that we shall succeed in our search. It does not then *directly* follow that, because there is no other way than the Reason by which we could attain that which the Understanding postulates, we can therefore attain it by means of the Reason. And this might have been a decisive consideration if Hegel had at-

[1] *op. cit.* II. B. 4.

tempted to prove the validity of the Reason to the Understanding in a positive manner. But to do this would have been unnecessary, and, indeed, self-destructive. For such a proof would have gone too far. It would have proved that there was nothing in the Reason which was not also in the Understanding —in other words, that there was no difference between them. If there are two varieties of thought, of which one is higher and more comprehensive than the other, it will be impossible from the nature of the case for the lower and narrower to be directly aware that the higher is valid. From the very fact that the higher will have canons of thought not accepted by the lower, it must appear invalid to the latter, which can only be forced to accept it by external and indirect proof of its truth. And of this sort is the justification which the Reason does offer to the Understanding. It proves that we have a need which the Understanding must recognise, but cannot satisfy. This leaves the hearer with two alternatives. He may admit the need and deny that it can be satisfied in any way, which, in the case of a fundamental postulate of thought, would involve complete scepticism. If he does not do this, he must accept the validity of the Reason, as the only source by which the demand can be satisfied.

The first alternative, however, in a case like this, is only nominal. If we have to choose between a particular theory and complete scepticism, we have, in fact, no choice at all. For complete scepticism is impossible, contradicted as it would be by the very speech or thought which asserted it. If Hegel's demonstrations are correct, there is to be found in every thought something which for the Understanding is a contradiction. But to reject all thought as incorrect is impossible. There must therefore be some mode of thought, higher than the Understanding, and supplementary to it, by which we may be justified in doing continually that which the Understanding will not allow us to do at all. And this is the Reason.

78. We are thus enabled to reject Hartmann's criticism that the dialectic violates all the tendencies of modern thought, by sundering the mind into two parts, which have nothing in common with one another[1]. The Understanding and the

---

[1] op. cit. II. B. 3.

Reason have this in common, that the Reason is the only method of solving the problems which are raised by the Understanding, and therefore can justify its existence on the principles which the Understanding recognises. For the distinctive mark of the Reason is, as Hegel says, that "it apprehends the unity of the categories in their opposition," that it perceives that all concrete categories are made up of reconciled contradictions, and that it is only in these syntheses that the contradictory categories find their true meaning. Now this apprehension is not needed in order to detect the contradictions which the finite categories involve. This can be done by the Understanding. And when the Understanding has done this, it has at any rate proved its own impotence, and therefore can scarcely be said to be essentially opposed to Reason, since it has forfeited its claim to any thorough or consistent use at all.

The whole justification of the Reason, as the necessary complement of the Understanding, is repeated in each triad of the Logic. The fact that the thesis leads of necessity to the antithesis, which is its contrary, is one of the contradictions which prove the impotence of the Understanding. We are forced either to admit the synthesis offered by the Reason, or to deny the possibility of reconciling the thesis and antithesis. The thesis itself, again, was a modified form of the synthesis of a lower thesis and antithesis. To deny it will therefore involve the denial of them also, since it offers the only means of removing their contradiction. And thus we should be driven lower and lower, till we reach at last an impossible scepticism, the only escape from which is to accept the union of opposites which we find in the Reason.

Thus the Reason, though it does something which the Understanding cannot do, does not really do anything which the Understanding denies. What the Understanding denies is the possibility of combining two contrary notions as they stand, each independent and apparently self-complete. What the Reason does, is to merge these ideas in a higher one, in which their opposition, while in one sense preserved, is also transcended. This is not what is denied by the Understanding, for the Understanding is incapable of realising the position.

Reason is not contrary to, but beyond the Understanding. It is true that whatever is beyond the Understanding may be said to be in one sense contrary to it, since a fresh principle is introduced. But as the Understanding has proved that its employment by itself would result in chaos, it has given up its assertion of independence and leads the way naturally to Reason. Thus there are not two faculties in the mind with different laws, but two methods of working, the lower of which, though it does not of course contain the higher, yet leads up to it, postulates it, and is seen, in the light of the higher method, only to exist as leading up to it, and to be false in so far as it claims independence. The second appears as the completion of the first; it is not merely an escape from the difficulties of the lower method, but it explains and removes those difficulties; it does not merely succeed, where the Understanding had failed, in rationalising the universe, but it rationalises the Understanding itself. Taking all this into consideration the two methods cannot properly be called two separate faculties, however great may be the difference in their working.

79. We must now pass to the second of the three questions proposed at the beginning of this chapter—namely, the internal consistency of the system. And it will be necessary to consider in the first place what foundation is assumed, upon which to base our argument, and whether we are entitled to this assumption.

Now the idea from which the dialectic sets out, and in which it professes to show that all the other categories are involved, is the idea of Being. Are we justified in assuming the validity of this idea ? The ground on which we can answer this question in the affirmative is that the rejection of the idea as invalid would be self-contradictory, as was pointed out above[1]. For it would be equivalent to a denial that anything whatever existed. And in that case the denial itself could not exist, and the validity of the idea of Being has not been denied. But, on the other hand, if the denial does exist, then there is something whose existence we cannot deny. And the same dilemma applies to doubt, as well as to positive denial. If the doubt exists, then there is something of whose existence we

[1] Chap. i. Section 18.

are certain; if the doubt does not exist, then we do not doubt the validity of the category. And both denial and doubt involve the existence of the thinking subject.

We have thus as firm a base as possible for our transcendental argument. It is not only a proposition which none of our opponents do in fact doubt, but one which they cannot by any possibility doubt, one which is involved and postulated in all thought and in all action. Whatever may be the nature of the superstructure, the foundation is strong enough to carry it.

80. The next consideration must be the validity of the process by which we conclude that further categories are involved in the one from which we start. In this process there are three steps. We go from thesis to antithesis, from thesis and antithesis to synthesis, and from synthesis again to a fresh thesis. The distinctness of the separate steps becomes somewhat obscured towards the end of the Logic, when the importance of negation, as the means by which the imperfect truth advances towards perfection, is considerably diminished. It will perhaps be most convenient to take the steps here in the form in which they exist at the beginning of the Logic. The effect produced on the validity of the process by the subsequent development of the method will be discussed in the next chapter.

It is not necessary to say much of the transition from the synthesis to the fresh thesis. It is, in fact, scarcely a transition at all. It is, as can be seen when Becoming passes into Being Determinate, rather a contemplation of the same truth from a fresh point of view—immediacy in the place of reconciling mediation—than an advance to a fresh truth. Whether in fact this new category is always the same as the previous synthesis, looked at from another point of view, is a question of detail which must be examined independently for each triad of the Logic, and which does not concern us here, as we are dealing only with the general principles of the system. But if the old synthesis and the new thesis *are* really only different expressions of the same truth, the passage from the one to the other is valid even according to formal Logic. Since nothing new is added at all, nothing can be added improperly.

81. Our general question must be put in a negative form

to suit the transition between thesis and antithesis. It would be misleading to ask whether we were justified in assuming that, since the thesis is valid, the antithesis is valid too. For the result of the transition from thesis to antithesis is to produce, till the synthesis is perceived, a state of contradiction and scepticism, in which it will be doubted if either category is valid at all, since they lead to contradictions. Our question should rather be, Are we justified in assuming that, unless the antithesis is valid, the thesis cannot be valid?

The ground of this assumption is that the one category implies the other. If we examine attentively what is meant by pure Being, we find that it cannot be discriminated from Nothing. If we examine Being-for-self, we find that the One can only be defined by its negation and repulsion, which involves the category of the Many.

It is objected that these transitions cannot be justified, because they profess to be acts of pure thought, and it is impossible to advance by pure thought alone to anything new. To this an answer was indicated in the last chapter, where we found that the motive to the whole advance is the presence in experience, and in our minds as they become conscious of themselves in experience, of the concrete reality, of which all categories are only descriptions, and of which the lower categories are imperfect descriptions[1]. Since pure thought has a double ground from which it may work—the abstract and imperfect explicit idea from which the advance is to be made, and the concrete and perfect implicit idea towards which the explicit idea gradually advances—real progress is quite compatible with pure thought. Because it has before it a whole which is so far merely implicit, and has not been analysed, it can arrive at propositions which were not contained, according to the rules of formal logic, in the propositions from which it starts, but are an advance upon the latter. On the other hand, the process remains one of pure thought only, because this whole is not empirically given. It is not empirically given, although it could not be given if experience did not exist. For it is necessarily in all experience; and being the essential nature of all reality, it can be deduced from any piece of

[1] Section 32.

experience whatever. Our knowledge of it is dependent, not on experience being thus and thus, but only on experience existing at all. And the existence of experience cannot be called an empirical fact. It is the presupposition alike of all empirical knowledge, and of all pure thought. We should not be aware even of the existence of the laws of formal logic without the existence of experience. Yet those laws are not empirical, because, although they have no meaning apart from experience, they are not dependent on any one fact of experience, but are the only conditions under which we can experience anything at all. And for a similar reason, we need not suppose that dialectic thought need be sterile because it claims to be pure.

82. From another point of view, it is sometimes said that the transitions of the dialectic only exist because the connection between the two categories has been demonstrated by means of facts taken from experience. In that case the dialectic, whatever value it might have, could not possess the inherent necessity, which characterises the movements of pure thought, and which its author claimed for it. It could at most be an induction from experience, which could never rise above probability, nor be safely applied beyond the sphere in which it had been verified by experience. I have endeavoured to show above that, since thought can be pure without being sterile, it does not follow that an advance must be empirical because it is real. Whether it is in fact empirical or not, is another matter. If we can conceive any change in the nature of the manifold of sensations, as distinct from the categories by which they are built up, which would invalidate any of the transitions of the dialectic, then no doubt we should have to admit that the system had broken down. It is of course impossible to prove generally and à priori that no such flaw can be found in any part of the system. The question must be settled by an investigation of each category independently, showing that the argument in each depends upon the movement of the pure notion, and not on any particulars of sense. To do this would be beyond the scope of my present essay, but the special importance of the idea of Motion renders it necessary to discuss Trendelenburg's theory that it has been

illegitimately introduced into the dialectic by the observation
of empirical facts[1].

83. The remaining transition is that from thesis and
antithesis to synthesis. We have seen above[2] that if the
synthesis *does* reconcile the contradictions, we are bound to
accept it as valid, unless we can find some other means of
reconciling them. For otherwise, since we cannot accept
unreconciled contradictions as true, we should have to deny the
validity of thesis and antithesis. And since the thesis itself
was the only reconciliation possible for a lower thesis and
antithesis, we should have also to deny the validity of the
latter, and so on until, in the denial of Being, we reached a
reductio ad absurdum. All that remains, therefore, is to
consider whether the synthesis is a satisfactory reconciliation of
contradictions.

With regard to the general possibility of transcending
contradictions, we must remember that the essence of the
whole dialectic lies in the assertion that the various pairs of
contrary categories are only produced by abstraction from the
fuller category in which they are synthesised. We have not,
therefore, to find some idea which shall be capable of reconciling
two ideas which had originally no relation to it. We are merely
restoring the unity from which those ideas originally came. It
is not, as we might be tempted to think, the reconciliation of
the contradiction which is an artificial expedient of our minds
in dealing with reality. It is rather the creation of the
contradiction which was artificial and subjective. The synthesis is the logical *prius* of its moments. Bearing this in
mind, we shall see that the possibility of transcending contradictions is a simpler question than it appears to be. For all
that has to be overcome is a mistake about the nature of
reality, due to the incomplete insight of the Understanding.
The contradiction has not so much to be conquered as to be
disproved.

84. Hartmann objects that the only result of the union of
two contraries is a blank, and not a richer truth[3]. This is
certainly true of the examples Hartmann takes, $+y$ and $-y$, for

---

[1] Sections 91–94.   [2] Section 78.
[3] *op. cit.* II. B. 7.

these, treated as mathematical terms, do not admit of synthesis, but merely of mechanical combination.

Hegel never maintained that two such terms as these, opposed in this way, could ever produce anything but a blank. Hartmann appears to think that he endeavoured to synthesise them in the passage in the Greater Logic [1], when he makes $+y$ and $-y$ equal to y and again to $2y$. But clearly neither y nor $2y$ could be a synthesis of $+y$ and $-y$, for a synthesis must introduce a new and higher idea. All Hegel meant here was that both $+y$ and $-y$ are of the nature of y, and that they are also both quantities, so that from one point of view they are both simply y (as a mile east and a mile west are both a mile) and from another point of view they are $2y$ (as in going a mile east, and then returning westwards for the same distance, we walk two miles). This gives us no reason to suppose that Hegel did not see that if we oppose $+y$ to $-y$, taking the opposition of the signs into consideration, the result will be 0.

But this tells us nothing about the possibility of synthesis. For Hegel does not, to obtain a synthesis, simply predicate the two opposite categories of the same subject,—a course which he, like everyone else, would admit to be impossible. He passes to another category, in which the two first are contained, yet in such a way that the incompatibility ceases. The result here is by no means an empty zero, because the synthesis is not a mere mechanical junction of two contradictory categories, but is the real unity, of which the thesis and antithesis are two aspects, which do not, however, exhaust its meaning. Whether the attempt to find such syntheses has in fact been successful all through the Logic, is, of course, another question. Such a solution however would meet Hartmann's difficulty, and he has given no reason why such a solution should be impossible. The nature of his example in itself proves that he has failed to grasp the full meaning of the process. In algebra there is no richer notion than that of quantity, in which $+y$ and $-y$ are directly opposed. No synthesis is therefore possible, and the terms cannot be brought together, except in that external unity which produces a mere blank. But such a case, which can only be dealt with by the most abstract of all sciences,

[1] *Werke*, Vol. IV. p. 53.

cannot possibly be a fair example of a system whose whole life consists in the gradual removal of abstractions.

85. We have seen that the cogency of the entire process rests mainly on the fact that the system is analytic as well as synthetic, and that it does not evolve an entirely new result, but only renders explicit what was previously implicit in all experience. On the ground of this very characteristic of the dialectic, Trendelenburg denies that it can have any objective validity. It may be convenient to quote his account of the dialectic process, which Professor Seth translates as follows[1]: "The dialectic begins according to its own declaration with abstraction; for if 'pure being' is represented as equivalent to 'nothing' thought has reduced the fulness of the world to the merest emptiness. But it is the essence of abstraction that the elements of thought which in their original form are intimately united are violently held apart. What is thus isolated by abstraction, however, cannot but strive to escape from this forced position. Inasmuch as it is a part torn from a whole, it cannot but bear upon it the traces that it is only a part; it must crave to be completed. When this completion takes place, there will arise a conception which contains the former in itself. But inasmuch as only one step of the original abstraction has been retraced, the new conception will repeat the process; and this will go on until the full reality of perception has been restored....Plainly a whole world may develop itself in this fashion, and, if we look more narrowly, we have discovered here the secret of the dialectic method. That method is simply the art by which we undo or retrace our original abstraction. The first ideas, because they are the products of abstraction, are recognised on their first appearance as mere parts or elements of a higher conception, and the merit of the dialectic really lies in the comprehensive survey of these parts from every side, and the thereby increased certainty we gain of their necessary connection with one another[2]." And he immediately continues, "What meanwhile happens in this progress is only a history of subjective knowledge, no development of the reality itself from its elements. For there is nothing corresponding in reality

---

[1] *Hegelianism and Personality*, p. 92.
[2] *Logische Untersuchungen*, Vol. I. p. 94.

which answers to the first abstraction of pure being. It is a strained image, produced by the analysing mind, and no right appears anywhere to find in pure being the first germ of an objective development."

In answer to this objection I may quote Mr F. H. Bradley, "you make no answer to the claim of Dialectic, if you establish the fact that external experience has already given it what it professes to evolve, and that no synthesis comes out but what before has gone in. All this may be admitted, for the question at issue is not, What can appear, and How comes it to appear? The question is as to the *manner* of its appearing, when it is induced to appear, and as to the special mode in which the mind recasts and regards the matter it may have otherwise acquired. To use two technical terms which I confess I regard with some aversion—the point in dispute is not whether the product is *a posteriori*, but whether, being *a posteriori*, it is not *a priori* also and as well[1]." And in the previous Section, speaking of the difference between common recognition and the dialectic, he says "The content in one case, itself irrational, seems to come to our reason from a world without, while in the other it appears as that natural outcome of our inmost constitution, which satisfies us because it is our own selves."

86. The process is more than is expressed by Trendelenburg's phrase "the art by which we retrace or undo our original abstractions," ("die Kunst wodurch die ursprüngliche Abstraction zurückgethan wird"). For the abstractions are not passively retraced by us, but insist on retracing themselves on pain of contradiction. Doubtless, as Trendelenburg says, to do this belongs to the nature of abstractions from a concrete whole. But then the significance of the dialectic might not unfairly be said to lie in the fact that it proved that our more abstract thought-categories *were* abstractions in this sense—a truth which without the dialectic we should not have known. All analysis results, no doubt, in ideas more or less abstract, but not necessarily in abstractions which spontaneously tend to return to the original idea analysed. The idea of a living foot apart from the idea of a body does contain a contradiction. We know that a living foot can only exist in connection with

---

[1] *Logic,* Book III. Part I. Chap II. Section 20.

a living body, and if we grant the first to exist at any given time and place we know that we also admit, by implication, the other. Now the idea of a steam flour-mill can in like manner be separated into two parts—that it is moved by steam, and that its object is to grind corn. But to admit that one of these ideas can be applied as a predicate to any given subject is not equivalent to admitting that the other can be applied to it also, and that the subject is a steam flour-mill. For a machine moved by steam can be used to weave cotton, and water-power can be used to grind corn. We have formed from our original idea two which are more abstract—the idea of a machine moved by steam, and the idea of a machine which grinds corn. But neither of them shows the least impulse to "retrace or undo our original abstraction."

The important question is, then, of which sort are the abstractions of which Hegel treats in the dialectic? It would, probably, be generally admitted that those which he ranks as the lower categories are more abstract, that is to say have less content, than those which he considers higher. But they may be, for anything that superficial observation can tell us, the real units, of which the higher categories are mere combinations. No one will deny that the idea of Causality includes the idea of Being. But it might contain it only as the idea of a steam flour-mill contains the idea of steam-power, so that it would not at all follow that the category of Causality is applicable to all being, any more than that all steam-power is used for grinding corn. And we should not be able, from this inclusion of the idea of Being in the idea of Causality, to conclude that the law of Causality was applicable anywhere at all, even if the validity of the idea of Being was admitted. For the particular case in which Being was combined with Causality might be one which never really occurred, just as there might be machines moved by steam-power without any of them being flour-mills.

87. The dialectic, however, puts us in a different position. From that we learn that Being is an abstraction, the truth of which can be found only in Causality, and in the higher categories into which Causality in turn develops. Being, therefore, inevitably leads us on to Causality, so that, to

whatever subject-matter we can apply the first as a predicate, to that we must necessarily apply the other.

The same change takes place in the relations of all the other categories. Without the dialectic we might suppose Life to be an effect of certain chemical combinations; with it we find that Chemism is an abstraction from Life, so that, wherever there is Chemism there must be Life also. Without the dialectic, again, we might suppose self-consciousness to be a mere effect of animal life; with it, we are compelled to regard all life as merely relative to some self-consciousness.

The result of the dialectic is thus much more than "the increased certainty we gain of the necessary connection" of parts of thought "with one another." For it must be remembered that organic wholes are not to be explained by their parts, but the reverse, while on the other hand merely composite wholes can be best explained from the units of which they are made up. We cannot explain a living body by putting together the ideas of the isolated limbs, though we might, if our knowledge was sufficiently complete, explain a limb by the idea of the body as a whole. But we cannot explain the sizes and shapes of stones from the idea of the beach which they make up, while, on the other hand, if we knew the sizes, shapes, and positions of all the stones, we should have complete knowledge of the beach. And the dialectic professes to show that the lower categories are contained in the higher in a manner more resembling that in which a foot is related to a body, than that in which a stone is related to a beach. The success of the dialectic, therefore, means no less than this—that, for purposes of ultimate explanation, we reverse the order of science and the understanding, and, instead of attempting to account for the higher phenomena of nature (i.e. those which *prima facie* exhibit the higher categories) by means of the laws of the lower, we account for the lower by means of the laws of the higher. The interest of this for the theoretical reason is obvious, and its importance for the practical reason is no less, since the lower categories are those of matter and the higher those of spirit.

88. So also it is not fair to say that the process is only one of subjective thought. It is doubtless true that the various

abstractions which form the steps of the dialectic have no separate existence corresponding to them in the world of reality, where only the concrete notion is to be found. But the result is one which has validity for objective thought. For it is by that result that we learn that the notion is really a concrete unity, and that there is nothing corresponding in the outside world to the separated fragments of the notion which form the stages of finite thought. This is the same conclusion from another point of view as the one mentioned in the preceding paragraph, and it is surely both objective and important.

Moreover the objective significance of the dialectic process is not confined to this negative result. For the different imperfect categories, although they have no *separate* objective existence, yet have an objective existence, as elements in the concrete whole, which is made up of them. If we ask what is the nature of the Absolute Idea, we must, from one side, answer that "its true content is only the whole system, of which we have been hitherto studying the development[1]." Since the one absolute reality may be expressed as the synthesis of these categories, they have reality in it.

Besides this, in the sphere of our ordinary finite thought, in which we use the imperfect categories as stable and permanent, the dialectic gives us objective information as to the relative amounts of truth and error which may be expected from the use of various categories, and as to the comparative reality and significance of different ways of regarding the universe,—as, for example, that the idea of Life goes more deeply into the nature of reality than the idea of Mechanism.

89. We are now in a position to meet the dilemma with which Trendelenburg challenges the dialectic. "Either" he says "the dialectic development is independent, and only conditioned by itself, then in fact it must know everything for itself. Or it assumes finite sciences and empirical knowledge, but then the immanent process and the unbroken connection are broken through by what is assumed from outside, and it relates itself to experience quite uncritically. The dialectic can choose. We see no third possibility[2]." And just before he

---

[1] *Enc.* Section 237, lecture note.   [2] *op. cit.* Vol. I. pp. 91, 92.

gives a further description of the second alternative. "It works then only in the same way and with the same means as the other sciences, only differing from them in its goal,—to unite the parts to the idea of the whole."

Neither of these two alternatives is valid. The dialectic development is only so far "independent and only conditioned by itself," that it does not depend on any particular sensuous content of experience, and would develop in the same way, whatever that content might be. But it does not follow that it knows everything for itself. All that part of knowledge which depends upon one content rather than another—the whole, that is, of what is ordinarily called science—certainly cannot be reached from the dialectic alone in the present state of our knowledge, and perhaps never will be [1]. Nor does the dialectic, as we have seen, assume finite sciences and empirical knowledge. In one sense, indeed, their subject-matter is the condition of its validity, for it endeavours to analyse the concrete idea which is implicit in all our experience. The dialectic may be said therefore, in a sense, to depend on the fact that we have empirical knowledge, without which we should be conscious of nothing, not even of ourselves (since it is only in experience that we become self-conscious), and in that case there would be no chance of the complete and concrete idea being implicitly in our minds, which is a necessary preliminary to our subsequently making it explicit in the dialectic.

This however does not make it depend upon the finite sciences and empirical knowledge. It is dependent for its existence on the existence of empirical knowledge, but its nature does not at all depend on the nature of our empirical knowledge. And it would only be this latter relation which would "break through the immanent process by what is assumed from outside." The process can be, and is, one of pure thought, although pure thought is only given as one element in experience.

The dialectic retraces the steps of abstraction till it arrives at the concrete idea. If the concrete idea were different, the dialectic process would be different. The conditions of the dialectic are therefore that the concrete idea should be what it

---

[1] Cp. Chap. II. Section 59.

is, and that there should be experience in which we may
become conscious of that idea. But it is *not* a condition of the
dialectic that all the contingent facts which are found in
experience should be what they are, and not otherwise. So
far as we know, the relation of the categories to one another
might be the same, even if sugar, for example, was bitter to
the taste, and hare-bells had scarlet flowers. And if such
particulars ever *should* be deducible from the pure idea, so that
they could not be otherwise than they are without some
alteration in the nature of the pure idea, then they would cease
to be merely empirical knowledge. In our present state the
particulars of sense are only empirically and contingently
connected with the idea under which they are brought. And
although, if the dialectic is to exist, the idea must be what it
is, and must have some sensations to complement it, yet the
particular nature of those sensations is entirely indifferent to
the dialectic, which is not dependent upon it in any sense of
the word.

90. It is no doubt the case that an advanced state of the
finite sciences is a considerable help to the *discovery* of the
dialectic process, and this for several reasons. In the first place
the labour is easier because it is slighter. To detect the
necessary relation between two categories will be easier when
both are already explicitly before us in consciousness than
when only one is given in this way, and the other has to be
constructed. The inadequacy, for example, of the category of
Teleology would be by itself logically sufficient ground for
discovering the category of Life. But it is much easier to see,
when that idea is necessarily before us in biological science,
that it is the necessary consequence of the idea of Teleology,
than it would be to construct it by the dialectic, although that
would be possible for a sufficiently keen observer. In the
second place, the more frequently, and the more keenly, the
finite categories are used in finite science, the more probable it
will be that the contradiction involved in their use will have
become evident, on some occasion or the other, to some at
least of those who use them, and the easier will it be, therefore,
to point out the various inadequacies of each category in
succession, which are the stepping stones of the dialectic. But

all this only shows that the appearance of the theory of the dialectic in a philosophical system is partly determined by empirical causes, which surely no one ever denied. It is possible that we might have had to wait for the theory of gravitation for some time longer, if it had not been for the traditional apple, and no one could go beyond a certain point in mathematical calculation without the help of pens and paper. But the logical validity of the theory of gravitation, when once discovered, does not come as a deduction from the existence of the apple, or of writing materials. With sufficient power, any of the calculations could have been made without the help of writing. Any other case of gravitation would have done as well as the apple, if it had happened to suggest to Newton the problem which lay in it as much as in the other. And, in the same way, with sufficient mental acuteness the whole dialectic process could have been discovered, by starting from any one piece of experience, and without postulating any other empirical knowledge whatever. For the whole concrete idea lies behind experience, and manifests itself in every part of it. Any fragment of experience, therefore, would be sufficient to present the idea to our minds, and thus give us implicitly the concrete truth, whose presence in this manner is the real source of our discontent with the lower categories, and consequently is the spring of the dialectic process. In any single fact in experience, however trifling and wherever selected, the dialectic could find all the basis of experience that it needs. Doubtless it would have been a task beyond even Hegel's strength to evolve the dialectic without a far larger basis, and without the aid of specially suggestive portions of experience. But this, while it may have some interest for empirical psychology, can have none for metaphysics.

91. I have thus endeavoured to show that the dialectic process is related to experience in such a way as to avoid sterility, and at the same time not necessarily to fall into empiricism. We have now to consider Trendelenburg's contention[1] that at one point an idea of great importance, the idea of Motion, has in fact been introduced from experience in a

[1] *op. cit.* Vol. I. p. 38.

merely empirical manner, thus destroying the value of the Logic as a theory of the nature of pure thought.

He points out that Hegel endeavours to deduce the category of Becoming, which involves the idea of Motion, from the two categories of Being and Not-Being, which are ideas of rest. His inference is that the idea of Motion has been uncritically imported from experience, and breaks the connection of the Logic. Certainly no flaw could be more fatal than this, for it occurs at the second step in the dialectic, and, if it is really a flaw, must make everything beyond this point useless.

It is certainly true that the category of Becoming involves the idea of Motion, and that neither the category of Being, nor the category of Not-Being, do so. There is something in the synthesis which is in neither the thesis nor the antithesis, if each of these is taken alone and separately. This, however, is the necessary result wherever the dialectic process is applied. That process does not profess to be merely analytic of the premises we start from, but to give us new truth. If it were not so, it could have no philosophical importance whatever, but would be confined to the somewhat sterile occupation of discovering what consequence could be drawn by formal logic from the assertion of the simple notion of pure Being—the only premise from which we start.

92. Whatever Hegel meant by his philosophy, he certainly meant more than this. We must presume then that he had faced the fact that his conclusions contained more than his premises. And there is nothing unjustifiable,—nothing which necessitates the illegitimate introduction of an empirical element—in this. For we must recollect that the dialectic process has not merely as its basis the consciously accepted premises, from which it proceeds synthetically, but also the implicit concrete and complete idea which it analyses and brings into distinct consciousness. There is, therefore, nothing unjustifiable in the synthesis having more in it than both the thesis and antithesis, for this additional element is taken from the concrete idea which is the real motive power of the dialectic advance. As this concrete idea is pure thought, no introduction of an empirical element is necessary.

And, if we examine the process in detail, we shall find that no such empirical element has been introduced. The first point at which Motion is involved in the dialectic is not that at which the category of Becoming is already recognised explicitly as a category, and as the synthesis of the preceding thesis and antithesis. Before we have a category of motion, we perceive a motion of the categories; we are forced into the admission that Becoming is a fundamental idea of the universe because of the tendency we find in the ideas already accepted as fundamental to become one another. There is therefore no illegitimate step in the introduction of the synthesis, for the idea of Motion is already involved in the relation of the two lower categories to each other, and the synthesis only makes this explicit.

The introduction of empirical matter must come then, if it comes at all, in the recognition of the fact that Being is just as much Nothing, and Nothing is just as much Being. If we start by positing the first, we find ourselves also positing the second. The one standpoint cannot be maintained alone, but if we start from it, we find ourselves at the other. To account for this it is not necessary to bring in any empirical element. For although neither of the two categories has the idea of Motion explicitly in it, each of them is, of its own nature, forced into the movement towards the other, by reason of its own incompleteness and inadequacy. Now in this there is nothing that requires any aid from empirical observation. For Trendelenburg remarks himself, in the passage quoted above, that all abstractions "cannot but strive to escape from this false position." It is thus simply as the result of the nature of pure thought that we arrive at the conclusion that there is a motion of the categories. And, having discovered this, we are only using the *data* fairly before us when we recognise a category of motion, and so reconcile the contradiction which arises from the fact that two categories, which profess, as all terms must, to have a fixed and constant meaning, are nevertheless themselves in continual motion.

Of course all this can only take place on the supposition that experience does exist. For, in the first place, since pure thought is only an abstraction, and never really exists except as an element in experience, it is impossible to come across the ideas of Being and Not-Being at all, except in experience. And, secondly, it is only in experience that the concrete idea is implicit, which brings about the transition from category to category, and so first introduces the idea of Motion. But this, as was pointed out above [1], involves no dependence on empirical data. All that is required for the purpose is that element in experience which is called pure thought, and, although this cannot be present without the empirical element, the argument does not in the least depend on the nature of the latter.

93. We are told also that Becoming involves time and space, which Hegel admits not to be elements of pure thought, but to belong to the world of nature. Now in the first place it does not seem necessary that the Becoming referred to here should be only such as must take place in time or space. It no doubt includes Becoming in time and space. But it would seem to include also a purely logical Becoming—where the transition is not from one event in time to a subsequent event, nor from one part of space to another, but from one idea to another logically connected with it. The movement is here only the movement of logic, such as may be said to take place from the premises to the conclusion of a syllogism. This involves neither space nor time. It is, of course, true that this process can only be perceived by us by means of a process in time. We have first to think the premises and then the conclusion. But this does not make the syllogism itself a process in time. The validity of the argument does not depend upon the fact that we have perceived it; and the movement of attention from one step to another of the process—a movement which is certainly in time—must not be confounded with the logical movement of the argument itself, which is not in time.

It is again, no doubt, true that if we wish to *imagine* the process of Becoming, we cannot imagine it, except as taking place in time. But this is no objection. Imagination is a sensuous process, and involves sensuous elements. It does not follow that it is impossible to *think* Becoming except as in time.

If then the Becoming of the Logic includes a species of

[1] Chap. I. Section 15.

Becoming which does not take place in time or space, it follows, of course, that the introduction of that category does not involve the introduction of time and space into the dialectic. But even if we leave out this point, and confine ourselves to those species of Becoming which can only take place in time and space, it would not follow that these notions have been introduced into the dialectic. For, even on this hypothesis, Becoming only involves time and space in the sense that it cannot be represented without them. It could still be distinguished from them, and its nature as a pure category observed. If indeed the argument by which we are led on from Becoming to the next category was based on anything in the nature of time and space, Trendelenburg's objection would doubtless be made good. But it is no more necessary that this should be the case, because time and space are the necessary medium in which we perceive the idea of Becoming, than that every step of the whole dialectic process should be tainted with empiricism, because every category can only be perceived in the whole of experience, in which it is bound up with empirical elements. And the transition which Hegel gives to the category of Being-determinate does not seem in any way to depend upon the nature of time and space, but rather on the nature of Becoming, as a determination of thought.

And, again, is the connection, which pure thought has with time and space, introduced for the first time in the category of Becoming? That category surely does not require *both* time and space, for we are able to apply it to the passage of our thoughts, when space is out of the question. And, on the other hand, is it possible for pure Being to exist except either in time or space? What sort of reality could be supposed to belong to immediate being apart from both these determinations, I am unable to see. And if it does require at least one of them, it would seem to follow that the transition to Becoming involves no other connection with the matter of intuition than is involved in the categories from which it is deduced. (I do not mean to suggest that no reality can be conceived as existing except in time or space, but only that it must be conceived as existing in time or space unless it is considered under some higher category than pure Being.)

94. Again, it is said that Being and Not-Being are abstractions, while Becoming is a "concrete intuition ruling life and death[1]." It is no doubt true that we never encounter, and cannot imagine, a case of Becoming without sensuous intuition. But the same might be said of any other category. Thought can never exist without sensation. And the quality of Becoming itself is not sensation, but thought. *What* becomes, indeed, must be told us by sensation, but that it becomes is as much a conception of pure thought as that it is, or is not. And the ideas of Being and Not-Being are scarcely more abstractions than Becoming is. For they also cannot come into consciousness without the presence of intuition. They are doubtless abstractions in the sense that we feel at once their inadequacy to any subject-matter. But this is the case to almost the same extent with Becoming, if we take it strictly. As a general rule, when we talk in ordinary discourse of Becoming, or of any other of the lower categories, we do not take it by itself, but mix it up with higher categories, such as Being-determinate, Substance, and Cause. If we do this, Being and Not-Being may pass as concrete. If we do not do it, but confine ourselves to the strict meaning of the category, Becoming shows itself to be almost as abstract and inadequate as pure Being. The philosophy which corresponds to Becoming is the doctrine of the eternal flux of all things, and it is difficult to see how this represents reality much more adequately than the Eleatic Being, or the Buddhist Nothing. Of course Becoming is to some extent more adequate than the categories that precede it, but this is the natural and inevitable result of the fact that it is a synthesis of them.

95. We must, in conclusion, consider the claims of the Hegelian system to ontological validity. This subject divides itself into two parts. In the first place Hegel denies the Kantian restriction of knowledge to mere phenomena, behind which lie things in themselves which we cannot know and he asserts that the laws of thought traced in the logic, as applicable to all possible knowledge, are applicable also to all reality. In the second place he deduces from the Logic the philosophies of Nature and Spirit.

[1] Trendelenburg, *op. cit.* Vol. I. p. 38.

Now as to the first of these two points, I have already endeavoured to show that any denial of it involves a contradiction [1]. We are told by those who attempt this denial that there are or may be things which we cannot know. But to know of the actuality or possibility of such things is to know them—to know that of which knowledge is impossible. Of course to know only that things are possible, or even that they actually exist, and to know nothing else about them, is very imperfect and inadequate knowledge of them. But it is knowledge. It involves a judgment, and a judgment involves a category. It is thus impossible to say that the existence of anything which does not conform to the universal laws of knowledge is either actual or possible. If the supporters of things-in-themselves were asked for a defence of their doctrine, they would be compelled to relate these things with our sensuous intuitions, through which alone *data* can be given to our minds. And this relation would bring them in connection with the world of knowledge, and destroy their asserted independence.

In fact the question whether there is any reality outside the world which we know by experience is unmeaning. There is much reality which we do not know; it is even possible that there is much reality which we never shall know. But it must, if we are to have any right to speak of it at all, belong to the same universe as the facts which we do know—that is, be connected with them by the same fundamental laws as those by which they are connected with one another. Otherwise we can have no justification for supposing that it exists, since all such suppositions must rest on some connection with the world of reality. We are not even entitled to say that it is possible that there may exist a world unconnected with the world of experience. For possibility is a phrase which derives all its meaning to us from its use in the world of experience, and beyond that world we have no right to use it, since anything brought under that, or any other predicate, is brought thereby into the world of the knowable. And a mere empty possibility, not based on the known existence of at least one of the necessary conditions, is too indefinite to possess any

---

[1] Chap. i. Section 25.

significance. Anything, however impossible, may be pronounced possible, if we are only ignorant enough of the subject-
matter, for if our ignorance extends to all the circumstances
incompatible with the truth of the proposition, all evidence of
impossibility is obviously beyond our reach. But the more
ignorance is involved in such a conclusion, the less valuable it
is, and when it is based on complete ignorance, as any
proposition relating to the possibility of a world outside
knowledge must inevitably be, the judgment becomes entirely
frivolous. It is merely negative and does not, as a real
judgment of possibility does, create the slightest expectation of
reality, but is devoid of all rational interest. Such a judgment,
as Mr Bradley points out "is absurd, because a privative
judgment, where the subject is left entirely undetermined in
respect of the suggestion, has no kind of meaning. Privation
gets a meaning where the subject is determined by a quality or
an environment which we have reason to think would give
either the acceptance or the rejection of X. But if we keep
entirely to the bare universal, we cannot predicate absence,
since the space we call empty has no existence[1]." And as
Hegel's theory, if valid at all, covers the whole sphere of actual
and possible knowledge, any speculations on the nature of
reality outside its sphere are meaningless, and the results of
the dialectic may be predicated of all reality.

96. The demand that the dialectic shall confine itself to
a purely subjective import, and not presume to limit reality by
its results, has been made from a fresh point of view by Mr
F. C. S. Schiller. He says "It does not follow that because all
truth in the narrower sense is abstract, because all philosophy
must be couched in abstract terms, therefore the whole truth
about the universe in the wider sense, i.e. the ultimate account
that can be given of it, can be compressed into a single abstract
formula, and that the scheme of things is nothing more than,
e.g., the self-development of the Absolute Idea. To draw this
inference would be to confuse the thought-symbol, which is,
and must be, the instrument of thought, with that which the
symbol expresses, often only very imperfectly, viz. the reality
which is 'known' only in experience and can never be evoked

_____
[1] *Logic*, Book I. Chap. VII. Section 30.

by the incantations of any abstract formula. If we avoid this confusion, we shall no longer be prone to think that we have disposed of the thing symbolized when we have brought home imperfection and contradiction to the formulas whereby we seek to express it...to suppose, e.g., that Time and Change cannot really be characteristic of the universe, because our thought, in attempting to represent them by abstract symbols, often contradicts itself. For evidently the contradiction may result as well from the inadequacy of our symbols to express realities of whose existence we are directly assured by other factors in experience, and which consequently are *data* rather than problems for thought, as from the 'merely apparent' character of their reality, and the moral to be drawn may only be the old one, that it is the function of thought to mediate and not to create [1]."

It is no doubt true that there is something else in our experience besides pure thought—namely, the immediate data of sensation. And these are independent of thought in the sense that they cannot be deduced from it, or subordinated to it, but must be recognised as a correlative and indispensable factor in experience. But it is not an independent element in the sense that it can exist or express reality *apart* from thought. And it would have, it seems to me, to be independent in this sense before we could accept Mr Schiller's argument.

97. Sensation without thought could assure us of the existence of nothing. Not of any objects outside the sentient being—for these objects are for us clearly ideal constructions. Not of the self who feels sensation—for a self is not itself a sensation, and the assurance of its reality must be an inference. Nay, sensation cannot assure us of its own existence. For the very terms existence, reality, assurance, are all terms of thought. To appeal (as Mr Schiller wishes to do, if I have understood him rightly) from a dialectic which shows, e.g. that Time cannot be real, to an experience which tells us that it *is* real, is useless. For our assurance of reality is itself an act of thought, and anything which the dialectic has proved about the nature of thought would be applicable to that assurance.

[1] "The Metaphysics of the Time-Process," *Mind*, n. s. Vol. iv. No. 14. p. 40.

It is difficult to see how sensations could even exist without thought. For sensations certainly only exist for consciousness, and what could a consciousness be which was nothing but a chaotic mass of sensations, with no relations among them, and consequently no unity for itself? But, even if they could exist without thought, they could tell us nothing of reality or existence, for reality and existence are not themselves sensations, and all analysis or inference, by which they might be reached from sensations, must be the work of thought.

By the side of the truth that thought without *data* can never make us aware of reality, we must place the corresponding truth that nothing can make us aware of reality without thought. Any law therefore which can be laid down for thought, must be a law which imposes itself on all reality which we can either know or imagine—and a reality which we can neither know nor imagine is, as I fancy Mr Schiller would admit, a meaningless abstraction.

To the demand then that we should admit the reality of anything although "we have brought home imperfection and contradiction to the formulas whereby we seek to express it," I should answer that it is only by the aid of these formulas that we can pronounce it real. If we cannot think it, we have no right to pronounce it real, for to pronounce it real is an act of thought. We should not, therefore, by pronouncing it real, be appealing from thought to some other means of knowledge. We should be thinking it, at the same time, to be real and to be self-contradictory. To say that a thing whose notion is self-contradictory is real, is to say that two or more contradictory propositions are true—that is, to violate the law of contradiction. If we do this we put an end to all possibility of coherent thought anywhere. If a contradiction is not a sign of error it will be impossible to make any inference whatever.

And so it seems to me, in spite of Mr Schiller's arguments, that if we find contradictions in our notion of a thing, we must give up its reality. This does not mean, of course, that we are to say that there was nothing real behind the contradictory appearance. Behind all appearance there is some reality. But this reality, before we can know it, must be re-thought in terms which are mutually coherent, and although we certainly have not "disposed of the thing symbolized when we have brought home imperfection and contradiction to the formulas whereby we seek to express it," we can only retain our belief in the thing's existence by thinking it under some other formula, by which the imperfection and the contradiction are removed.

98. There remains only the transition from Logic to Nature and Spirit. From what has been said in Chapters I and II, it will be seen that the validity of this transition must be determined by the same general considerations as determine the validity of the transitions from one category to another within the Logic. For the motive power of the transition was the same—the impatience of its incompleteness felt by an abstraction, since the whole of thought, even when it has attained the utmost completeness of which it is capable, is only an abstraction from the fuller whole of reality. And the method of the transition is also the same—the discovery of a contradiction arising from the inadequacy of the single term, which leads us on to the opposite extreme, which is also found to be contradictory, and so leaves us no refuge but a synthesis which comprehends and reconciles both extremes. I have endeavoured to show in the last Chapter that this was all that Hegel ever intended to do, and that no other deduction of Nature and Spirit from pure thought can be attributed to him. We have now to consider whether he was justified in proceeding in this manner.

Is thought incomplete as compared with the whole of reality? This can scarcely be denied. To admit it does not involve any scepticism as to the adequacy of knowledge. Thought may be perfectly capable of expressing the whole of reality, all that is real may be rational, but it will nevertheless remain true that all that is real cannot be merely reasoning. For all reasoning as such is merely mediate, and it is obvious that a mediation without something which it mediates is a contradiction. This something must be given immediately. It is true that thought itself, as an event in our consciousness, may be given immediately, and may be perceived by inner sense, in the same way that colours, sounds, and the like, may be perceived by outer sense. But this means that thought, considered as it is in the Logic (i.e. not as a *datum*, but as an activity), can never be self-subsistent, but must always depend on something (even if that something is other thought), which presents itself immediately. And thus the Logic, which only deals with the forms by which we may mediate what is immediately given, does not by itself contain the whole of reality.

99. This is obviously the case while, as at present, a large amount of experience is concerned with physical data apparently entirely contingent to the idea, and with mental *data* scarcely less contingent. It is quite clear that the Logic does not as yet express the whole universe, while we still find ultimate and unexplained such facts as that one particular number of vibrations of ether in a second gives us the sensation of blue, and that another particular number gives us the sensation of red. But even if the process of rationalisation was carried as far as it could by any possibility go, if all matter was reduced to spirit, and every quality of spirit was deduced from the Logic, nevertheless to constitute experience something would have to be immediately given, and the Logic contemplates nothing but thought as it deals with something given already. The existence of thought requires the existence of something given. It is undeniable that we think. But we could not think unless there were something to think about. Therefore there must be something. This is all of the world of Nature and Spirit which we can deduce from the Logic. Logic must have its complement and correlative, and the two must be united in one whole. This, as I have tried to show, is all Hegel did attempt to deduce from the Logic. But whether this is so or not, we must admit that it is all that he has a right to deduce from it. The concrete whole towards which we are working is the universalised particular, the mediated immediate, the rationalised *datum*. Logic is the universal, the mediating, the rationalising element. There must therefore be a particular, immediate, given element, and the two must be reconciled. So much we can deduce by pure thought. But if this other element has any other qualities except those just mentioned which make it correlative to Logic, we cannot deduce them. We must treat them as contingent, and confine ourselves to pointing out the way in which the Logic is incarnate in Nature and Spirit, piercing through these contingent particulars.

Philosophy can tell us *à priori* that Nature and Spirit do exist, and that all the categories of the Logic must be realised in them, but *how* they are realised in the midst of what seem, at any rate at present, to be contingent particulars, must be a matter for empirical observation, and not for deduction from Logic.

100. In what way does the transition from Logic take place? The suggestion which most naturally occurs to us is that the element which supplements the deficiency of Logic should be its antithesis, and the combination of the two in a concrete whole should form the synthesis. In this case the antithesis would be the mere abstract and unconnected particularity, which is really unnameable, since all names imply that the matter of discourse has been qualified by some judgment. With the very beginnings of Nature, on this view, we pass to the synthesis, for in Nature we have already the idea as immediate, as given, as realised in fact. Spirit and Nature together would thus form the synthesis, Spirit being distinguished from Nature only as being a more complete and closer reconciliation of the two elements. It makes explicit the unity which in Nature is only implicit. But it does not add any aspect or element which is not in Nature, it is more elaborated, but not more comprehensive.

This, however, is not the course of the transition which is actually adopted by Hegel. In this, while the Logic is the thesis, the antithesis is Nature, and the synthesis is Spirit. The bond of connection here is that they are the universal, the particular, and the individual, and that the individual is the synthesis of the universal and the particular. If it should be objected to this that there is more in Nature than mere particularity, since the idea is realised, though imperfectly realised, in Nature, and the idea is the universal. Hegel's reply, I suppose, would be that this is the case also with every particular thing, since mere particularity is an abstraction. We can never perceive anything without a judgment, and a judgment involves a category. Indeed the very phrase " thing" implies this.

The difference between the two methods is thus very marked, not only because of the different place assigned to

Nature in them, but because in the second the antithesis marks a distinct advance upon the thesis, as a concrete reality, though an imperfect one, while in the first the thesis and antithesis are both alike mere abstractions and aspects which require a reconciliation before anything concrete is reached.

Here we have two examples of the dialectic process, each starting from the same point—the Logic—and each arriving at the same point—Absolute Spirit—but reaching that point in different ways. What are we to say about them? Is one wrong and the other right? Or can we argue, from the fact that the principles of the dialectic would seem to justify either of them, to the conclusion that there must be some error in those principles, since they lead to two inconsistent results? Or, finally, can we pronounce them both to be correct? To these questions Hegel, as far as I can find, affords no definite answer, but one may, I think, be found by following up some indications which he gives. This I shall endeavour to do in the next chapter[1].

101. Before leaving this part of the subject, we must consider some criticisms which have been passed by Lotze on Idealism, the most important and elaborate of which occurs in the Microcosmus[2]. In this he considers the assertion, which he attributes to Idealism, that Thought and Being are identical. He does not mention Hegel by name here, but it would seem, from the nature of the criticisms, and from scattered remarks in other parts of his writings, that he held his criticisms to apply to the Hegelian dialectic.

Now in what sense does Hegel say that Thought and Being are identical? In the first place we must carefully distinguish, from such an assertion of identity, another assertion which he does make,—namely, that Being is a category, and therefore a determination of thought, and that, in consequence, even the mere recognition that a thing is, can only be effected by thought. He uses this undeniable truth as an argument against appeals from the results of thought to immediate facts. For it means that we can only know that a thing is a fact by means of thought, and that it is impossible to find any ground, upon which we can base a proposition, which does not involve

---

[1] Sections 131—138.   [2] Book VIII. Chap. I. towards the end.

thought, and which is not subject to all the general laws which we can obtain by analysing what is involved in thinking.

This, however, is not what is meant by Lotze. That the predicate of Being can only be applied by us to a subject by means of thought, is a statement which Lotze could not have doubted, and which he had no reason to wish to deny. He attacks a very different proposition—that everything which is included under the predicate of Being, that is, everything in the universe, is identical with thought.

This, again, may have two very different meanings. If we call the particular reality, of which we are speaking, *A*, then we may mean, in the first place, that *A's* being is identical with *B's* thought, when *B* is thinking about *A*,—or would be so, if *B's* thought was in a state of ideal perfection. Or we may mean, in the second place, that *A's* being is identical with his own thought, i.e. that his only nature is to be a thinking being, and his only activity is to think. The first view is that *A* is identical with what may be thought about him, the second is that *A* is identical with what he thinks. These are clearly very different.

102. It is the first of these meanings, it seems, which Lotze supposes his Idealist to adopt. This appears from his considering that he has refuted it by showing that there is always in our knowledge of anything an immediate *datum*, which thought must accept as given, and without which it cannot act at all. "Thought," he says, "is everywhere but a mediating activity moving hither and thither, bringing into connection the original intuitions of external and internal perception, which are predetermined by fundamental ideas and laws the origin of which cannot be shown; it develops special and properly logical forms peculiar to itself, only in the effort to apply the idea of truth (which it finds in us) to the scattered multiplicity of perceptions, and of the consequences developed from them. Hence nothing seems less justifiable than the assertion that this Thinking is identical with Being, and that Being can be resolved into it without leaving any residuum; on the contrary, everywhere in the flux of thought there remain quite insoluble those individual nuclei which represent the several aspects of that important content which we designate

by the name of Being[1]." The fact that there are immediate
elements in our knowledge of other things could be no reason
for doubting that our nature—and theirs also—lay in thinking,
as we shall see later on.   But it would doubtless be an
excellent reason for denying that our thought of the object
could ever be identical with the object itself. And it is this
last theory which Lotze must have had in view.

103. No doubt Hegel would have been wrong if he had
asserted that Thought and Being were identical in this sense.
But, as I have tried to show in the last chapter[2], there is no
reason to suppose that he failed to appreciate the fact that
there is an element of immediacy in all knowledge, and that
thought, without such *data*, would not only be inadequate, but
completely impotent. The passage which I then quoted from
the Philosophy of Spirit[3], declares that Spirit is the logical
prius, not only of Nature but of Logic.   Now Spirit differs
from Logic by reason of the element of immediacy, introduced
in Nature, and completely harmonised with Logic in Spirit.
It seems clear then that Hegel can never have imagined that
pure thought could dispense with the element of immediacy.
And, if so, our pure thought by itself could never have been
identical with the content of its object.

104. The necessity of immediacy for thought, however,
does not prevent the identity of Thought and Being in the
second sense mentioned above. If all reality in the universe
consisted simply of thinking beings there would be no lack of
immediate *data* for them to mediate. For thought itself can
be observed, and, when observed, forms itself a *datum* for
thought. And a universe of thinking beings, in connection
with one another, would find their immediate *data*, A in B, and
B in A.

In this sense it seems that Hegel did hold the identity of
Thought and Being—though the phrase is not a very happy
one. That is to say, he held that all reality consisted of
self-conscious beings; and it appears from the Philosophy of
Spirit that he also held that the highest—the only ultimate—

---

[1] *loc. cit.* (English Translation, Vol. II. p. 354, 4th ed.)
Sections 56, 57.   [3] *Enc.* Section 381, lecture note.

activity of Spirit, in which all others are transcended and swallowed up, is that of pure thought.

In doing this, he ignored a fact which is made prominent by Lotze in many parts of his system, though not in the chapter from which I have quoted. This is, that Spirit has two other aspects besides thought—namely, volition and feeling—which are as important as thought, and which cannot be deduced from it, nor explained by it. I shall have to consider this point at greater length in Chapter VI, and shall there endeavour to show that, while Hegel was justified in identifying all Being with Spirit, he was not justified in taking the further step of identifying the true nature of Spirit exclusively with pure thought.

105. Such a conclusion, no doubt, would make a considerable change in the Hegelian system. But it would not involve that Hegel had ignored the immediate aspect of reality, nor would it prove that he was wrong in asserting all being to be Spirit. Nor would it make his philosophy less thoroughly Idealistic. For the essence of Idealism does not lie in the assertion of the identity of Thought and Being, though it does lie very largely in the assertion of a relation between them. That relation may be expressed by saying that Thought is adequate to express Being, and Being adequate to embody Thought. On the one hand, no reality exists beyond the sphere of actual or possible knowledge, and no reality, when known as completely as possible, presents any contradiction or irrationality. On the other hand, there is no postulate which Thought demands in order to construct a harmonious and self-consistent system of knowledge, which is not realised in Being.

Hegel, as we have seen, establishes this by demonstrating that the higher categories are so involved in the lower that, if we say a thing exists at all, we are obliged to bring it under predicates which ensure that it will answer completely to the demands of our reason. In doing this, he arrives at the conclusions that the true nature of all Being is Spirit, and that the true nature of all Spirit is Thought. But important as these results,—true or false—are, they are only subsidiary as compared with the more general result that Thought and

Being—whether identical or not—are yet in complete harmony. From the point of view of theory, we thus know that reality is rational. From the point of view of practice, we know that reality is righteous, since the only view of reality which we can consider as completely rational, is shown to be one which involves our own complete self-realization. And it is this assertion that reality is both rational and righteous which is the distinguishing mark of Idealism.

CHAPTER IV.

106. MY object in this chapter will be to show that the method, by which Hegel proceeds from one category to another in his Logic, is not the same throughout, but changes materially as the process advances. I shall endeavour to show that this change may be reduced to a general law, and that from this law we may derive important consequences with regard to the nature and validity of the dialectic.

The exact relation of these corollaries to Hegel's own views is rather uncertain. Some of them do not appear to be denied in any part of the Logic, and, since they are apparently involved in some of his theories, may be supposed to have been recognised and accepted by him. On the other hand, he did not explicitly state and develope them anywhere, which, in the case of doctrines of such importance, is some ground for supposing that he did not hold them. Others, again, are certainly incompatible with his express statements. I desire, therefore, in considering them, to leave on one side the question of how far they were believed by Hegel, and merely to give reasons for thinking that they are necessary consequences of his system, and must be accepted by those who hold it.

107. The passage in which Hegel sums up his position on this point most plainly runs as follows: "The abstract form of the advance is, in Being, an other and transition into an other; in Essence, showing a reflection in the opposite; in notion, the distinction of individual from universality, which continues itself as such into, and is as an identity with, what is distinguished from it[1]."

The difference between the procedure in the doctrine of Being and in the doctrine of Essence is given in more detail earlier. "In the sphere of Essence one category does not pass into another, but refers to another merely. In Being the form of reference is simply due to our reflection on what takes place; but this form is the special and proper characteristic of Essence. In the sphere of Being, when somewhat becomes another, the somewhat has vanished. Not so in Essence: here there is no real other, but only diversity, reference of the one to its other. The transition of Essence is therefore at the same time no transition; for in the passage of different into different, the different does not vanish: the different terms remain in their relation. When we speak of Being and Nought, Being is independent, so is Nought. The case is otherwise with the Positive and the Negative. No doubt these possess the characteristic of Being and Nought. But the positive by itself has no sense; it is wholly in reference to the negative. And it is the same with the negative. In the Sphere of Being the reference of one term to another is only implicit; in Essence, on the contrary, it is explicit. And this in general is the distinction between the forms of Being and Essence: in Being everything is immediate, in Essence everything is relative[2]."

And again, in describing the transition from Essence to the Notion, he says: "Transition into something else is the dialectical process within the range of Being; reflection (bringing something else into light) in the range of Essence. The movement of the Notion is *development*; by which that only is explicitly affirmed which is already implicitly speaking present. In the world of nature, it is organic life that corresponds to the grade of the notion. Thus, e.g., the plant is developed from its germ. The germ virtually involves the whole plant, but does so only ideally or in thought; and it would therefore be a mistake to regard the development of the root, stem, leaves, and other different parts of the plant as meaning that they were *realiter* present, but in a very minute form, in the germ.

[1] *Enc.* Section 240.
[2] *Enc.* Section 111, lecture note.

That is the so-called 'box-within-box' hypothesis; a theory which commits the mistake of supposing an actual existence of what is at first found only in the shape of an ideal. The truth of the hypothesis on the other hand lies in its perceiving that, in the process of development, the notion keeps to itself, and only gives rise to alteration of form without making any addition in point of content. It is this nature of the notion—this manifestation of itself in its process as a development of its own self—which is chiefly in view by those who speak of innate ideas, or who, like Plato, describe all learning as merely reminiscence. Of course that again does not mean that everything which is embodied in a mind, after that mind has been formed by instruction, had been present in that mind beforehand in a definitely expanded shape.

"The movement of the notion is after all to be looked on only as a kind of play. The other which it sets up is in reality not another. Or, as it is expressed in the teaching of Christianity, not merely has God created a world which confronts Him as another; He has also from all eternity begotten a Son, in whom He, a Spirit, is at home with Himself[1]."

108. The result of this process may be summed up as follows: The further the dialectic goes from its starting point the less prominent becomes the apparent stability of the individual finite categories, and the less do they seem to be self-centred and independent. On the other hand, the process itself becomes more clearly self-evident, and is seen to be the only real meaning of the lower categories. In Being each category appears, taken by itself, to be permanent and exclusive of all others, and to have no principle of transition in it. It is only outside reflection which examines and breaks down this pretence of stability, and shows us that the dialectic process is inevitable. In Essence, however, each category by its own import refers to that which follows it, and the transition is seen to be inherent in its nature. But it is still felt to be, as it were, only an external effect of that nature. The categories have still an inner nature, as contrasted with the outer relations which they have with other categories. So far as they have

---

[1] *Enc.* Section 161, lecture note.

this inner nature, they are still conceived as independent and self-centred. But with the passage into the notion things alter; that passage "is the very hardest, because it proposes that independent actuality shall be thought as having all its substantiality in the passing over and identity with the other independent actuality[1]." Not only is the transition now necessary to the categories, but the transition *is* the categories. The reality in any finite category, in this stage, consists only in its summing up those which went before, and in leading on to those which come after.

109. Another change can be observed as the process continues. In the categories of Being the typical form is a transition from a thesis to an antithesis which is merely complementary to it, and is in no way superior to it in value or comprehensiveness. Only when these two extremes are taken together is there for the first time any advance to a higher notion. This advance is a transition to a synthesis which comes as a consequence of the thesis and antithesis jointly. It would be impossible to obtain the synthesis, or to make any advance, from either of the two complementary terms without the other. Neither is in any respect more advanced than the other, and neither of them can be said to be more closely connected than the other with the synthesis, in which both of them alike find their explanation and reconciliation. But when we come to Essence the matter is changed. Here the transition from thesis to antithesis is still indeed from positive to negative, but it is more than merely this. The antithesis is not merely complementary to the thesis, but is a correction of it. It is consequently more concrete and true than the thesis, and represents a real advance. And the transition to the synthesis is not now made so much from the comparison of the other two terms as from the antithesis alone. For the antithesis does not now merely oppose a contrary defect to the original defect of the thesis. It corrects, to some degree, that original mistake, and therefore has—to use the Hegelian phraseology—"the truth" of the thesis more or less within itself. As the action of the synthesis is to reconcile the thesis and the antithesis it

[1] *Enc.* Section 159.

can only be deduced from the comparison of the two. But if the antithesis has—as it has in Essence—the thesis as part of its own significance, it will present the whole of the data which the synthesis requires, and it will not be necessary to recur to the thesis, before the step to the synthesis is taken.

But although the reconciliation can be inferred from the second term, apart from the first, a reconciliation is still necessary. For, while the antithesis is an advance upon the thesis, it is also opposed to it. It is not simply a completion of it, but also a denial, though a denial which is already an approximation to union. This element of opposition and negation tends to disappear in the categories of the Notion. As these approach the end of the whole process, the steps are indeed discriminated from one another, but they can scarcely be said to be in opposition. For we have now arrived at a consciousness more or less explicit that in each category all that have gone before are summed up, and all that are to come after are contained implicitly. "The movement of the Notion is after all to be looked on only as a kind of play. The other which it sets up is in reality not another." And, as a consequence, the third term merely completes the second, without correcting one-sidedness in it, in the same way as the second term merely expands and completes the first. As this type is realised, in fact, the distinctions of the three terms gradually lose their meaning. There is no longer an opposition produced between two terms and mediated by a third. Each term is a direct advance on the one before it. The object of the process is not now to make the one-sided complete, but the implicit explicit. For we have reached a stage when each side carries in it already more or less consciousness of that unity of the whole which is the synthesis, and requires development rather than refutation.

110. It is natural that these changes should accompany the one first mentioned. For, as it is gradually seen that each category, of its own nature, and not by mere outside reflection on it, leads on to the next, that next will have inherent in it its relation to the first. It will not only be the negation and complement of the thesis, but will know that it is so. In so far as it does this, it will be higher than the thesis. It is true

that the thesis will see in like manner that it must be connected with the category that succeeds it. But this knowledge can only give a general character of transition to the thesis, for it only knows that it is connected with something, but does not yet know with what. But the antithesis does know with what it is connected, since it is connected with a term which precedes it in the dialectic process. And to see how it is inseparably connected with its opposite, and defined by its relation to it, is an important step towards the reconciliation of the opposition. A *fortiori* the greater clearness and ease of the transition will have the same effect in the case of the Notion. For there we see that the whole meaning of the category lies in its passage to another. The second therefore has the whole meaning of the first in it, as well as the addition that has been made in the transition, and must therefore be higher than the first.

From this follows naturally the change in the relation of the terms to their synthesis. We have seen that, in proportion as the meaning of the thesis is completely included in the meaning of the antithesis, it becomes possible to find all the *data* required for the synthesis in the antithesis alone. And when each term has its meaning completely absorbed in the one which follows it, the triple rhythm disappears altogether, in which case each term would be a simple advance on the one below it, and would be deduced from that one only.

111. While Hegel expressly notices, as we have seen, the increasing freedom and directness of the dialectic movement, he makes no mention of the different relation to one another assumed by the various members of the process, which I have just indicated. Traces of the change may, however, be observed in the detail of the dialectic. The three triads which it will be best to examine for this purpose are the first in the doctrine of Being, the middle one in the doctrine of Essence, and the last in the doctrine of the Notion. For, if there is any change within each of these three great divisions (a point we must presently consider), the special characteristics of each will be shown most clearly at that point at which it is at the greatest distance from each of the other divisions. The triads in question are those of Being, Not-Being, and Becoming; of the

World of Appearance, Content and Form, and Ratio[1]; and of Life, Cognition, and the Absolute Idea[2].

Now, in the first of these, thesis and antithesis are on an absolute level. Not-Being is no higher than Being: it does not contain Being in any sense in which Being does not contain it. We can pass as easily from Not-Being to Being as *vice versa.* And Not-Being by itself is helpless to produce Becoming—as helpless as Being is. The synthesis can only come from the conjunction of both of them. On the other hand the idea of Content and Form, according to Hegel, is a distinct advance on the idea of the World of Appearance, since in Content and Form "the connection of the phenomenon with self is completely stated." Ratio, again, although the synthesis of the two previous terms, is deduced from the second of them alone, while it could not be deduced from the first alone. It is the relation of Content and Form to one another which leads us on to the other relation which is called ratio. The idea of Cognition, also, is a distinct advance upon the idea of Life, since the defect in the latter, from which Hegel explains the existence of death, is overcome as we pass to Cognition. And it is from Cognition alone, without any reference back to Life, that we reach the Absolute Idea.

112. Another point arises on which we shall find but little guidance in Hegel's own writings. To each of the three great divisions of the dialectic he has ascribed a particular variation of the method. Are we to understand that one variety changes into another suddenly at the transition from division to division, or is the change continuous, so that, while the typical forms of each division are strongly characterised, the difference between the last step in one and the first step in the next is no greater than the difference between two consecutive steps in the same division? Shall we find the best analogy in the distinction between water and steam—a qualitative change suddenly brought about when a quantitative change has reached a certain degree—or in the distinction between youth and man-

---

[1] I follow the divisions of Essence as given in the *Encyclopaedia.*

[2] Cognition is used by Hegel in two senses. Here it is to be taken as Cognition in general, of which Cognition proper and Volition are species.

hood, which at their most characteristic points are clearly distinct, but which pass into one another imperceptibly.

On this point Hegel says nothing. Possibly it had never presented itself to his mind. But there are signs in the Logic which may lead us to believe that the change of method is gradual and continuous.

In the first place we may notice that the absolutely pure type of the process in Being, is not to be met with in any triad of Quality or Quantity except the first. Being and Not-Being are on a level. But if we compare Being *an sich* with Being for another, the One with the Many, and mere Quantity with Quantum, we observe that the second category is higher than the first in each pair, and that it is not merely the complement of the first, but to a certain degree transcends it. The inherent relation of thesis to antithesis seems to develop more as we pass on, so that before Essence is reached its characteristics are already visible to some extent, and the mere passivity and finitude of Being is partly broken down.

If, again, we compare the first and last stages of Essence, we shall find that the first approximates to the type of Being, while the last comes fairly close to that of the Notion, by substituting the idea of development for the idea of the reconciliation of contradictions. Difference, as treated by Hegel, is certainly an advance on Identity, and not a mere opposite, but there is still a good deal of opposition between the terms. The advance is shown by the fact that Difference contains Likeness and Unlikeness within itself, while the opposition of the two categories is clear, not only in common usage, but from the fact that the synthesis has to reconcile them, and balance their various deficiencies. But when we reach Substance and Causality we find that the notion of contradiction is subordinated to that of development, nearly as fully as if we were already at the beginning of the doctrine of the Notion.

So, finally, the special features of the doctrine of the Notion are not fully exhibited until we have come to its last stage. In the transitions of the Notion as Notion, of the Judgment, and of the Syllogism, we have not by any means entirely rid ourselves of the elements of opposition and negation. It is not until we reach the concluding triad of the Logic that we are able fully to see the typical progress of the Notion. In the transition from Life to Cognition, and from Cognition to the Absolute Idea, we perceive that the movement is all but completely direct, that the whole is seen to be in each part, and that there is no longer a contest, but only a development.

It is not safe, however, to place much weight on all this. In the first place, while Hegel explicitly says that each of the three doctrines has its special method, he says nothing about any development of method within each doctrine. In the second place the difficulty and uncertainty of comparing, quantitatively and exactly, shades of difference so slight and subtle, must always be very great. And, so far as we can compare them, there seem to be some exceptions to the rule of continuous development. We find some triads which approximate more closely to the pure Being-type than others which precede them, and we find some which approximate more closely to the pure Notion-type than others which follow them. But that there are some traces of continuous development cannot, I think, be denied, and this will become more probable if we see reason to think that, in a correct dialectic, the development would be continuous.

113. Before we consider this question we must first enquire whether the existence of such a development of any sort, whether continuous or not, might be expected from the nature of the case. We shall see that there are reasons for supposing this to be so, when we remember what we must regard as the essence of the dialectic. The motive power of all the categories is the concrete absolute truth, from which all finite categories are mere abstractions and to which they tend spontaneously to return. Again, two contradictory ideas cannot be held to be true at the same time. If it ever seems inevitable that they should be, this is a sign of error somewhere, and we cannot feel satisfied with the result, until we have transcended and synthesised the contradiction. It follows that in so far as the finite categories announce themselves as permanent, and as opposed in pairs of unsynthesised contradictories, they are expressing falsehood and not truth. We gain the truth by transcending the contradictions of the categories and by demonstrating their instability. Now the change in the method, of which we are speaking, indicates a clearer perception of this truth. For we have seen that the process becomes more spontaneous and more direct. As it becomes more spontaneous, as each category is seen to lead on of its own nature to the next, and to have its meaning only in the transition, it brings out more fully what lies at the root of the whole dialectic—namely that the truth of the opposed categories lies only in the synthesis. And as the process becomes more direct and leaves the opposition and negation behind, it also brings out more clearly what is an essential fact in every stage of the dialectic,—that is, that the impulse of imperfect truth, as we have it, is not towards self-contradiction as such, but towards self-completion. The essential nature of the whole dialectic is thus more clearly seen in the later stages, which approximate to the type of the Notion, than in the earlier stages which approximate to the type of Being.

This is what we might expect *a priori*. For the content of each stage in the dialectic is nearer to the truth than that of the stage before it. And each stage forms the starting-point from which we go forward again to further truth. At each step, therefore, in the forward process, we have a fuller knowledge of the truth than at the one before, and it is only natural that this fuller knowledge should react upon the manner in which the next step is made. The dialectic is due to the relation between the concrete whole, implicit in consciousness, and the abstract part of it which has become explicit. Since the second element alters at every step, as the categories approximate to the complete truth, it is clear that its relation to the unchanging whole alters also, and this would naturally affect the method. And, since the change in the relation will be one which will make that relation more obvious and evident, we may expect that every step which we take towards the full truth will render it possible to proceed more easily and directly to the next step.

Even without considering the special circumstance that each step in the process will give us this deeper insight into the meaning of the work we are carrying on, we might find other reasons for supposing that the nature of the dialectic process is modified by use. For the conception of an agent which is purely active, acting on a material which is purely passive, is a mere abstraction, and has a place nowhere in reality. Even in the case of matter, we find that this is true. An axe has not the same effect at its second blow as at its first, for it is more or less blunted. A violin has not the same tone the second time it is played on, as it had the first. And it would be least of all in the work of the mind that a rigid distinction could be kept up between form and matter, between the tool and the materials.

114. Now these arguments for the existence of change in the method are also arguments for supposing that the change will be continuous. There is reason to expect a change in the method whenever we have advanced a step towards truth. But we advance towards truth, not only when we pass from one chief division of the Logic to another, but whenever we pass from category to category, however minute a subdivision of the process they may represent. It would therefore seem that it is to be expected that the method would change after each category, and that no two transitions throughout the dialectic would present quite the same type. However continuous the change of conclusions can be made, it is likely that the change of method will be equally continuous.

It may also be noted that the three doctrines themselves form a triad, and that in the same way the three divisions of each doctrine, and the three subdivisions of each division, form a triad. The similarity of constitution which exists between the larger and smaller groups of categories may perhaps be some additional reason for anticipating that the smaller transitions will exert on the method an influence similar to that of the larger transitions, although, of course, less in amount.

115. We may therefore, I think, fairly arrive at the conclusion, in the first place, that the dialectic process does and must undergo a progressive change, and, in the second place, that this change is as much continuous as the process of the dialectic itself. Another question now arises. Has the change in the method destroyed its validity? The ordinary proofs

relate only to the type characteristic of Being, which, as
we have now found reason to believe, is only found in its
purity in the very first triad of all. Does the gradual
change to the types characteristic of Essence and the Notion
make any difference in the justification of the method as a
whole?

This question must be answered in the negative. The
process has lost none of its cogency. It consisted, according
to the earliest type, of a search for completeness, and of a
search for harmony between the elements of that completeness, the two stages being separate. Later on we have the
same search for completeness and for harmony, but both objects
are attained by a single process. In Being, the inadequacy
of the thesis led on to the antithesis. Each of these ideas
was regarded as an immediate and self-centred whole. On
the other hand each of them implied the other, since they
were complementary and opposite sides of the truth. This
brought about a contradiction, which had to be reconciled by
the introduction of the synthesis. Now the change in the
process has the effect of gradually dropping the intermediate
stage, in which the two sides of the whole are regarded as
incompatible and yet as inseparably connected. In the stage
of Essence, each category has a reference in its own nature
to those which come before and after it. When we reach the
antithesis therefore, we have already a sort of anticipation of the
synthesis, since we recognise that the two sides are connected
by their own nature, and not merely by external reasoning. Thus
the same step by which we reach the idea complementary to
our starting-point, and so gain completeness, does something
towards joining the two extremes in the harmony which we
require of them. For, when we have seen that the categories
are inherently connected, we have gone a good way towards
the perception that they are not incompatible. The harmony
thus attained in the antithesis is however only partial, and
leaves a good deal for the synthesis to do. In the Notion, the
change is carried further. Here we see that the whole meaning
of the category resides in the transition, and the whole thesis
is really summed up in the antithesis, for the meaning of the
thesis is now only the production of the antithesis, and it is

absorbed and transcended in it. In fact the relation of thesis, antithesis and synthesis would actually disappear in the typical form of process belonging to the Notion, for each term would be the completion of that which was immediately before it, since all the reality of the latter would be seen to be in its transition to its successor. This never actually happens, even in the final triad of the whole system. For the characteristic type of the Notion represents the process as it would be when it started from a perfectly adequate premise. When however the premise, the explicit idea in the mind, became perfectly adequate and true, we should have rendered explicit the whole concrete idea, and the object of the dialectic process would be attained, so that it could go no further. The typical process of the Notion is therefore an ideal, to which the actual process approximates more and more closely throughout its course, but which it can only reach at the moment when it stops completed.

116. The process always seeks for that idea which is logically required as the completion of the idea from which it starts. At first the complementary idea presents itself as incompatible with the starting-point, and has to be independently harmonised with it. Afterwards the complementary idea is at once presented as in harmony with the original idea in which it is implied. All the change lies in the fact that two operations, at first distinct, are fused into one. The argument of the dialectic all through is, If we start with a valid idea, all that is implied in it is valid, and also everything is valid that is required to avoid a contradiction between the starting-point and that which we reach by means of the starting-point. As we approximate to the end of the process, we are able to see, implied in the idea before us, not merely a complementary and contradictory idea on the same level, but an idea which at once complements and transcends the starting-point. The second idea is here from the first in harmony with the idea which it complements. But its justification is exactly the same as that of the antithesis in the Being-type of the process—that is, that its truth is necessarily involved in the truth of an idea which we have already admitted to be valid. And thus if we are satisfied with the cogency of the earlier forms of the process, we shall have no reason to modify our belief on account of the change of method.

117. We may draw several important conclusions with regard to the general nature of the dialectic, from the manner in which the form changes as it advances towards completion. The first of these is one which we may fairly attribute to Hegel himself, since it is evident from the way in which he deals with the categories, although it is not explicitly noticed by him. This is the subordinate place held by negation in the whole process. We have already observed that the importance of negation in the dialectic is by no means primary[1]. In the first place Hegel's Logic is very far from resting, as is supposed by some critics, on the violation of the law of contradiction. It rather rests on the impossibility of violating that law, and on the necessity of finding, for every contradiction, a reconciliation in which it vanishes. And not only is the idea of negation destined always to vanish in the synthesis, but even its temporary introduction is an accident, though an inevitable accident. The motive force of the process lies in the discrepancy between the concrete and perfect idea implicitly in our minds, and the abstract and imperfect idea explicitly in our minds, and the essential characteristic of the process is in the search of this abstract and imperfect idea, not after its negation as such, but after its complement as such. Its complement is, indeed, its contrary, because a relatively concrete category can be analysed into two direct contraries, and therefore the process does go from an idea to its contrary. But it does not do so because it seeks denial, but because it seeks completion.

But this can now be carried still further. Not only is the presence of negation in the dialectic a mere accident, though a necessary one, of the gradual completion of the idea. We are now led to consider it as an accident which is necessary indeed in the lower stages of the dialectic, but which is gradually eliminated in proportion as we proceed further, and in proportion as the materials from which we start are of a concrete and adequate character. For in so far as the process ceases to be from one extreme to another extreme equally one-sided, both of

----

[1] Chap. I. Section 9.

which regard themselves as permanent, and as standing in a relation of opposition towards one another, and in so far as it becomes a process from one term to another which is recognised as in some degree mediated by the first, and as transcending it—in so far the negation of each category by the other disappears. For it is then recognised that in the second category there is no contradiction to the first, because, in so far as the change has been completed, the first is found to have its meaning in the transition to the second.

The presence of negation, therefore, is not only a mere accident of the dialectic, but an accident whose importance continuously decreases as the dialectic progresses, and as its subject-matter becomes more fully understood.

118. We now come to a fresh question, of very great importance. We have seen that in the dialectic the relation of the various finite ideas to one another in different parts of the process is not the same—the three categories of Being, Not-Being, and Becoming standing in different relations among themselves to those which connect Life, Cognition, and the Absolute Idea. Now the dialectic process professes to do more than merely describe the stages by which we mount to the Absolute Idea—it also describes the nature of that Idea itself. In addition to the information which we gain about the latter by the definition given of it at the end of the dialectic, we also know that it contains in itself as elements or aspects all the finite stages of thought, through which the dialectic has passed before reaching its goal. It is not something which is reached by the dialectic, and which then exists independently of the manner in which it was reached. It does not reject all the finite categories as absolutely false, but pronounces them to be partly false and partly true, and it sums up in itself the truth of all of them. They are thus contained in it as moments. What relation do these moments bear to one another in the Absolute Idea?

We may, in the first place, adopt the easy and simple solution of saying that the relation they bear to one another, as moments in the Absolute Idea, is just the same as that which they bear to one another, as finite categories in the dialectic process. In this case, to discover their position in the Absolute

Idea, it is only necessary to consider the dialectic process, not as one which takes place in time, but as having a merely logical import. The process contemplated in this way will be a perfect and complete analysis of the concrete idea which is its end, containing about it, the truth, the whole truth, and nothing but the truth. And this, apparently, would have been Hegel's answer, if the question had been explicitly proposed to him. For he undoubtedly asserts that the dialectic expresses the deepest nature of objective thought.

119. But this conclusion seems open to doubt. For the change of method results, as we have seen, from a gradually growing perception of the truth which is at the bottom of the whole dialectic—the unreality of any finite category as against its synthesis, since the truth and reality of each category consists only in its reference to the next, and in its passage onwards to it. If this was not true all through the dialectic, there could be no dialectic at all, for the justification of the whole process is that the truth of the thesis and the antithesis is contained in the synthesis, and that in so far as they are anything else but aspects of the synthesis they are false and deceptive. This then must be the true nature of the process of thought, and must constitute the real meaning and essence of the dialectic. Yet this is only explicitly perceived in the Notion, and at the end of the Notion—or rather, as I pointed out above, we never attain to complete perception of it, but only approximate towards it as our grasp of the subject increases. Before this the categories appear always as, in their own nature, permanent and self-centred, and the breaking down of this self-assertion, and the substitution for it of the knowledge that truth is only found in the synthesis, appears as opposed to what went before, and as in contradiction to it, although a necessary and inevitable consequence of it. But if this were really so, the dialectic process would be impossible. If there really were any independent element in the lower categories, or any externality in the reconciliation, that reconciliation could never be complete and the dialectic could never claim, as it un-doubtedly does claim, to sum up *all* the lower elements of truth.

The very existence of the dialectic thus tends to prove that it is not in every sense objectively correct. For it would be impossible for any transition to be made, at any point in the process, unless the terms were really related according to the type belonging to the Notion. But no transition in the dialectic does take place exactly according to that type, and most of them according to types substantially different. We must therefore suppose that the dialectic does not exactly represent the truth, since if the truth were as it represents it to be, the dialectic itself could not exist. There must be in the process, besides that element which actually does express the real notion of the transition, another element which is due to the inadequacy of our finite thought to express the character of the reality which we are trying to describe.

This agrees with what was said above—that the change of method is no real change, but only a rearrangement of the elements of the transition. It is, in fact, only a bringing out explicitly of what is implicitly involved all along. In the lower categories our data, with their false appearance of independence, obscure and confuse the true meaning of the dialectic. We can see that the dialectic *has* this true meaning, even among these lower categories, by reflecting on what is implied in its existence and success. But it is only in the later categories that it becomes explicit. And it must follow that those categories in which it is not yet explicit do not fully represent the true nature of thought, and the essential character of the transition from less perfect to more perfect forms.

120. The conclusion at which we are thus compelled to arrive must be admitted, I think, to have no warrant in Hegel. Hegel would certainly have admitted that the lower categories, regarded in themselves, gave views of reality only approximating, and, in the case of the lowest, only very slightly approximating, to truth. But the procession of the categories, with its advance through oppositions and reconciliations, he apparently regarded as presenting absolute truth—as fully expressing the deepest nature of pure thought. From this, if I am right, we are forced, on his own premises, to dissent. For the true process of thought is one in which each category springs out of the one before it, not by contradicting it, but as an expression of its truest significance, and finds its own truest significance, in turn, by

passing on to another category. There is no contradiction, no opposition, and, consequently, no reconciliation. There is only development, the rendering explicit what was implicit, the growth of the seed to the plant. In the actual course of the dialectic this is never attained. It is an ideal which is never quite realised, and from the nature of the case never can be quite realised. In the dialectic there is always opposition, and therefore always reconciliation. We do not go straight onward, but more or less from side to side. It seems inevitable, therefore, to conclude that the dialectic does not completely and perfectly express the nature of thought.

This conclusion is certainly startling and paradoxical. For the validity of the dialectic method for any purpose, and its power of adequately expressing the ultimate nature of thought, appear to be so closely bound up together, that we may easily consider them inseparable. The dialectic process is a distinctively Hegelian idea. Doubtless the germs of it are to be found in Fichte and elsewhere; but it was only by Hegel that it was fully worked out and made the central point of a philosophy. And in so far as it has been held since, it has been held substantially in the manner in which he stated it. To retain the doctrine, and to retain the idea that it is of cardinal importance while denying that it adequately represents the nature of thought, looks like a most unwarranted and gratuitous distinction between ideas which their author held to be inseparable.

Yet I cannot see what alternative is left to us. For it is Hegel himself who refutes his own doctrine. The state to which the dialectic, according to him, gradually approximates, is one in which the terms thesis, antithesis, and synthesis can have no meaning. For in this state there is no opposition to create the relation of thesis and antithesis, and, therefore, no reconciliation of that opposition to create a synthesis. "The elements distinguished are without more ado at the same time declared to be identical with one another, and with the whole. ...The other which the notion sets up is in reality not another[1]." Now, nowhere in the dialectic do we entirely get rid of the relation of thesis, antithesis, and synthesis; even in the final

---

[1] *Enc.* Section 161.

triad of the process there are traces of it. The inference seems inevitable that the dialectic cannot fully represent, in any part of its movement, the real and essential nature of pure thought. The only thing to be done is to consider whether, with this important limitation, the process has any longer a claim to any real significance, and, if so, to how much? I shall endeavour to show that its importance can scarcely be said to have diminished at all.

121. Since the dialectic, if the hypothesis I have advanced be correct, does not adequately represent the nature of pure thought itself, although it does represent the inevitable course our minds are logically bound to follow, when they attempt to deal with pure thought, it follows that it must be in some degree subjective. We have now to determine exactly the meaning in which we are using this rather ambiguous word. On the one hand it is clear that the dialectic is not subjective in that sense in which the word has been defined as meaning "that which is mine *or* yours." It is no mere empirical description or generalisation. For, whatever view we may hold with regard to the success or failure of the dialectic in apprehending the true nature of thought, it will not at all affect the question of its internal necessity, and of its cogency for us. The dialectic is not an account of what men have thought, or may think. It is a demonstration of what they must think, provided they wish to deal with Hegel's problem at all, and to deal with it consistently and truly.

On the other hand, we must now pronounce the dialectic process to be subjective in this sense—that it does not fully express the essential nature of thought, but obscures it more or less under characteristics which are not essential. It may not seem very clear at first sight how we can distinguish between the necessary course of the mind when engaged in pure thought, which the dialectic method, according to this hypothesis, is admitted to be, and the essential nature of thought, which it is not allowed that it can adequately express. What, it may be asked, is the essential nature of thought, except that course which it must and does take, whenever we think?

We must remember, however, that according to Hegel thought can only exist in its complete and concrete form—that is, as the Absolute Idea. The import of our thought may be, and of course often is, a judgment under some lower category, but our thought itself, as an existent fact, distinguished from the meaning it conveys, must be concrete and complete. For to stop at any category short of the complete whole involves a contradiction, and a contradiction is a sign of error. Now our judgments can be, and often are, erroneous. And so we can, and do, make judgments which involve a contradiction. But there would be no meaning in saying that a fact is erroneous, and therefore, if we find a contradiction in any judgment, we know that it cannot be true of facts. It follows that, though it is unquestionably true that we can predicate *in* thought categories other than the highest, and even treat them as final, it is no less certain that we cannot, with complete truth, explain thought, any more than any other aspect of reality, by any category but the Absolute Idea.

This explains how it is possible for the actual and inevitable course of thought not to express fully and adequately its own nature. For thought may be erroneous or deceptive, when it is treating of thought, as much as when it is treating of any other reality. And it is possible that under certain circumstances the judgment expressed in our thoughts may be inevitably erroneous or deceptive. If these judgments have thought as their subject-matter we shall then have the position in question—that the necessary course of thought will fail to express properly its own nature.

122. The mistake, as we have already noticed, comes from the fact that, whereas the logical relations, which form the content of the Absolute Idea, and express the true nature of thought, consist in a direct development in which each term only exists in the transition to another, the actual process, on the other hand, is one from contradictory to contradictory, each of which is conceived as possessing some stability and independence. The reason of this mistake lies in the nature of the process, which is one from error to truth. For while error remains in our conclusions, it must naturally affect our comprehension of the logical relations by which those conclusions are connected, and induce us to suppose them other than they are. In particular, the mistake may be traced to the circum-

stance that the dialectic starts with the knowledge of the part, and from this works up to the knowledge of the whole. This method of procedure is always inappropriate in anything of the nature of an organism. Now the relation of the moments of the Absolute Idea to the whole of which they are parts is still more close and intimate than is the relation of the parts of a living organism to the organism itself. And here, therefore, even more than with organisms, will it be inadequate and deceptive to endeavour to comprehend the whole from the standpoint of the part. And this is what the dialectic, as it progresses, must necessarily do. Consequently, not only are the lower categories of the dialectic inadequate when taken as ultimate, but their relation to each other is not the relation which they have in the Absolute Idea, and consequently in all existence. These relations, in the dialectic, represent more or less the error through which the human mind is gradually attaining to the truth. They do not adequately represent the relations existing in the truth itself. To this extent, then, the dialectic is subjective.

123. And the dialectic is also to be called subjective because it not only fails to show clearly the true nature of thought, but, as we noticed above, does not fully express its own meaning—the meaning of the process forwards. For the real meaning of the advance, if it is to have any objective reality at all—if it is to be a necessary consequence of all attempt at thorough and consistent thinking, must be the result of the nature of thought as it exists. Our several judgments on the nature of thought have not in themselves any power of leading us on from one of them to another. It is the relation of these judgments to the concrete whole of thought, incarnate in our minds and in all our experience, which creates the dialectic movement. Since this is so, it would seem that the real heart and kernel of the process is the movement of abstractions to rejoin the whole from which they have been separated, and that the essential part of this move- ment is that by which we are carried from the more abstract to the more concrete. This will be determined by the relations in which the finite categories stand to the concrete idea, when they are viewed as abstractions from it and aspects of it—the

only sense in which they have any truth. But the true relation of the abstractions to the concrete idea is, as we have already seen, that to which the dialectic method gradually approximates, but which it never reaches, and not that with which it starts, and which it gradually, but never entirely, discards. And so the dialectic advance has, mixed up with it, elements which do not really belong to the advance, nor to the essence of pure thought, but are merely due to our original ignorance about the latter, of which we only gradually get rid. For all that part of the actual advance in the dialectic, which is different from the advance according to the type characteristic of the Notion, has no share in the real meaning and value of the process, since it does not contribute to what alone makes that meaning and value, namely the restoration of the full and complete idea. What this element is, we can learn by comparing the movement of the dialectic which is typical of Being, with that which is typical of the Notion. It is the opposition and contradiction, the immediacy of the finite categories, and the way in which they negate their antitheses, and resist, until forced into submission, the transition to their syntheses. It is, so to speak, the transverse motion as opposed to the direct motion forward. The dialectic always moves onwards at an angle to the straight line which denotes advance in truth and concreteness. Starting unduly on one side of the truth, it oscillates to the other, and then corrects itself. Once more it finds that even in its corrected statement it is still one-sided, and again swings to the opposite extreme. It is in this indirect way alone that it advances. And the essence of the process is the direct part alone of the advance. The whole point of the dialectic is that it gradually attains to the Absolute Idea. In so far then as the process is not direct advance to the absolute, it does not express the essence of the process only, but also the inevitable inadequacies of the human mind when considering a subject-matter which can only be fully understood when the consideration has been completed.

And, as was remarked above, it also fails to express its own meaning in another way. For the imperfect type of transition, which is never fully eliminated, represents the various categories as possessing some degree of independence and self-subsistence.

If they really possessed this, they could not be completely absorbed in the syntheses, and the dialectic could not be successful. The fact that it is successful proves that it has not given a completely correct account of itself, and, for this reason also, it deserves to be called subjective, since it does not fully express the objective reality of thought.

124. Having decided that the dialectic is to this extent subjective, we have to consider how far this will reduce its cardinal significance in philosophy, or its practical utility. I do not see that it need do either. For all that results from this new position is that the dialectic is a process through error to truth. Now we knew this before. For on any theory of the dialectic it remains true that it sets out with inadequate ideas of the universe and finally reaches adequate ideas. We now go further and say that the relation of these inadequate ideas to one another does not completely correspond to anything in the nature of reality. But the general result is the same—that we gain the truth by the dialectic, but that the steps by which we reach it contain imperfections. We shall see that our new view does not destroy the value of the dialectic, if we consider in more detail in what that value consists.

The importance of the dialectic is threefold. The first branch of it depends chiefly on the end being reached, and the other two chiefly on the means by which it is reached. The first of these lies in the conclusion that if we can predicate any category whatever of a thing, we are thereby entitled to predicate the Absolute Idea of it. Now we can predicate some category of anything whatever, and the Absolute Idea is simply the description in abstract terms of the human spirit, or, in other words, the human spirit is the incarnation of the Absolute Idea. From this it follows that the mind could, if it only saw clearly enough, see a nature like its own in everything. The importance of this conclusion is obvious. It gives the assurance of that harmony between ourselves and the world for which philosophy always seeks, and by which alone science and religion can be ultimately justified.

Hegel was entitled, on his own premises, to reach this conclusion by means of the dialectic. And the different view of the relation of the dialectic to reality, which I have ventured to put forward, does not at all affect the validity of the dialectic for this purpose. For the progress of the dialectic remains as necessary as before. The progress is indirect, and we have come to the conclusion that the indirectness of the advance is not in any way due to the essential nature of pure thought, but entirely to our own imperfect understanding of that nature. But the whole process is still necessary, and the direct advance is still essential. And all that we want to know is that the direct advance is necessary. We are only interested, for this particular purpose, in proving that from any possible stand-point we are bound in logical consistency to advance to the Absolute Idea. In this connection it is not of the least importance what is the nature of the road we travel, provided that we must travel it, nor whether the process expresses truth fully, provided that the final conclusion does so. Now the theory propounded above as to the dialectic process leaves the objectivity and adequacy of the result of the dialectic unimpaired. And therefore for this function the system is as well adapted as it ever was.

125. The second ground of the importance of the Hegelian logic consists in the information which it is able to give us about the world as it is here and now for us, who have not yet been able so clearly to interpret all phenomena as only to find our own most fundamental nature manifesting itself in them. As we see that certain categories are superior in concreteness and truth to others, since they come later in the chain and have transcended the meaning of their predecessors, we are able to say that certain methods of regarding the universe are more correct and significant than others. We are able to see that the idea of organism, for example, is a more fundamental explanation than the idea of causality, and one which we should prefer whenever we can apply it to the matter in hand.

Here also the value of the dialectic remains unimpaired. For whether it does or does not express the true nature of thought with complete correctness; it certainly, according to this theory, does show the necessary and inevitable connection of our finite judgments with one another. The utility which we are now considering lies in the guidance which the dialectic can give us to the relative validity and usefulness of these finite judgments. For it is only necessary to know their relations to one another, and to know that as the series goes further, it goes nearer to the truth. Both these things can be learnt from the dialectic. That it does not tell us the exact relations which subsist in reality is unimportant. For we are not here judging reality, but the judgments of reason about reality.

126. The third function of the dialectic process is certainly destroyed by the view of it which I have explained above. The dialectic showed, for Hegel, the relation of the categories to one another, as moments in the Absolute Idea, and in reality. We are now forced to consider those moments as related in a way which is inadequately expressed by the relation of the categories to one another. We are not however deprived of anything essential to the completeness of the system by this. In the first place, we are still able to understand completely and adequately what the Absolute Idea is. For although one definition was given of it by which "its true content is only the whole system of which we have been hitherto studying the development," yet a more direct and independent one may also be found[1]. Our inability to regard the process any longer as an adequate analysis of the Absolute Idea will not leave us in ignorance of what the Absolute Idea really is.

And, in the second place, we are not altogether left in the dark even as regards the analysis of the Absolute Idea. The dialectic, it is true, never fully reveals the true nature of thought which forms its secret spring, but it gives us data by which we can discount the necessary error. For the connection of the categories resembles the true nature of thought (which is expressed in the typical transition of the Notion), more and more closely as it goes on, and at the end of the Logic it differs from it only infinitesimally. By observing the type to which the dialectic method approximates throughout its course, we are thus enabled to tell what element in it is that which is due to the essential nature of thought. It is that element which alone is left when, in the typical movement of the Notion, we see how the dialectic would act if it could act with full self-con-

---

[1] "Der Begriff der Idee, dem die Idee als solche der Gegenstand, dem das Objekt sie ist."—*Enc.* Section 236. The definition quoted in the text is in Section 237, lecture note.

sciousness. It is true that in the lower categories we can never see the transition according to this type, owing to the necessary confusion of the subject-matter in so low a stage, which hides the true nature of the process to which the dialectic endeavours to approximate. But we can regard the movement of all the categories as compounded, in different proportions according to their positions in the system, of two forces, the force of opposition and negation, and the force of advance and completion, and we can say that the latter is due to the real nature of thought, and the former to our misconceptions about it. In other words, the element of imperfection in the dialectic is inevitable, but its amount can be ascertained, and it need not therefore introduce any doubt or scepticism into the conclusions to which the dialectic may lead us.

127. What then is this real and essential element in the advance of thought which is revealed, though never completely, in the dialectic? In the first place, it is an advance which is direct. The element of indirectness which is introduced by the movement from thesis to antithesis, from opposite to opposite, diminishes as the dialectic proceeds, and, in the ideal type, wholly dies away. In that type each category is seen to carry in itself the implication of the next beyond it, to which thought then proceeds. The lower is only lower because part of its meaning is still implicit; it is no longer one-sided, requiring to be corrected by an equal excess on the other side of the truth. And, therefore, no idea stands in an attitude of opposition to any other; there is nothing to break down, nothing to fight. All that aspect of the process belongs to our misapprehension of the relation of the abstract to the concrete. While looking up from the bottom, we may imagine the truth is only to be attained by contest, but in looking down from the top—the only true way of examining a process of this sort—we see that the contest is only due to our misunderstanding, and that the growth of thought is really direct and unopposed.

The movement of the dialectic may perhaps be compared to that of a ship tacking against the wind. If we suppose that the wind blows exactly from the point which the ship wishes to reach, and that, as the voyage continues, the sailing powers of the ship improve so that it becomes able to sail closer and closer to the wind, the analogy will be rather exact. It is impossible for the ship to reach its destination by a direct course, as the wind is precisely opposite to the line which that course would take, and in the same way it is impossible for the dialectic to move forward without the triple relation of its terms, and without some opposition between thesis and antithesis. But the only object of the ship is to proceed towards the port, as the only object of the dialectic process is to attain to the concrete and complete idea, and the movement of the ship from side to side of the direct line is labour wasted, so far as the end of the voyage is concerned, though necessarily wasted, since the forward movement would, under the circumstances, be impossible without the combination with it of a lateral movement. In the same way, the advance in the dialectic is merely in the gradually increasing completeness of the ideas. The opposition of one idea to another, and the consequent negation and contradiction, do not mark any real step towards attaining the knowledge of the essential nature of thought, although they are necessary accompaniments of the process of gaining that knowledge. Again, the change in the ship's sailing powers which allows it to go nearer to the wind, and so reduces the distance which it is necessary to travel in order to accomplish the journey, will correspond to the gradual subordination of the elements of negation and opposition, which we have seen to take place as we approach the end of the dialectic.

128. Not the whole, then, of each category represents the objective nature of the dialectic, but only a certain element in it. And this is the element of unity and continuity. The element which keeps the categories apart, and gives them the appearance of distinction and stability, is just the element which we are now led to believe is due to our incapacity to grasp the nature of thought until we arrive at the end of the dialectic.

This would seem to render it probable that the dialectic may be looked on primarily as continuous and not discrete. The categories, if this view is right, should not be taken as ultimate units, which are combined in groups of three, and these again in larger groups of three, till at last the whole dialectic is in this manner built up. On the contrary the whole dialectic should be looked on as primarily a unity, which can be analysed into three members, each of which can again be analysed into three members, and so on, as long as our interest and insight are sufficient to induce us to pursue the division.

This theory is confirmed by two other characteristics of the dialectic. The first of these is the great difference in the lengths to which the sub-division of the categories is carried in different parts of the system. If, for example, in the Smaller Logic, we take the first division of Essence, which is named Essence as Ground, we find that its first two sub-divisions are called, respectively, Primary Characteristics of Reflection, and Existence. In the latter there is no trace of further sub-division, while the former is divided again into Identity, Difference, and Ground, and in Difference, once more, we find distinguished Diversity, Likeness and Unlikeness, and Positive and Negative. Similar differences are to be found at other points of the system, and also in the Greater Logic. If the individual categories were ultimate units, such discrepancies in their size and importance would be strange and inexplicable. But if we regard the whole of the dialectic as logically prior to its parts, and the parts as produced by analysis, we have an easy and natural explanation of the inequality—namely, that it is due to some circumstance which rendered Hegel, or which perhaps renders all men, more interested or more acute when dealing with one part of the process than when dealing with another.

129. There is also a second characteristic of the dialectic which supports this theory. It is not necessary to descend to the lowest sub-divisions which Hegel gives, in order to observe the dialectic process. The larger divisions, also, lead on to one another by the same necessity as the smaller ones do. Reasons could be given, without going into greater detail, why Quality should involve Quantity, and both of them Measure; or, again, why Notion must lead us on to Judgment, and Judgment to Syllogism. An argument which confined itself to so few steps would be far more obscure, and consequently more dangerous and doubtful, than the argument which we actually have in the Logic. But still such a chain of demonstrations could be formed, and in many places Hegel gives us part of it.

Now this is incompatible with the view of the dialectic as ultimately discrete. For then every larger division would be nothing but an aggregate of smaller ones. No such division could then be used as a transition from the one below it to the one above it, without descending into the lowest sub-divisions. Being an aggregate of separate units, it could not be treated as a coherent whole until all its separate parts had been demonstrated to be linked together. And the fact that the dialectic process can go from one to another of the larger divisions, ignoring their sub-divisions, will confirm us in supposing that the dialectic is not a chain of links, but rather a continuous flow of thought, which can be analysed into divisions and sub-divisions.

130. The belief that the dialectic is continuous may have an important influence on our position if we are led, on closer examination, to the conclusion that any of Hegel's transitions are erroneous and cannot be justified. On the hypothesis that the steps of the dialectic are discrete, one such error would destroy the validity of the whole process, beyond the point where it occurs, as completely as the two ends of a chain would be separated by the breaking of a single link, even if all the rest held fast. Our only reason for not considering the whole value of the process, beyond the faulty link, as absolutely destroyed, would rest on a rough argument from analogy. It might be said that, if there was a valid dialectic process up to a certain point, and again from that point onwards, it was not probable that there would, at that one point, be an absolute gulf, and we might therefore hope that a fresh transition might be discovered at this point, instead of the one which we had been compelled to reject. But such an analogy would not be very strong.

On the other hand, the theory of the continuity of the dialectic will make such a discovery much less serious. For if the larger division, in a sub-division of which the fault occurs, forms itself a valid transition from the division before it to the one which follows it, we shall be sure that to do this it must be a coherent whole, and capable, therefore, of being analysed into a coherent chain of sub-divisions. And therefore, though we cannot be satisfied with the dialectic until we have replaced the defective member with one that will stand criticism, we shall have good grounds for supposing that such a change can be effected.

131. The gradual change in the method of the dialectic can be well exemplified by examining the supreme and all-including triad, of which all the others are moments. This triad is given by Hegel as Logic, Nature, and Spirit.

If we enquire as to the form which the dialectic process is likely to assume here, we find ourselves in a difficulty. For the form of transition in any particular triad was determined by its place in the series. If it was among the earlier categories, it approximated to the character given as typical of Being; if it did not come till near the end, it showed more or less resemblance to the type of the Notion. And we were able to see that this was natural, because the later method, being more direct, and less encumbered with irrelevant material, was only to be attained when the work previously done had given us sufficient insight into the real nature of the subject-matter. This principle, however, will not help us here. For the transition which we are here considering is both the first and the last of its series, and it is impossible, therefore, to determine its characteristic features by its place in the order. The less direct method is necessary when we are dealing with the abstract and imperfect categories with which our investigations must begin, the more direct method comes with the more adequate categories. But this triad covers the whole range, from the barest category of the Logic—that of pure Being—to the culmination of human thought in Absolute Spirit.

Since it covers the whole range, in which all the types of the dialectic method are displayed, the natural conclusion would seem to be that one of them is as appropriate to it as another, that whichever form may be used will be more or less helpful and significant, because the process does cover the ground in which that form can appropriately be used; while, on the other hand, every form will be more or less inadequate, because the process covers ground on which it cannot appropriately be used. If we cast it in the form of the Notion, we shall ignore the fact that it starts at a point too early for a method so direct; if, on the other hand, we try the form of the categories of Being, the process contains material for which such a method is inadequate.

132. And if we look at the facts we shall find that they confirm this view, and that it is possible to state the relation of Logic, Nature, and Spirit to one another, in two different ways. Hegel himself states it in the manner characteristic of the Notion. It is not so much positive, negative, and synthesis, as universal, particular, and individual that he points out. In the Logic thought is to be found in pure abstraction from all particulars, (we cannot, of course, think it as abstracted from particulars, but in the Logic we attend only to the thought, and ignore the data it connects). In Nature we find thought again, for Nature is part of experience, and more or less rational, and this implies that it has thought in it. In Nature, however, thought is rather buried under the mass of data which appear contingent and empirical; we see the reason is there, but we do not see that everything is completely rational. It is described by Hegel as the idea in a state of alienation from itself. Nature is thus far from being the mere contrary and correlative of thought. It is thought and something more, thought incarnate in the particulars of sense. At the same time, while the transition indicates an advance, it does not indicate a pure advance. For the thought is represented as more or less overpowered by the new element which has been added, and not altogether reconciled to and interpenetrating it. In going forward it has also gone to one side, and this requires, therefore, the correction which is given to it in the synthesis, when thought; in Spirit, completely masters the mass of particulars which for a time had seemed to master it, and when we perceive that the truth of the universe lies in the existence of thought as fact, the incarnation of the Absolute Idea—in short, in Spirit.

Here we meet all the characteristics of the Notion-type. The second term, to which we advance from the first, is to some extent its opposite, since the particulars of sense, entirely wanting in the first, are in undue prominence in the second. But it is to a much greater extent the completion of the first, since the idea, which was taken in the Logic in unreal abstraction, is now taken as embodied in facts, which is the way it really exists. The only defect is that the embodiment is not yet quite complete and evident. And the synthesis which removes this defect does not, as in earlier types of the dialectic, stand impartially between thesis and antithesis, each as defective as the other, but only completes the process already begun in the antithesis. It is not necessary to compare the two lower terms, Logic and Nature, to be able to proceed to Spirit. The consideration of Nature alone would be sufficient to show that it postulated the existence of Spirit. For we have already in Nature both the sides required for the synthesis, though their connection is so far imperfect, and there is consequently no need to refer back to the thesis, whose meaning has been incorporated and preserved in the antithesis. The existence of the two sides, not completely reconciled, in the antithesis, in itself postulates a synthesis, in which the reconciliation shall be completed.

133. But it would also be possible to state the transition in the form which is used in the Logic for the lower part of the dialectic. In this case we should proceed from pure thought to its simple contrary, and from the two together to a synthesis. This simple contrary will be the element which, together with thought, forms the basis for the synthesis which is given in Spirit. And as Nature, as we have seen, contains the same elements as Spirit, though less perfectly developed, we shall find this contrary of thought to be the element in experience, whether of Nature or Spirit, which cannot be reduced to thought. Now of this element we know that it is immediate and that it is particular—not in the sense in which Nature is particular, in the sense of incompletely developed individuality, but of abstract particularity. It is possible to conceive that in the long run all other characteristics of experience except these might be reduced to a consequence of thought. But however far the process of rationalisation might be carried, and however fully we might be able to answer the question of why things are as they are and not otherwise, it is impossible to get rid of a *datum* which is immediate and therefore unaccounted for. For thought is only mediation, and therefore, taken apart from immediacy, is a mere abstraction. If nothing existed but thought itself, still the fact of its existence must be in the long run immediately given, and something for which thought itself could not account. This immediacy is the mark of the element which is essential to experience and irreducible to thought.

If then we wished to display the process from Logic to Spirit according to the Being-type of transition we should, starting from pure thought as our thesis, put as its antithesis the element of immediacy and "givenness" in experience. This element can never be properly or adequately described, since all description consists in predicating categories of the subject, and is therefore mediation; but by abstracting the element of mediation in experience, as in Logic we abstract the element of immediacy, we can form some idea of what it is like. Here we should have thought and immediacy as exactly opposite and counterbalancing elements. They are each essential to the truth, but present themselves as opposed to one another. Neither of them has the other as a part of itself, though they can be seen to be closely and intimately connected. But each of them negates the other as much as it implies it, and the relation, without the synthesis, is one of opposition and contradiction. We cannot see, as we can when a transition assumes the Notion-form, that the whole meaning of the one category lies in its transition to the other. The synthesis of our triad would be the notion of experience or reality, in which we have the given immediate mediated. This would contain both Nature and Spirit, the former as the more imperfect stage, the latter as the more perfect, culminating in the completely satisfactory conception of Absolute Spirit. Nature stands in this case in the same relation to Absolute Spirit as do the lower forms of Spirit,—as less perfectly developed forms of the concrete reality.

This triad could be proved as cogently as the other. It could be shown, in the first place, that mere mediation is unmeaning, except in relation to the merely immediate, since, without something to mediate, it could not act. In the same way it could be shown that the merely given, without any action of thought on it, could not exist, since any attempt to describe it, or even to assert its existence, involves the use of some category, and therefore of thought. And these two extremes, each of which negates the other, and at the same time demands it, are reconciled in the synthesis of actual experience, whether Nature or Spirit, in which the immediate is mediated, and both extremes in this way gain for the first time reality and consistency.

134. The possibility of this alternative arrangement affords, as I mentioned above, an additional argument in favour of the view that the change of method is essential to the dialectic, and that it is due to the progressively increasing insight into the subject which we gain as we pass to the higher categories and approximate to the completely adequate result. For, in this instance, when the whole ground from beginning to end of the dialectic process is covered in a single triad, we find that either method may be used,—a fact which suggests of itself that the two methods are appropriate to the two ends of the series, which are here, and here only, united by a single step. Independently of this, however, it is also worth while to consider the possibility of the double transition attentively, because it may help us to explain the origin of some of the misapprehensions of Hegel's meaning which are by no means uncommon.

135. We saw above that the dialectic represented the real nature of thought more closely in the later categories, when it appeared comparatively direct and spontaneous, than in the earlier stages, when it was still encumbered with negations and contradictions. It would appear probable, therefore, beforehand, that of the two possible methods of treating this particular triad, the one which Hegel has in fact adopted would be the more expressive and significant. On examination we shall find that this is actually the case. For there is no real separation between thought and immediacy ; neither can exist without the other. Now, in the method adopted by Hegel, the element of immediacy comes in first in Nature, and comes in, not as an element opposed to, though necessarily connected with, pure thought, but as already bound up with it in a unity. This expresses the truth better than a method which starts by considering the two aspects as two self-centred and independent realities, which have to be connected by reasoning external to themselves. For by this second method, even when the two terms are finally reconciled in a synthesis, it is done, so to speak, against their will, since their claims to independence are only overcome by the *reductio ad absurdum* to which they are brought, when they are seen, as independent, to be at once mutually contradictory and mutually implied in each other. In this method the transitory nature of the incomplete categories and the way in which their movement forward depends on their own essential nature, are not sufficiently emphasised.

And we shall find that the subject-matter of the transition is too advanced to bear stating according to the Being-type without showing that that type is not fully appropriate to it. Logic and Immediacy are indeed as much on a level as Being and Not-Being. There is no trace whatever in the former case, any more than in the latter, of a rudimentary synthesis in the antithesis. But the other characteristic of the lower type—that the thesis and the antithesis should claim to be mutually exclusive and independent—cannot be fully realised. Being and Nothing, although they may be shown by reasoning to be mutually implicated, are at any rate *primâ facie* distinct and independent. But mediation and immediacy, although opposed, are nevertheless connected, even *primâ facie*. It is impossible even to define the two terms without suggesting that each of them is, by itself, unstable, and that their only real existence is as aspects of the concrete whole in which they are united. The method is thus not sufficiently advanced for the matter it deals with.

136. It is, however, as I endeavoured to show above, probable *à priori* that neither method would completely suit this particular case. And not only the method which we have just discussed, but the one which Hegel preferred to it, will be found to some extent inadequate to its task here. Hegel's is, no doubt, the more correct and convenient of the two; yet its use alone, without the knowledge that it does not in this case exclude the concurrent use of the other as equally legitimate, may lead to grave miscomprehensions of the system.

For the use of that method which Hegel does not adopt—the one in which the terms are Logic, Immediacy, and Nature and Spirit taken together—has at any rate this advantage, that it brings out the fact that Immediacy is as important and ultimate a factor in reality as Logic is, and one which cannot be reduced to Logic. The two terms are exactly on a level. We begin with the Logic and go from that to Immediacy, because it is to the completed idea of the Logic that we come if we start from the idea of pure Being, and we naturally start from the idea of pure Being, because it alone, of all our ideas, is the one whose denial carries with it, at once and clearly, self-contradiction. But the transition from Immediacy to Logic is exactly the same as that from Logic to Immediacy. And as the two terms are correlative in this way, it would be comparatively easy to see, by observing them, that neither of them derived its validity from the other, but both from the synthesis.

137. This is not so clear when the argument takes the other form. The element of Immediacy here never appears as a separate and independent term at all. It appears in Nature for the first time, and here it is already in combination with thought. And Nature and Logic are not correlative terms, from either of which we can proceed to the other. The transition runs from Logic to Nature—from thought by itself, to thought in union with immediacy. It is not unnatural, therefore, to suppose that immediacy is dependent on pure thought, and can be deduced from it, while the reverse process is not possible. The pure reason is supposed to make for itself the material in which it is embodied. "The logical bias of the Hegelian philosophy," says Professor Seth, "tends ... to reduce things to mere types or 'concretions' of abstract formulæ[1]." It might, I think, be shown that other considerations conclusively prove this view to be incorrect. In the first place, throughout the Logic there are continual references which show that pure thought requires some material, other than itself, in which to work. And, secondly, the spring of all movement in the dialectic comes from the synthesis towards which the process is working, and not from the thesis from which the start is made. Consequently, progress from Logic to Nature could, in any case, prove, not that the additional element in nature was derived from thought, but that it

[1] *Hegelianism and Personality*, p. 126.

co-existed with thought in the synthesis which is their goal. But although the mistake might have been avoided, even under the actual circumstances, it could scarcely have been made if the possibility of the alternative method of deduction had been recognised. Immediacy would, in that case, have been treated as a separate element in the process, and as one which was correlative with pure thought, so that it could scarcely have been supposed to have been dependent on it.

138. The more developed method, again, tends rather to obscure the full meaning and importance of the synthesis, unless we realise that, in this method, part of the work of the synthesis is already done in the second term. This is of great importance, because we have seen that it is in their synthesis alone that the terms gain full reality and validity, which they did not possess when considered in abstraction. In the earlier method we see clearly that pure thought is one of these abstractions, as mere immediacy is the other. It is, therefore, clear that each of these terms, taken by itself, is a mere aspect, and could not possibly, out of its own nature, produce the other aspect, and the reality from which they both come. From this standpoint it would be impossible to suppose that out of pure thought were produced Nature and Spirit.

Now, in the type characteristic of the Notion, the same element appears both in thesis and antithesis, although in the latter it is in combination with a fresh element. There is, therefore, a possibility of misunderstanding the process. For an element which was both in thesis and antithesis might appear not to be merely a one-sided abstraction, but to have the concreteness which is to be found in the synthesis, since it appears in both the extremes into which the synthesis may be separated. When, for example, we have Logic, Nature, and Spirit, we might be tempted to argue that pure thought could not be only one side of the truth, since it was found in each of the lower terms—by itself in Logic and combined with immediacy in Nature—and hence to attribute to it a greater self-sufficiency and importance than it really possesses.

This mistake will disappear when we realise that the only reason that pure thought appears again in the second term of the triad is that the synthesis, in transitions of this type, has already begun in the second term. It is only in the synthesis that thought appears in union with its opposite, and, apart from the synthesis, it is as incomplete and unsubstantial as immediacy is.

But the change in the type of the process is not sufficiently emphasised in Hegel, and there is a tendency on the part of observers to take the type presented by the earliest categories as that which prevails all through the dialectic. And as, in the earlier type, one of the extremes could not have been found both in the first and second terms of a triad, it is supposed that pure thought cannot be such an extreme, cannot stand in the same relation to Spirit, as Being does to Becoming, and is rather to be looked on as the cause of what follows it, than as an abstraction from it.

139. I have endeavoured to show that the view of the dialectic given in this chapter, while we cannot suppose it to have been held by Hegel, is nevertheless not unconnected with his system. The germs of it are to be found in his exposition of the changes of method in the three great divisions of the process, and the observation of the details of the system confirm this. But it was not sufficiently emphasised, nor did Hegel draw from it the consequences, particularly as regards the subjective element in the dialectic, which I have tried to show are logically involved in it.

But there is, nevertheless, justification for our regarding this theory as a development and not a contradiction of the Hegelian system, since it is only by the aid of some such theory that we can regard that system as valid at all. And we have seen that such a modification will not affect either of the great objects which Absolute Idealism claims to have accomplished— the demonstration, namely, that the real is rational and the rational is real, and the classification, according to their necessary relations and intrinsic value, of the various categories which we use in ordinary and finite thought.

CHAPTER V.

140. ONE of the most interesting and important questions which can arise in connexion with Hegel's philosophy is the question of the relation between the succession of the categories in the dialectic and the succession of events in time. Are we to regard the complex and concrete Absolute Idea, in which alone true reality is to be found, as gradually growing up in time by the evolution of one category after another? Or are we to regard the Absolute Idea as existing eternally in its full completeness, and the succession of events in time as something which has no part as such in any ultimate system of the universe?

The succession of categories in Hegel's Logic is, of course, not primarily a temporal succession. We pass from one to another because the admission of the first as valid requires logically the admission of the second as valid. At the same time there are various reasons for accepting the view that one category succeeds another in time. One of the facts of the universe which requires explanation is the existence of time, and it seems at first sight a simple and satisfactory explanation to account for it by the gradual development of the Notion from Pure Being to the Absolute Idea. And Hegel certainly explains the past to some extent by bringing the successive events under successive categories.

Nevertheless, it seems to me that such a view is incompatible with the system. There are doubtless difficulties in either interpretation of Hegel's meaning, but there seems no doubt that we must reject the development of the process in time.

In the first place, the theory that time is an ultimate reality would lead to insoluble difficulties as to the commencement of the process. Secondly, the Absolute Idea must be held to be the presupposition and the logical *prius* of the lower categories. It follows that a theory which makes the appearance of the lower category the presupposition of the appearance of the higher one, cannot fully represent the ultimate reality of the process. And, finally, Hegel's language seems to be decisively on the side of the interpretation that the Absolute Idea exists eternally in its full perfection, and the movement from the lower to the higher is reconstruction and not construction.

141.   Let us consider the first of these points. Hegel, of course, maintains that the universe is fully rational. Can we regard as fully rational a universe in which a process in time is fundamentally real? The theory before us maintains that the universe starts with a minimum of reality, corresponding only to the category of Pure Being. From this point it develops by the force of the dialectic. Gradually each of the higher categories becomes real, and this gradual evolution of logical completeness makes the process which constitutes the life of the universe. All the facts around us are to be attributed to the gradually developing idea, and when the development is complete, and reality has become an incarnation of the Absolute Idea, then the process will end in perfection. The spiritual character of the universe, up till then explicit and partial, will have become complete and explicit. The real will be completely rational, and the rational will be completely real.

On this we must remark, in the first place, that the process in time by which the dialectic develops itself must be regarded as finite and not as infinite. Neither in experience nor in *à priori* criticism can we find any reason to believe that infinite time really exists, or is anything more than an illegitimate inference from the infinite extensibility of time. Nor, if it did exist, could it form part of an ultimate rational explanation of the universe. An unending regress, whether it is true or not, is certainly not a solution which meets the demands of reason. More especially is it impossible that it should be accepted as part of an Hegelian theory. For infinite time would be the strongest possible example of the "false infinite" of endless aggregation, which Hegel invariably condemns as a mere mockery of explanation.

And, independently of this, it is clear that an infinite series in time would not be an embodiment of the dialectic. For the dialectic is most emphatically a process with a beginning and an end, and any series which embodies it must have a beginning and an end also. If the dialectic has any truth, there can be no steps before Pure Being, nor any steps after the Absolute Idea. As the number of steps is finite, either the time taken by each of them is infinite,—and in that case there would be no process at all—or the time taken by the whole series must be finite.

We may consider, then, that any theory which imagines the dialectic to develop itself in time at all, will regard it as doing so in a limited time. What follows from this hypothesis?

142. The first difficulty which arises is that every event in time requires a previous event as its cause. How then shall we be able to explain the first event of the complete series? The first event, like all the others, is an event in time, that is, it had a beginning, before which it did not exist. What determined the change which brought it into existence? Whatever determined it must be itself an event in time, for if the cause had not a definite place in the time series it could not account for its effect having one. But in this case it will itself need a determining cause, which will also be an event, and we have thus lost our finite series with a definite beginning, and embarked on an infinite series, which cannot, as we have seen, be of any assistance to us in our present purpose.

On the other hand, to deny that the first term of such a series requires a determining cause is impossible. It is perhaps not impossible that our minds should form the conception of something on which other things depend, while it depends itself on nothing. But an event in time could never hold such a place. For an event in time has always before it a time when it was not, and this coming into existence deprives it of the possibility of being self-subsistent. Time, as Hegel says, is still outside itself[1]. It has no principle of unity or

---

[1] *Enc.* Section 257.

coherence. It can only be limited by something external to it. Our finite series in time can only have the definite beginning which it requires by means of further time beyond it. To fix any point in time is to imply the existence of time upon both sides of it. And thus no event in time could be accepted as an ultimate beginning. On the other hand, some such event would have to be accepted as the ultimate beginning, if a finite series were to be accepted as an ultimate explanation.

If we apply this to the particular problem before us, we shall find that the theory that the Absolute Idea develops in time lands us in a hopeless difficulty. Let us suppose that all the phenomena of the universe have been accounted for as the manifestations of the gradually developing Idea, and let us suppose that each of these manifestations of the Idea has been shown to be the logical consequence of the existence of the previous manifestation. Then the final and ultimate fact upon which our explanation will depend will be that, at the beginning of time, the first of the categories—the category of Pure Being—manifested itself in reality. And for this fact itself an external explanation is required. No such explanation, indeed, would be required for the deduction of the universe from the idea of Pure Being. If the system is correct, the categories are so inseparably connected that the existence of one stage in the dialectic process implies the existence of all, and the existence of any reality, again, implies the existence of the categories. The category of Pure Being can thus be deduced from the fact that the universe exists, and the fact that the universe exists does not require, as it does not admit, any outside cause. But here, to account for the existence of the universe in time, we have taken as our ultimate fact the realisation of the first category at a particular time. Time is in itself quite empty and indifferent to its content. No possible reason could be given why the process should not have begun a hundred years later than it did, so that we should be at the present moment in the reign of George III. The only way of fixing an event to a particular time is by connecting it with some other event which happened in a particular time. This would lead here to an infinite regress, and, independently of this, would be impracticable. For, by the hypothesis, the dialectic development was to account for the entire universe, and there can, therefore, be no event outside it to which it can be referred in order that it can be accounted for itself. And yet the question—why it happened now and not at another time—is one which we cannot refrain from asking, since time must be regarded as infinitely extensible.

143. Various attempts have been made to evade this difficulty. It has been suggested that the temporal process has its root in a timeless state. If we ask what determined the first event, we are referred to the timeless state. If we ask what caused the latter, we are answered that it had no beginning, and consequently required no cause.

But how could a timeless reality be the cause of a succession in time? It could, no doubt, be the cause of everything else in a series of successive events, except of the fact that they did take place in time. But how are we to account for that? No reconciliation and no mediation is possible upon the hypothesis with which we are here dealing. According to some views of the question, time might be regarded as nothing but a form assumed by eternity, or time and the timeless might be regarded as forms of a higher reality. But such a view is impossible here. The theory which we are here considering had to explain the fact of a succession in the universe, and did so by making the central principle of the universe to be the realisation of the dialectic in time. The realisation in time, according to this theory, is as much part of the ultimate explanation of the universe as the dialectic itself. By making time ultimate we certainly get rid of the necessity for explaining it. But, on the other hand, we lose the possibility of treating time as a distinction which can be bridged over, or explained away, when we wish to make a connection between time and the timeless. If time is an ultimate fact, then the distinction between that which does, and that which does not, happen in time must be an ultimate distinction; and how are we to make, if this is so, a transition from the one to the other?

So far as a thing is timeless, it cannot change, for with change time comes necessarily. But how can a thing which does not change produce an effect in time? That the effect

11—2

was produced in time implies that it had a beginning. And if the effect begins, while no beginning can be assigned to the cause, we are left to choose between two alternatives. Either there is something in the effect—namely, the quality of coming about as a change—which is altogether uncaused. Or the timeless reality is only a partial cause, and is determined to act by something which is not timeless. In either case, the timeless reality fails to explain the succession in time, and we are no better off than we were before. It would be equally available as an explanation if the process had begun at any point besides the one at which it actually did begin, and a cause which can remain the same while the effect varies, is obviously unsatisfactory.

144. It may be objected to this that, if the dialectic process is the ultimate truth of all change, the point in time at which it is to begin is determined by the nature of the case. For time only exists when change exists. The changeless would be the timeless. Therefore the beginning of the change must come at the beginning of time, and there can be no question why it should come at one moment rather than another.

This, however, will not remove one difficulty. Actual time, no doubt, only began with actual change. But possible time stretches back indefinitely beyond this. It is part of the essential nature of time that, beyond any given part of it, we can imagine a fresh part—that, indeed, we must do so. We cannot conceive time as coming to an end. And with this indefinite stretch of possible time the question again arises— what determined the timeless to first produce change at the point it did, and not in the previous time, which we now regard as possible only, but which would have become actual by the production of change in it? And again there is no reason why the series of actual time should not have been placed later in the series of possible time than it actually was. Actual time begins whenever change begins, and so cannot be regarded as a fixed point, by which the beginning of change can be deter-mined. A certain amount of the dialectic process has now been realised in time. Can we give any reason why the amount should not have been greater or less? Yet, if no such reason can be given, the present state of the universe is left unaccounted for by our system.

The difficulty lies in the fact that we are compelled by the nature of time to regard the time series as indefinitely extended, and to regard each member of it as, in itself, exactly like each other member. We may call that part of the series which is not occupied by actual change, possible time, but the very name implies that there is no reason why it should not have been occupied by events, as much as the actual time which really is occupied by them. And, as possible time is indefinite, it is indefinitely larger than any finite time. The question we have been discussing will then take the form—why is this particular part of the time series filled with reality rather than any other part? And since, apart from its contents, one moment of time is exactly like another, it would seem that the question is insoluble.

145. It has sometimes been attempted to ignore on general grounds all endeavours to show that development throughout a finite period in time cannot be accepted. Time, it has been said, must be either finite or infinite. If we accept the objections to taking finite time as part of our ultimate explanation, it can only be because we are bound to an infinite regress. An infinite regress involves infinite time. But infinite time is impossible—an unreal abstraction, based on the impossibility of limiting the regress in thought. Any argument which involves its real existence is thereby reduced to an absurdity. And, since the objections to finite time as part of our ultimate explanation do involve the real existence of infinite time, we may, it is asserted, safely ignore the objections and accept the principle.

The answer which we must make to this, in the first place, is that the argument might as well be reversed. If the difficulties in the way of infinite time are to be taken as a reason for ignoring all difficulties in the way of finite time, why should we not make the difficulties in the way of finite time a ground for accepting with equally implicit faith the existence of infinite time?

Nor can we escape by saying that we do know finite time to exist, and that therefore we are entitled to ignore the objections to it, while we must accept the objections to infinite time. For we have no more experience of finite time, in the sense in which the phrase is used in this argument, than we have of infinite time. What we meet in experience is a time series, extending indefinitely both before and after our immediate contact with it, out of which we can cut finite portions. But for a theory which makes the development of the Notion in time part of its ultimate formula, we require a time which is not merely limited in the sense of being cut off from other time, but in the sense of having none before it and none after it. Of this we have no more experience than we have of infinite time, and if there are difficulties in the way of both, we have no right to prefer the one to the other.

146. Since either hypothesis as to the extension of time leads us into equal difficulties, our course should surely be, not to accept either, but to reject both. Time must, we are told, be either finite or infinite. But there is a third alternative. There may be something wrong in our conception of time, or rather, to speak more precisely, there may be something which renders it unfit, in metaphysics, for the ultimate explanation of the universe, however suited it may be to the finite thought of every-day life. If we ask whether time, as a fact, is finite or infinite, we find hopeless difficulties in the way of either answer. Yet, if we take time as an ultimate reality, there seems no other alternative. Our only resource is to conclude that time is not an ultimate reality.

This is the same principle which is at work in the dialectic itself. When we find that any category, if we analyse it sufficiently, lands us, in its application to reality, in contradictions, we do not accept one contradictory proposition and reject the other. We conclude the category in question to be an inadequate way of looking at reality, and we try to find a higher conception, which will embrace all the truth of the lower one, while it will avoid the contradictions. This is what we ought, it would seem, to do with the idea of time. If it only presents us with a choice between impossibilities, we must regard it as an inadequate way of looking at the universe. And in this case we cannot accept the process in time as part of our ultimate solution.

147. We now come to the second objection to the development of the dialectic in time. That which we have just been discussing would equally perplex any other idealistic system which should adopt a time process as an original element. The new difficulty belongs specially to the dialectic. It appears, as we have seen[1], to be essential to the possibility of a dialectic process that the highest term, in which the process ends, should be taken as the presupposition of all the lower terms. The passage from category to category must not be taken as an actual advance, producing that which did not previously exist, but as an advance from an abstraction to the concrete whole from which the abstraction was made—demonstrating and rendering explicit what was before only implicit and immediately given, but still only reconstructing, and not constructing anything fresh.

This view of Hegel's system becomes inevitable when we consider, on the one hand, that his conclusion is that all that is real is rational, and, on the other hand, that his method consists in proving that each of the lower steps of the dialectic, taken by itself, is not rational. We cannot then ascribe reality to any of these steps, except in so far as they lose their independence and become moments of the Absolute Idea.

We are compelled, according to Hegel, to pass from each thesis and antithesis to their synthesis, by discovering that the thesis and antithesis, while incompatible with one another, nevertheless involve one another. This produces a contradiction, and this contradiction can only be removed by finding a term which reconciles and transcends them.

Now if we suppose that the dialectic process came into existence gradually in time, we must suppose that all the contradictions existed at one time or another independently, and before reconciliation, *i.e.*, as contradictions. Indeed, as the time process is still going on, all the reality round us at the present day must consist of unreconciled contradictions.

Such an assertion, however, would, it is clear, be absolutely untenable. To say that the world consists of reconciled contradictions would produce no difficulty, for it means nothing more than that it consists of things which only appear contradictory

---

[1] Chap. I. Section 6.

when not thoroughly understood. But to say that a contradiction can exist as such would plunge us in utter confusion. All reasoning, and Hegel's as much as anybody else's, involves that two contradictory propositions cannot both be true. It would be useless to reason, if, when you had demonstrated your conclusion, it was as true to assert the opposite of that conclusion.

And, again, if contradictory propositions could both be true, the special line of argument which Hegel follows would have lost all its force. We are enabled to pass on from the thesis and antithesis to the synthesis just because a contradiction cannot be true, and the synthesis is the only way out of it. But if contradictions are true, there is no necessity to find a way out of it, and the advance of the dialectic is no longer valid. If the contradictions exist at all, there seems no reason that they should not continue to do so. We should not be able to avoid this by saying that they are real, but that their imperfection made them transitory. For the dialectic process, even if we suppose it to take place in time, is not a mere succession in time, but essentially a logical process. Each step has to be proved to follow from those before it by the nature of the latter. It is clear that it would be impossible, by consideration of the nature of a logical category, to deduce the conclusion that for some time it could exist independently, but that, after that, its imperfection would drive it on to another stage.

148. It is, too, only on the supposition that reality always corresponds to the Absolute Idea, and is not merely approximating to it, that we can meet another difficulty which is propounded by Trendelenburg. Either, he says, the conclusion of the whole process can be obtained by analysis of the original premise, or it cannot. The original premise of the whole process is nothing but the validity of the idea of Pure Being. If the whole conclusion can be got out of this, we learn nothing new, and the whole dialectic process is futile. If, on the other hand, we introduce anything not obtained from our original premise, we fail in our object—which was to prove that the whole system followed, when that premise was admitted.

We considered this difficulty above [1], and came to the con-

---

[1] Chap. II. Section 32.

clusion that the answer was contained in Mr Bradley's statement of the true nature of dialectic.   The passage in which he
dealt with the matter was, it will be remembered, as follows,
" An idea prevails that the Dialectic Method is a sort of experiment with conceptions *in vacuo*.   We are supposed to have
nothing but one single isolated abstract idea, and this solitary
monad then proceeds to multiply by gemmation from or by
fission of its private substance, or by fetching matter from the
impalpable void.   But this is a mere caricature, and it comes
from confusion between that which the mind has got before it
and that which it has within itself.   Before the mind there is a
single conception, but the whole mind itself, which does not
appear, engages in the process, operates on the *datum*, and
produces the result.   The opposition between the real, in that
fragmentary character in which the mind possesses it, and the
true reality felt within the mind, is the moving cause of that
unrest which sets up the dialectical process."   And again:
" The whole, which is both sides of this process, rejects the
claim of a one-sided *datum*, and supplements it by that other
and opposite side which really is implied—so begetting by
negation a balanced unity.   This path once entered on, the
process starts afresh with the whole just reached.   But this
also is seen to be the one-sided expression of a higher synthesis;
and it gives birth to an opposite which co-unites with it into a
second whole, a whole which in its turn is degraded into a
fragment of truth.   So the process goes on till the mind,
therein implicit, finds a product which answers its unconscious
idea; and here, having become in its own entirety a *datum* to
itself, it rests in the activity which is self-conscious in its
object [1]."

If we hold, according to this view, that the dialectic process
depends on the relation between the concrete whole and the
part of it which has so far become explicit, it is clear that we
cannot regard the concrete whole as produced out of the incomplete and lower category by means of the dialectic process,
since the process cannot possibly produce its own presupposition.

149.   And finally Hegel's own language appears to be

[1] *Logic;* Book III. Part I. Chap. II. Sections 20 and 21.

clearly incompatible with the theory that the dialectic is gradually evolved in time. It is true that, in the Philosophy of Religion, the Philosophy of History, and the History of Philosophy, he explains various successions of events in time as manifestations of the dialectic. But this proves nothing as to the fundamental nature of the connection of time with the universe. The dialectic is the key to all reality, and, therefore, whenever we do view reality under the aspect of time, the different categories will appear as manifesting themselves as a process in time. But this has no bearing on the question before us—whether they first came into being in time, or whether they have a timeless and eternally complete existence.

Even in this part of his work, too, Hegel's adherence to the eternal nature of the dialectic becomes evident in a manner all the more significant, because it is logically unjustifiable. In several places he seems on the point of saying that all dissatis-faction with the existing state of the universe, and all efforts to reform it, are futile and vain, since reason is already and always the sole reality. This conclusion cannot be fairly drawn from the eternity of the dialectic process. For if we are entitled to hold the universe perfect, the same arguments lead us to consider it also timeless and changeless. Imperfection and progress, then, may claim to share whatever reality is to be allowed to time and change, and no conclusion can be drawn, such as Hegel appears at times to suggest, against attempting to make the future an improvement on the past. Neither future and past, nor better and worse, can be really adequate judgments of a timeless and perfect universe, but in the sense in which there is a future it may be an improvement on the past. But the very fact that Hegel has gone too far in his application of the idea that reality is timeless, makes it more clear that he did hold that idea.

There are not, I believe, any expressions in the Logic which can be fairly taken as suggesting the development of the dialectic in time. It is true that two successive categories are named Life and Cognition, and that science informs us that life existed in this world before cognition. But the names of the categories must be taken as those of the facts in which the idea in question shows itself most clearly, and not as indicating the only form in which the idea can show itself at all. Otherwise we should be led to the impossible result that Notions, Judgments, and Syllogisms existed before Cognition.

A strong assertion of the eternal nature of the process is to be found in the Doctrine of the Notion. "Die Vollführung des unendlichen Zwecks ist so nur die Täuschung aufzuheben, als ob er noch nicht vollführt sey. Das Gute, das absolute Gute, vollbringt sich ewig in der Welt und das Resultat ist, dass es schon an und für sich vollbracht ist und nicht erst auf uns zu warten braucht[1]."

Another important piece of evidence is his treatment of his own maxim: "All that is real is rational." To the objections to this he replies by saying that reality does not mean the surface of things, but something deeper behind them. Besides this he admits occasionally, though apparently not always, that contingency has rights within a sphere of its own, where reason cannot demand that everything should be explained. But he never tries to meet the attacks made on his principle by drawing a distinction between the irrational reality of the present and the rational reality of the future. Such a distinction would be so natural and obvious, and would, for those who could consistently make use of it, so completely remove the charge of a false optimism about the present, that we can scarcely doubt that Hegel's neglect of it was due to the fact that he saw it to be incompatible with his principles.

Hegel's treatment of time, moreover, confirms this view. For he considers it merely as a stage in the Philosophy of Nature, which is only an application of the Logic. Now if the realisation of the categories of the Logic only took place in time, time would be an element in the universe correlative with those categories, and of equal importance with them. Both would be primary elements in a concrete whole. Neither could be looked on as an application of, or deduction from, the other. But the treatment of time as merely one of the phenomena which result from the realisation of the Logic, is incompatible with such a theory as this, and we may fairly conclude that time had not for Hegel this ultimate importance.

---

[1] *Enc.* Section 212, lecture note.

150. We have thus arrived at the conclusion that the dialectic is not for Hegel a process in time, but that the Absolute Idea must be looked on as eternally realised. We are very far, however, from having got rid of our difficulties. It looks, indeed, as if we were brought, at this point, to a *reductio ad absurdum*. For if the other theory was incompatible with Hegel, this seems to be incompatible with the facts.

The dialectic process is one from incomplete to complete rationality. If it is eternally fulfilled, then the universe must be completely rational. Now, in the first place, it is certain that the universe is not completely rational for us. We are not able to see everything round us as a manifestation of the Absolute Idea. Even those students of philosophy who believe on general grounds that the Absolute Idea must be manifested in everything are as unable as the rest of us to see *how* it is manifested in a table or a thunder-storm. We can only explain these things—at present, at any rate—by much lower categories, and we cannot, therefore, explain them completely. Nor are we by any means able, at present, to eliminate completely the contingency of the data of sense, which are an essential element in reality, and a universe which contains an ultimately contingent element cannot be held to be completely rational. It would seem, too, that if we are perfectly rational in a perfectly rational universe, there must always be a complete harmony between our desires and our environment. And this is not invariably the case.

But if the universe appears to us not to be perfect, can it be so in reality? Does not the very failure to perceive the perfection destroy it? In the first place, the Absolute Idea, as defined by Hegel[1], is one of self-conscious rationality—the Idea to which the Idea itself is "Gegenstand" and "Objekt." If any part of reality sees anything, except the Absolute Idea, anywhere in reality, this ideal can scarcely be said to have been fulfilled.

And, more generally, if the universe appears to us to be only imperfectly rational, we must be either right or wrong. If we are right, the world is not perfectly rational. But if we

---

[1] *Enc.* Section 236.

are wrong, then it is difficult to see how *we* can be perfectly
rational. And we are part of the world. Thus it would seem
that the very opinion that the world is imperfect must, in one
way or another, prove its own truth.

151. If this is correct, we seem to be confronted with a
difficulty as hopeless as those which encountered us when we
supposed the dialectic to develop itself in time. These, we saw,
were due to our hypothesis being found incompatible with the
system, while our present view appears untenable because,
though a logical development from the system, it is incompatible with the facts. The result with regard to the first is that
we come to the conclusion that the development in time cannot
be part of Hegel's philosophy. The result of the second would
at first sight seem to be that Hegel's philosophy must be
abandoned, since it leads to such untenable conclusions.

We rejected the hypothesis of the development of the
Absolute Idea in time upon two grounds. The first was that
we had to choose between a false infinite and an uncaused
beginning. Each of these hypotheses left something unexplained and contingent, and was consequently incompatible
with a system which demanded above all things that the
universe should be completely rationalised, and which believed
itself to have accomplished its aim. Our second objection was
due to the fact that the development of the dialectic at all,
upon Hegel's principles, presupposed the existence of its goal,
which could not therefore be supposed to be reached for the
first time by the process. But our difficulty now is not at all
incompatible with the system. It is one which must arise
from it, and which must, in some form or another, arise in any
system of complete idealism. Every such system must declare
that the world is fundamentally rational and righteous throughout, and every such system will be met by the same difficulty.
How, if all reality is rational and righteous, are we to explain
the irrationality and unrighteousness which are notoriously part
of our every-day life? We must now consider the various
attempts which have been made to answer this question.

152. Hegel's answer has been indicated in the passage
quoted above[1]. The infinite end is really accomplished eter-

---

[1] *Enc.* Section 212, lecture note.

nally. It is only a delusion on our part which makes us suppose otherwise. And the only real progress is the removal of the delusion. The universe is eternally the same, and eternally perfect. The movement is only in our minds. They trace one after another in succession the different categories of the Logic, which in reality have no time order, but continually coexist as elements of the Absolute Idea which transcends and unites them.

This solution can, however, scarcely be accepted, for the reasons given above. How can we account for the delusion that the world is partially irrational, if, as a matter of fact, it is completely rational? How, in particular, can we regard such a delusion as compatible with our own complete rationality?

To this it may be possibly objected that our argument is based on a confusion. That a thought is a delusion need not imply that it, or the being who thinks it, is irrational. Everything which, like a thought, is used as a symbol, can be viewed in two aspects—firstly as a fact, and secondly as representing, as a symbol, some other fact. In the first aspect we say that it is real or unreal; in the second that it is true or false. These two pairs of predicates have no intrinsic connection. A false judgment is just as really a fact as a true one.

Now the conclusion from the Hegelian dialectic was that whatever was real was rational. We are, therefore, compelled to assert that every thought, and every thinking being, is completely rational—can be explained in a way which gives entire rest and satisfaction to reason. But, it may be said, this is not in the least interfered with by the fact that many real thoughts are defective symbols of the other reality which they profess to represent. The false can be, and, indeed, must be, real, for a thought cannot misrepresent reality unless it is itself real. Till it is real it can do nothing. And if the false can be real, why can it not be rational? Indeed we often, in every-day life, and in science, do find the false to be more or less rational. It is as possible to account, psychologically, for the course of thought which brings out an erroneous conclusion as for the course of thought which brings out a correct one. We can explain our failures to arrive at the truth as well as our successes. It would seem then that there is nothing to prevent ourselves and our thoughts being part of a completely rational universe, although our thoughts are in some respects incorrect symbols.

153. But it must be remembered that the rationality which Hegel requires of the universe is much more than complete determination under the category of cause and effect —a category which the dialectic maintains to be quite insufficient, unless transcended by a higher one. He requires, among other things, the validity of the idea of final cause. And if this is brought in, it is difficult to see how delusions can exist in a rational world. For a delusion involves a thwarted purpose. If a man makes a mistake, it means that he wishes to know the truth, and that he does not know it. Whether this is the case or not, with regard to simple perception of the facts before us, it cannot be denied that wherever there is a long chain of argument, to which the mind is voluntarily kept attentive, there must be a desire to know the truth. And if this desire is unsuccessful, the universe could not be, in Hegel's sense, completely rational.

This becomes more evident if we look at Hegel's definition of complete rationality, as we find it in the Absolute Idea. The essence of it is that reality is only completely rational in so far as it is conscious of its own rationality. The idea is to be "Gegenstand" and "Objekt" to itself. If this is the case, it follows that the rationality of Spirit, as an existent object, depends upon its being a faithful symbol of the rationality expressed in other manifestations of Spirit. The delusion by which Hegel explains all imperfection will of course prevent its being a faithful symbol of that rationality, and will therefore destroy the rationality itself. In so far as we do not see the perfection of the universe, we are not perfect ourselves. And as we are part of the universe, that too cannot be perfect. And yet its perfection appears to be a necessary consequence of Hegel's position.

154. Hegel's attempt to make the imperfection which is evident round us compatible with the perfection of the universe must, then, be rejected. Can we find any other solution which would be more successful? One such solution suggests itself. It was the denial of the ultimate reality of time which caused

our difficulty, since it forced us to assert that the perfect
rationality, which idealism claims for the universe, cannot be
postponed to the future, but must be timelessly and eternally
present. Can the denial of the reality of time be made to
cure the wound, which it has itself made? Would it not be
possible, it might be said, to escape from our dilemma as
follows? The dialectic itself teaches us that it is only the
concrete whole which is completely rational, and that any
abstraction from it, by the very fact that it is an abstraction,
must be to some extent false and contradictory. An attempt
to take reality moment by moment, element by element, must
make reality appear imperfect. The complete rationality is
only in the whole which transcends all these elements, and
any one of them, considered as more or less independent, must
be false. Now, if we look at the universe as in time, it will
appear to be a succession of separate events, so that only part
of it is existing at any given instant, the rest being either
past or future. Each of these events will be represented as
real in itself, and not merely a moment in a real whole. And
in so far as events in time are taken to be, as such, real, it
must follow that reality does not appear rational. If an organic
whole is perfect, then any one of its parts, taken separately
from the whole, cannot possibly be perfect. For in such a
whole all the parts presuppose one another, and any one, taken
by itself, must bear the traces of its isolation and incompleteness. Now the connection of the different parts of the universe,
viewed in their ultimate reality, is, according to the dialectic,
even closer than the connection of the parts of an organism.
And thus not only each event, but the whole universe taken
as a series of separate events, would appear imperfect. Even
if such a series could ever be complete, it could not fully
represent the reality, since the parts would still, by their
existence in time, be isolated from one another, and claim
some amount of independence. Thus the apparent imperfection
of the universe would be due to the fact that we are regarding
it *sub specie temporis*—an aspect which we have seen reason
to conclude that Hegel himself did not regard as adequate to
reality. If we could only see it *sub specie aeternitatis*, we
should see it in its real perfection.

155. It is true, I think, that in this way we get a step nearer to the goal required than we do by Hegel's own theory, which we previously considered. Our task is to find, for the apparent imperfection, some cause whose existence will not interfere with the real perfection. We shall clearly be more likely to succeed in this, in proportion as the cause we assign is a purely negative one. The appearance of imperfection was accounted for by Hegel as a delusion of our own minds. Now a delusion is as much a positive fact as a true judgment is, and requires just as much a positive cause. And, as we have seen, we are unable to conceive this positive cause, except as something which will prevent the appearance from being a delusion at all, since it will make the universe really imperfect. On the theory just propounded, however, the cause of the imperfection is nothing but the fact that we do not see everything at once. Seen as we see things now, reality must be imperfect. But if we can attain to the point of looking at the whole universe *sub specie aeternitatis*, we shall see just the same subject-matter as in time ; but it will appear perfect, because seen as a single concrete whole, and not as a succession of separated abstractions. The only cause of the apparent imperfection will be the negative consideration that we do not now see the whole at once.

156. This theory would be free from some of the objections which are fatal to a rather similar apology for the universe which is often found in systems of optimism. It is admitted in such apologies that, from the point of view of individuals, the world is imperfect and irrational. But, it is asserted, these blemishes would disappear if we could look at the world as a whole. The part which, taken by itself, is defective, may we are told, be an element in a perfect harmony. Such a theory, since it declares that the universe can be really perfect, although imperfect for individuals, implies that some individuals, at any rate, can be treated merely as means, and not as ends in themselves. Without enquiring whether such a view is at all tenable, it is at any rate clear that it is incompatible with what is usually called optimism, since it would permit of many—indeed of all—individuals being doomed to eternal and infinite misery. We might be led to the formula in which Mr Bradley sums up optimism :—"The world is the best of all possible worlds, and everything in it is a necessary evil[1]." For if the universal harmony can make any evil to individuals compatible with its own purposes, there is no principle upon which we can limit the amount which it can tolerate. It is more to our present purpose to remark that such a view could not possibly be accepted as in any way consistent with Hegel's system. It would be in direct opposition to its whole tendency, which is to regard the universal as only gaining reality and validity when, by its union with the particular, it becomes the individual. For Hegel the ideal must lie, not in ignoring the claims of individuals, but in seeing in them the embodiment of the universal.

Mr Bradley's own treatment of the problem is, as far as I can see, of a rather similar type. He has to reconcile the harmony which he attributes to the Absolute, with the disharmony which undoubtedly prevails, to some extent, in experience. This he does by taking the finite individual to be, as such, only appearance and not reality, from which it follows that it must distort the harmony of the Absolute, and cannot adequately manifest it. It may be doubted whether we do not fall into more difficulties than we avoid by this low estimate of the conscious individual. But, at any rate, such a solution would be impracticable for anyone who accepted Hegel's version of the Absolute Idea, to which the individual is the highest form that the universal can take.

Some of the objections which apply to such attempts to save the perfection of the Absolute by ignoring the claims of individuals will not hold against our endeavour to escape from our difficulty by ignoring, so to speak, the claims of particular moments of time. None of those considerations which make us consider each separate person as an ultimate reality, whose claims to self-realisation must be satisfied and cannot be transcended, lead us to attribute the same importance to separate periods of time. Indeed the whole drift of Hegel's system is as much against the ultimate reality of a succession of phenomena, as such, as it is in favour of the ultimate reality of individual persons, as such. To deny *any* reality in what

---

[1] *Appearance and Reality*, Preface, p. xiv.

now presents itself to us as a time-series would indeed be suicidal. For we have no *data* given us for our thought, except in the form of a time-series, and to destroy our *data* would be to destroy the super-structure. But while philosophy could not start if it did not accept its *data*, it could not proceed if it did not alter them. There is then nothing obviously impossible in the supposition that the whole appearance of succession in our experience is, as such, unreal, and that reality is one timeless whole, in which all that appears successive is really co-existent, as the houses are co-existent which we see successively from the windows of a train.

157. It cannot, however, be said that this view is held by Hegel himself. In the Philosophy of Nature he treats time as a stage in the development of nature, and not as a cause why there is any appearance of successive development at all. Indeed he says there that things are not finite because they are in time, but are in time because they are finite[1]. It would be thus impossible, without departing from Hegel, to make time the cause of the apparent imperfection of the universe.

Everything else in the Hegelian philosophy may indeed be considered as of subordinate importance to the Dialectic, and to its goal, the Absolute Idea. If it were necessary, we might, to save the validity of the Dialectic, reject Hegel's views even on a subject so important as time, and yet call ourselves Hegelians. But we should not gain much by this reconstruction of the system. For it leaves the problem no more solved than it was before. The difficulty which proved fatal to Hegel's own attempt to explain the imperfection comes back as surely as before, though it may not be quite so obvious. However much we may treat time as mere appearance, it must, like all other appearance, have reality behind it. The reality, it may be answered, is in this case the timeless Absolute. But this reality will have to account, not merely for the facts which appear to us in time, but for the appearance of succession which they do undoubtedly assume. How can this be done? What reason can be given why the eternal reality should manifest itself in a time process at all? If we tried to find the reason outside the nature of the eternal reality, we should

---

[1] *Enc.* Section 258, lecture note.

be admitting that time had some independent validity, and we should fall back into all the difficulties mentioned in the earlier part of this chapter. But if we try to find the reason inside the nature of the eternal reality, we shall find it to be incompatible with the complete rationality which, according to Hegel's theory, that reality must possess. For the process in time is, by the hypothesis, the root of all irrationality, and how can it spring from anything which is quite free of irrationality? Why should a concrete and perfect whole proceed to make itself imperfect, for the sake of gradually getting rid of the imperfection again? If it gained nothing by the change, could it be completely rational to undergo it? But if it had anything to gain by the change, how could it previously have been perfect?

158. We have thus failed again to solve the difficulty. However much we may endeavour to make the imperfection of the universe merely negative, it is impossible to escape from the fact that, as an element in presentation, it requires a positive ground. If we denied this, we should be forced into the position that not only was our experience of imperfection a delusion, but that it was actually non-existent. And this, as was mentioned above, is an impossibility. All reasoning depends on the fact that every appearance has a reality of which it is the appearance. Without this we could have no possible basis upon which to rest any conclusion.

Yet, on the other hand, so long as we admit a positive ground for the imperfection, we find ourselves to be inconsistent with the original position from which we started. For that position asserted that the sole reality was absolutely perfect. On this hangs the appearance of imperfection, and to this real perfection as cause we have to ascribe apparent imperfection as effect. Now it is not impossible, under certain circumstances, to imagine a cause as driven on, by a dialectic necessity, to produce an effect different from itself. But in this case it does seem impossible. For any self-determination of a cause to produce its effect must be due to some incompleteness in the former without the latter. But if the cause, by itself, was incomplete, it could not, by itself, be perfect. If, on the other hand it was perfect, it is impossible to see how it could produce anything else as an effect. Its perfection makes it in complete harmony with itself. And, since it is all reality, there is nothing outside it with which it could be out of harmony. What could determine it to production?

Thus we oscillate between two extremes, each equally fatal. If we endeavour to treat evil as absolutely unreal, we have to reject the one basis of all knowledge—experience. But in so far as we accept evil as a manifestation of reality, we find it impossible to avoid qualifying the cause by the nature of the effect which it produces, and so contradicting the main result of the dialectic—the harmony and perfection of the Absolute.

159. We need not, after all, be surprised at the apparently insoluble problem which confronts us. For the question has developed into the old difficulty of the origin of evil, which has always baffled both theologians and philosophers. An idealism which declares that the universe is in reality perfect, can find, as most forms of popular idealism do, an escape from the difficulties of the existence of evil, by declaring that the world is as yet only growing towards its ideal perfection. But this refuge disappears with the reality of time, and we are left with an awkward difference between what our philosophy tells us must be, and what our life tells us actually is.

The aim of the dialectic was to prove that all reality was completely rational. And Hegel's arguments led him to the conclusion that the universe as a whole could not be rational, except in so far as each of its parts found its own self-realisation. It followed that the universe, if harmonious on the theoretical side, would be harmonious also in a practical aspect—that is, would be in every respect perfect. This produces a dilemma. Either the evil round us is real, or it is not. If it is real, then reality is not perfectly rational. But if it is absolutely unreal, then all our finite experience—and we know of no other—must have an element in it which is absolutely irrational, and which, however much we may pronounce it to be unreal, has a disagreeably powerful influence in moulding the events of our present life. Nor can we even hope that this element is transitory, and comfort ourselves, in orthodox fashion, with the hope of a heaven in which the evil shall have died away, while the good remains. For we cannot assure ourselves of such a result by any empirical arguments from particular *data*, which would be hopelessly inadequate to support such a conclusion. The only chance would be an *a priori* argument founded on the essential rationality of the universe, which might be held to render the imperfection transitory. But we should have no right to use such an argument. To escape the difficulties involved in the present coexistence of rationality and irrationality, we have reduced the latter to such complete unreality that it is not incompatible with the former. But this cuts both ways. If the irrationality cannot interfere with the rationality so as to render their present coexistence impossible, there can be no reason why their future coexistence should ever become impossible. If the irrational is absolutely unreal now, it can never become less real in the future. Thus our ascription of complete rationality to the universe leads us to a belief that one factor in experience, as it presents itself to us, is fundamentally and permanently irrational—a somewhat singular conclusion from such a premise.

To put the difficulty from a more practical point of view, either the imperfection in experience leaves a stain on the perfection of the Absolute, or it does not. If it does, there is no absolute perfection, and we have no right to expect that the imperfection around us is a delusion or a transitory phase. But if it does not, then there is no reason why the perfection should ever feel intolerant of it, and again we have no right to hope for its disappearance. The whole practical interest of philosophy is thus completely overthrown. It asserts an abstract perfection beyond experience, but that is all. Such a perfection might almost as well be a Thing-in-itself, since it is unable to explain any single fact of experience without the aid of another factor, which it may call unreal, but which it finds indispensable. It entirely fails to rationalise reality or to reconcile it with our aspirations.

160. The conclusion we have reached is one which it certainly seems difficult enough to reconcile with continued adherence to Hegelianism. Of the two possible theories as to the relation of time to the dialectic process, we have found that one, besides involving grave difficulties in itself, is quite inconsistent with the spirit of Hegel's system. The other, again, while consistent with that system, and, indeed, appearing to be its logical consequence, has landed us in what seems to be a glaring contradiction to the facts. Is it not inevitable that we must reject a system which leads us to such a result?

Before deciding on such a course, however, it might be wise to see if we can really escape from the difficulty in such a way. If the same problem, or one of like nature, proves equally insoluble in any possible system, we may be forced to admit the existence of an incompleteness in our philosophy, but we shall no longer have any reason to reject one system in favour of another. Now, besides the theory which has brought us into this trouble—the theory that reality is fundamentally rational—there are, it would seem, three other possibilities. Reality may be fundamentally irrational. (I shall use "irrational" here to signify anything whose nature and operation are not merely devoid of reason, but opposed to it, so that its influence is always in the opposite direction to that exercised by reason.) Or reality may be the product of two independent principles of rationality and irrationality. Or it may be the work of some principle to which rationality and irrationality are equally indifferent—some blind fate, or mechanical chance.

These possibilities may be taken as exhaustive. It is true that, on Hegelian principles, a fifth alternative has to be added, when we are considering the different combinations in which two predicates may be asserted or denied of a subject. We may say that it is also possible that the two predicates should be combined in a higher unity. This would leave it scarcely correct to say, without qualification, that either is asserted or either denied of the subject. But synthesis is itself a process of reasoning, and unites its two terms by a category in which we recognise the nature of each extreme as a subordinate moment, which is harmonised with the other. The harmony involves that, wherever a synthesis is possible, reason is supreme. And so, if the truth were to be found in a synthesis of the rational and irrational, that synthesis would itself be rational—resolving, as it would, the whole universe into a unity expressible by thought. Thus we should have come round again to Hegel's position that the world is fundamentally rational.

161. We need not spend much time over the supposition that the world is fundamentally irrational—not only regardless of reason, but contrary to reason. To begin with, such a hypothesis refutes itself. The completely irrational cannot be real, for even to say that a thing is real implies its determination by at least one predicate, and therefore its comparative rationality. And our hypothesis would meet with a difficulty precisely analogous to that which conflicts with Hegel's theory. In that case the stumbling-block lay in the existence of some irrationality, here it lies in the existence of some rationality. We can no more deny that there are signs of rationality in the universe, than we can deny that there are signs of irrationality. Yet it is at least as impossible to conceive how the fundamentally irrational should manifest itself as rationality, as it is to conceive the converse process. We shall gain nothing, then, by deserting Hegel for such a theory as this.

162. It might seem as if a dualistic theory would be well adapted to the chequered condition of the actual world. But as soon as we try to construct such a theory, difficulties arise. The two principles, of rationality and irrationality, to which the universe is referred, will have to be absolutely separate and independent. For if there were any common unity to which they should be referred, it would be that unity, and not its two manifestations, which would be the ultimate explanation of the universe, and the theory, having become monistic, resolves itself into one of the others, according to the attitude of this single principle towards reason, whether favourable, hostile, or indifferent.

We must then refer the universe to two independent and opposed forces. Nor will it make any important difference if we make the second force to be, not irrationality, but some blind force not in itself hostile to reason. For, in order to account for the thwarted rationality which meets us so often in the universe, we shall have to suppose that the result of the force is, as a fact, opposed to reason, even if opposition to reason is not its essential nature.

In the first place can there be really two independent powers in the universe? Surely there cannot. As Mr Bradley points out: "Plurality must contradict independence. If the beings are not in relation, they cannot be many; but if they are in relation, they cease forthwith to be absolute. For, on the one hand, plurality has no meaning, unless the units are somehow taken together. If you abolish and remove all relations, there seems no sense left in which you can speak of plurality. But, on the other hand, relations destroy the real's self-dependence. For it is impossible to treat relations as adjectives, falling simply inside the many beings. And it is impossible to take them as falling outside somewhere in a sort of unreal void, which makes no difference to anything. Hence ... the essence of the related terms is carried beyond their proper selves by means of their relations. And, again, the relations themselves must belong to a larger reality. To stand in a relation and not to be relative, to support it and yet not to be infected and undermined by it, seem out of the question. Diversity in the real cannot be the plurality of independent beings. And the oneness of the Absolute must hence be more than a mere diffused adjective. It possesses unity, as a whole, and is a single system[1]."

The argument has additional strength in this case. For the two forces which we are asked to take as absolutely opposed are, by the hypothesis which assumed them, indissolubly united. Both forces are regarded as all-pervading. Neither can exist by itself anywhere. Every fact in the universe is due to the interaction of the two. And, further, they can only be described and defined in relation to one another. If the dualism is between the rational and the irrational as such, it is obvious that the latter, at any rate, has only meaning in relation to its opposite. And if we assume that the second principle is not directly opposed to rationality, but simply indifferent to it, we shall get no further in our task of ex-plaining the imperfect rationality which appears in our data, unless we go on to assume that its action is contrary to that of a rational principle. Thus a reference to reason would be necessary, if not to define our second principle, at any rate to allow us to understand how we could make it available for our purpose.

We cannot, besides, describe anything as irrational, or as

[1] *Appearance and Reality*, Chap. 13, p. 141.

indifferent to reason, without ascribing to it certain predicates—Being, Substance, Limitation, for example. Nor can we refer to a principle as an explanation of the universe without attributing to it Causality. These determinations may be transcended by higher ones, but they must be there, at least as moments. Yet anything to which all these predicates can be ascribed cannot be said to be entirely hostile or indifferent to reason, for it has some determinations common to it and to reason, and must be, therefore, in more or less harmony with the latter. But if this is so, our complete dualism has been surrendered.

The two principles then can scarcely be taken as absolutely independent. But if they cannot our dualism fails to help us, and indeed vanishes. We were tempted to resort to it because the two elements in experience—the rationality and the want of rationality—were so heterogeneous as to defy reduction to a single principle. And if we cannot keep our two principles distinct, but are compelled to regard them as joined in a higher unity, we might as well return explicitly to monism.

163. But, even if we could keep the two principles independent, it seems doubtful if we should be able to reach, by means of this theory, a solution of our difficulty. The forces working for and against the rationality of the universe must either be in equilibrium or not. If they are not in equilibrium, then one must be gaining on the other. The universe is thus fundamentally a process. In this case we shall gain nothing by adopting dualism. For the difficulties attendant on conceiving the world as a process were just the reason which compelled us to adopt the theory that the universe was at present perfectly rational, and so produced the further difficulties which are now driving us to look round for a substitute for idealism. If we could have taken development in time as ultimately real, we should have found no hindrance in our way when we endeavoured to conceive the universe as the product of a single rational principle. But we could not do so then, and we shall find it as impossible now. The process must be finite in length, since we can attach no meaning to an actual infinite process. And, since it is still continuing, we shall have to suppose that the two principles came into operation at a given moment, and not before. And since these principles are, on the hypothesis, ultimate, there can be nothing to determine them to begin to act at that point, rather than any other. In this way we shall be reduced, as before, to suppose an event to happen in time without antecedents and without cause—a solution which cannot be accepted as satisfactory.

164. Shall we succeed any better on the supposition that the forces which work for and against rationality are exactly balanced? In the first place we should have to admit that the odds against this occurring were infinity to one. For the two forces are, by the hypothesis, absolutely independent of one another. And, therefore, we cannot suppose any common influence acting on both of them, which should tend to make their forces equal, nor any relationship between them, which should bring about this result. The equilibrium could only be the result of mere chance, and the probability of this producing infinitely exact equilibrium would be infinitely small. And the absence of any *a priori* reason for believing in such an equilibrium could not, of course, be supplied by empirical observation. For the equilibrium would have to extend over the whole universe, and we cannot carry our observations so far.

Nor can we support the theory by the consideration that it, and no other, will explain the undoubted co-existence of the rational and irrational in our present world. For it fails to account for the facts. It fails to explain the existence of change- -at any rate of that change which leaves anything more or less rational, more or less perfect, than it was before. It is a fact which cannot be denied that sometimes that which was good becomes evil, and sometimes that which was evil becomes good. Now, if the two principles are exactly balanced, how could such a change take place? Of course we cannot prove that the balance between the two forces does not remain the same, if we consider the whole universe. Every movement in the one direction, in one part of the whole, *may* be balanced by a corresponding move in the other direction somewhere else. As we do not know the entire universe in detail it is impossible for us to refute this supposition. But even this supposition will not remove the difficulty. We have two principles whose relations to one another are constant. Yet the facts around us, which are manifestations of these two principles, and of these two principles only, manifest them in proportions which constantly change. How is this change to be accounted for? If we are to take time and change as ultimate facts, such a contradiction seems insuperable. On the other hand, to deny the ultimate validity of time and change, commits us to the series of arguments, the failure of which first led us to doubt Hegel's position. If time could be viewed as a manifestation of the timeless, we need not have abandoned monism, for the difficulty of imperfection could then have been solved. If, however, time cannot be viewed in this way, the contradiction between the unchanging relation of the principles and the constant change of their effects appears hopeless.

165. There remains the theory that the world is exclusively the product of a principle which regards neither rationality nor irrationality, but is directed to some aim outside them, or to no aim at all. Such a theory might account, no doubt, for the fact that the world is not a complete and perfect manifestation either of rationality or irrationality. But it is hardly exaggerated to say that this is the only fact about the world which it would account for. The idea of such a principle is contradictory. We can have no conception of its operation, of its nature, or even of its existence, without bringing it under some predicates of the reason. And if this is valid, the principle is, to some extent at least, rational.

166. So far indeed, the rationality would be but slight. And it might be suggested that the solution of the difficulty would be found in the idea that reality was, if we might so express it, moderately rational. Up to this point we have supposed that our only choice was between a principle manifesting the complete and perfect rationality, which is embodied in Hegel's Absolute Idea, and a principle entirely hostile or indifferent to reason. But what if the ultimate principle of the universe was one of which, for example, the categories of Being and Essence were valid, while those of the Notion remained unjustified ideals? This would account, it might be said, at once for the fact that the universe was sufficiently in accord with our reason for us to perceive it and attempt to comprehend it, and also for the fact that we fail to comprehend it completely. It would explain the judgment that the world, as we see it, might be better and might also be worse, which common sense pronounces, and which philosophy, whether it accepts it or not, is bound to explain somehow.

The supporters of such a theory, however, would have a difficult task before them. They might claim to reject Hegel's general theory of the universe on the ground that, on this question of imperfection, it was hopelessly in conflict with the facts. But when they, in their turn, set up a positive system, and asserted the earlier categories to be valid of reality, while the later ones were delusions, they would have to meet in detail Hegel's arguments that the earlier categories, unless synthesised by the later ones, plunge us in contradictions. The dialectic, being now merely negative and critical of another system, could not be disposed of on the ground that its own system broke down as a whole. Its arguments against the independent validity of the earlier categories would have to be met directly. What the issue of the conflict would be cannot be considered here, as considerations of space have prevented me from including in this book any discussion of the steps of the dialectic in detail. It may be remarked in passing, however, that several of the commentators, who unhesitatingly reject the system as a whole, admit the cogency of the argument from step to step in the Logic—which is all that is wanted here.

This, at any rate, is certain, that the possibility of explaining the existence of imperfection by such a theory as we have been considering, can give us no grounds for rejecting Hegel's system which we did not possess before. For if the deduction of the categories is defective, Hegelianism must be rejected as unproved, independently of its success or failure in interpreting the facts. And if the deduction of the categories is correct, then the theory of the partial rationality of reality must be given up. For, in that case, to assert the validity of the lower categories without the higher would be to assert a contradiction, and to do this is to destroy all possibility of coherent thought.

167. It would seem then that any other system offers as many obstacles to a satisfactory explanation of our difficulty as were presented by Hegel's theory. Is the inquirer then bound

to take refuge in complete scepticism, and reject all systems of philosophy, since none can avoid inconsistencies or absurdities on this point? This might perhaps be the proper course to pursue, if it were possible. But it is not possible. For every word and every action implies some theory of metaphysics. Every assertion or denial of fact—including the denial that anything is certain—implies that something is certain; and a doubt, also, implies our certainty that we doubt. Now to admit this, and yet to reject all ultimate explanations of the universe, is a contradiction at least as serious as any of those into which we were led by our attempt to explain away imperfection in obedience to the demands of Hegel's system.

We find then as many, and as grave, difficulties in our way when we take up any other system, or when we attempt to take up no system at all, as met us when we considered Hegel's theory, and our position towards the latter must be to some degree modified. We can no longer reject it, because it appears to lead to an absurdity, if every possible form in which it can be rejected involves a similar absurdity. At the same time we cannot possibly acquiesce in an unreconciled contradiction. Is there any other course open to us?

168. We must remark, in the first place, that the position in which the system finds itself, though difficult enough, is not a *reductio ad absurdum*. When an argument ends in such a reduction, there can never be any hesitation or doubt about rejecting the hypothesis with which it started. It is desired to know if a certain proposition is true. The assumption is made that the proposition is true, and it is found that the assumption leads to a contradiction. Thus there is no conflict of arguments. The hypothesis was made, not because it had been proved true, but to see what results would follow. Hence there is nothing to contradict the inference that the hypothesis must be false, which we draw from the absurdity of its consequences. On the one side is only a supposition, on the other ascertained facts.

This, however, is not the case here. The conclusion, that the universe is timelessly perfect, which appears to be in conflict with certain facts, is not a mere hypothesis, but asserts itself to be a correct deduction from other facts as certain as those which oppose it. Hence there is no reason why one should yield to the other. The inference that the universe is completely rational, and the inference that it is not, are both deduced by reasoning from the facts of experience. Unless we find a flaw in one or the other of the chains of deduction, we have no more right to say that Hegel's dialectic is wrong because the world is imperfect, than to deny that the world is imperfect, because Hegel's dialectic proves that it cannot be so.

It might appear at first sight as if the imperfection of the world was an immediate certainty. But in reality only the *data* of sense, upon which, in the last resort, all propositions must depend for their connection with reality, are here immediate. All judgments require mediation. And, even if the existence of imperfection in experience was an immediate certainty, yet the conclusion that its existence was incompatible with the perfection of the universe as a whole, could clearly only be reached mediately, by the refutation of the various arguments by means of which a reconciliation has been attempted.

It is, no doubt, our first duty, when two chains of reasoning appear to lead to directly opposite results, to go over them with the greatest care, that we may ascertain whether the apparent discrepancy is not due to some mistake of our own. It is also true that the chain of arguments, by which we arrive at the conclusion that the world is perfect, is both longer and less generally accepted than the other chain by which we reach the conclusion that there is imperfection in the world, and that this prevents the world from being perfect. We may, therefore, possibly be right in expecting beforehand to find a flaw in the first chain of reasoning, rather than in the second.

This, however, will not entitle us to adopt the one view as against the other. We may expect beforehand to find an error in an argument, but if in point of fact we do not succeed in finding one, we are bound to continue to accept the conclusion. For we are compelled to yield our assent to each step in the argument, so long as we do not see any mistake in it, and we shall in this way be conducted as inevitably to the end of the long chain as of the short one.

169. We may, I think, assume, for the purposes of this paper, that no discovery of error will occur to relieve us from our perplexity, since we are endeavouring to discuss here, not the truth of the Hegelian dialectic, but the consequences which will follow from it if it is true. And we have now to consider what we must do in the presence of two equally authoritative judgments which contradict one another.

The only course which it is possible to take appears to me that described by Mr Balfour. The thinker must "accept both contradictories, thinking thereby to obtain, under however unsatisfactory a form, the fullest measure of truth which he is at present able to grasp[1]." Of course we cannot adopt the same mental attitude which we should have a right to take in case our conclusions harmonised with one another. We must never lose sight of the fact that the two results do *not* harmonise, and that there must be something wrong somewhere. But we do not know where. And to take any step except this, would imply that we did know where the error lay. If we rejected the one conclusion in favour of the other, or if we rejected both in favour of scepticism, we should thereby assert, in the first case, that there was an error on the one side and not on the other, in the second case that there were errors on both sides. Now, if the case is as it has been stated above, we have no right to make such assertions, for we have been unable to detect errors on either side. All that we can do is to hold to both sides, and to recognise that, till one is refuted, or both are reconciled, our knowledge is in a very unsatisfactory state.

At the same time we shall have to be very careful not to let our dissatisfaction with the conflict, from which we cannot escape, carry us into either an explicit avowal or a tacit acceptance of any form of scepticism. For this would mean more than the mere equipoise of the two lines of argument. It would mean the entire rejection, at least, of the one which asserts that the universe is completely rational. And, as has been said, we have no right to reject either side of the contradiction, for no flaw has been found in either.

170. The position in which we are left appears to be this: If we cannot reject Hegel's dialectic, our system of knowledge will contain an unsolved contradiction. But that contradiction

---

[1] *Defence of Philosophic Doubt*, p. 313.

gives us no more reason for rejecting the Hegelian dialectic than for doing anything else, since a similar contradiction appears wherever we turn.   We are merely left with the conviction that something is fundamentally wrong in knowledge which all looks equally trustworthy.   Where to find the error we cannot tell.   Such a result is sufficiently unsatisfactory. Is it possible to find a conclusion not quite so negative ?

We cannot, as it seems to us at present, deny that both the propositions are true, nor deny that they are contradictory. Yet we know that one must be false, or else that they cannot be contradictory.   Is there any reason to hope that the solution lies in the last alternative ?   This result would be less sceptical and destructive than any other.   It would not involve any positive mistake in our previous reasonings, as far as they went, such as would be involved if harmony was restored by the discovery that one of the two conclusions was fallacious. It would only mean that we had not gone on far enough.   The two contradictory propositions—that the world was fundamentally perfect, and that imperfection did exist—would be harmonised and reconciled by a synthesis, in the same way that the contradictions within the dialectic itself are overcome. The two sides of the opposition would not so much be both false as both true.   They would be taken up into a higher sphere where the truth of both is preserved.

Moreover, the solution in this case would be exactly what might be expected if the Hegelian dialectic were true.   For, as has been said, the dialectic always advances by combining on a higher plane two things which were contradictory on a lower one.   And so, if, in some way now inconceivable to us, the eternal realisation of the Absolute Idea were so synthesised with the existence of imperfection as to be reconciled with it, we should harmonise the two sides by a principle already exemplified in one of them.

171.   It must be noticed also that the contradiction before us satisfies at any rate one of the conditions which are necessary if a synthesis is to be effected.   It is a case of contrary and not merely of contradictory opposition.   The opposition would be contradictory if the one side merely denied the validity of the data, or the correctness of the inferences, of the other.

For it would not then assert a different and incompatible conclusion, but simply deny the right of the other side to come to its own conclusion at all.   But it is a contrary opposition, because neither side denies that the other is, in itself, coherent and valid, but sets up against it another line of argument, also coherent and valid, which leads to an opposite and incompatible conclusion.   We have not reasons for and against a particular position, but reasons for two positions which deny one another.

If the opposition had been contradictory, there could have been no hope of a synthesis.   We should have ended with two propositions, one of which was a mere denial of the other—the one, that the universe is eternally rational, the other, that this is not the case.   And between two merely contradictory propositions, as Trendelenburg points out, there can be no possible synthesis [1].   One only affirms, and the other only denies.   And, between simple affirmation and simple negation, we can find nothing which will succeed in reconciling them.   For their whole meaning is summed up in their denial of one another, and if, with their reconciliation, the reciprocal denial vanished, the whole meaning would vanish also, leaving nothing but a blank.   Instead of having equally strong grounds to believe two different things, we should have no grounds to believe either.   Any real opposition may conceivably be synthesised. But it is as impossible to get a harmony out of an absolute blank, as it is to get anything else.

Here, however, when we have two positive conclusions, which appear indeed to be incompatible, but have more in them than simple incompatibility, it is not impossible that a higher notion could be found, by which each should be recognised as true, and by which it should be seen that they were really not mutually exclusive.

The thesis and antithesis in Hegel's logic always stand to one another in a relation of contrary opposition.   In the higher stages, no doubt, the antithesis is more than a mere opposite of the thesis, and already contains an element of synthesis.   But the element of opposition, which is always there, is always an opposition of contraries.   Hence it does not seem impossible that this further case of contrary opposition should be dealt

[1] *Logische Untersuchungen*, Vol. i. p. 56.

with on Hegel's principle. Incompatible as the two terms seem at present, they can hardly seem more hopelessly opposed than many pairs of contraries in the dialectic seem, before their syntheses are found.

172. It is possible, also, to see some reasons why such a solution, if possible at all, should not be possible yet, and why it would be delayed till the last abstraction should be removed, as the dialectic process rebuilds concrete realities. Our aim is to reconcile the fact that the Absolute Idea exists eternally in its full perfection, with the fact that it manifests itself as something incomplete and imperfect. Now the Absolute Idea only becomes known to us through a process and consequently as something incomplete and imperfect. We have to grasp its moments successively, and to be led on from the lower to the higher. And, in like manner, all our knowledge of its manifestations must come to us in the form of a process, since it must come gradually. We cannot expect to see how all process should only be an element in a timeless reality, so long as we can only think of the timeless reality by means of a process. But, *sub specie aeternitatis*, it might be that the difficulty would vanish.

I am not, of course, trying to argue that there is such a reconciliation of these two extremes, or that there is the slightest positive evidence that a reconciliation can exist. As we have seen above, the eternal realisation of the Absolute Idea, and the existence of change and evil, are, for us as we are, absolutely incompatible, nor can we even imagine a way in which they should cease to be so. If we could imagine such a way we should have solved the problem, for, as it would be the only chance of rescuing our knowledge from hopeless confusion, we should be justified in taking it.

All I wish to suggest is that it is conceivable that there should be such a synthesis, although we cannot at present conceive what it could be like, and that, although there is no positive evidence for it, there is no evidence against it. And as either the incompatibility of the two propositions, or the evidence for one of them, must be a mistake, we may have at any rate a hope that some solution may lie in this direction.

173. If indeed we were absolutely certain that neither the

arguments for the eternal perfection of the Absolute Idea, nor
the arguments for the existence of process and change, were
erroneous, we should be able to go beyond this negative
position, and assert positively the existence of the synthesis,
although we should be as unable as before to comprehend of
what nature it could be.   We could then avail ourselves of Mr
Bradley's maxim, "what may be and must be, certainly is."
That the synthesis must exist would, on the hypothesis we are
considering, be beyond doubt.   For if both the lines of
argument which lead respectively to the eternal reality of the
Absolute Idea, and to the existence of change, could be known,
not merely to be at present unrefuted, but to be true, then they
must somehow be compatible.   That all truth is harmonious is
the postulate of reasoning, the denial of which would abolish
all tests of truth and falsehood, and so make all judgment
unmeaning.   And since the two propositions are, as we have
seen throughout this chapter, incompatible as they stand in
their immediacy, the only way in which they can possibly be
made compatible is by a synthesis which transcends them and
so unites them.

Can we then say of such a synthesis that it may be? Of
course it is only possible to do so negatively.   A positive
assertion that there was no reason whatever why a thing
should not exist could only be obtained by a complete knowledge of it, and, if we had a complete knowledge of it, it would
not be necessary to resort to indirect proof to discover whether
it existed or not.   But we have, it would seem, a right to say
that no reason appears why it should not exist.   If the Hegelian
dialectic is true (and, except on this hypothesis, our difficulty
would not have arisen), we know that predicates which seem to
be contrary can be united and harmonised by a synthesis.   And
the fact that such a synthesis is not conceivable by us need not
make us consider it impossible.   Till such a synthesis is found,
it must always appear inconceivable, and that it has not yet
been found implies nothing more than that the world, considered as a process, has not yet worked out its full meaning.

174.   But we must admit that the actual result is rather
damaging to the prospects of Hegelianism.   We may, as I
have tried to show, be sure, that, if Hegel's dialectic is true,

then such a synthesis must be possible, because it is the only way of harmonising all the facts. At the same time, the fact that the dialectic cannot be true, unless some synthesis which we do not know, and whose nature we cannot even conceive, relieves it from an obstacle which would otherwise be fatal, certainly lessens the chance that it is true, even if no error in it has yet been discovered. For our only right to accept such an extreme hypothesis lies in the impossibility of finding any other way out of the dilemma. And the more violent the consequences to which an argument leads us, the greater is the antecedent probability that some flaw has been left undetected.

Not only does such a theory lose the strength which comes from the successful solution of all problems presented to it, but it is compelled to rely, with regard to this particular proposition, on a possibility which we cannot at present fully grasp, even in imagination, and the realisation of which would perhaps involve the transcending of all discursive thought. Under these circumstances it is clear that our confidence in Hegel's system must be considerably less than that which was possessed by its author, who had not realised the tentative and incomplete condition to which this difficulty inevitably reduced his position.

The result of these considerations, however, is perhaps on the whole more positive than negative. They can scarcely urge us to more careful scrutiny of all the details of the dialectic than would be required in any case by the complexity of the subjects with which it deals. And, on the other hand, they do supply us, as it seems to me, with a ground for believing that neither time nor imperfection forms an insuperable objection to the dialectic. If the dialectic is not valid in itself, we shall any way have no right to believe it. And if it is valid in itself, we shall not only be entitled, but we shall be bound, to believe that one more synthesis remains, as yet unknown to us, which shall overcome the last and most persistent of the contradictions inherent in appearance.

175. NOTE.—After this chapter, in a slightly different form, had appeared in *Mind*, it was criticised by Mr F. C. S. Schiller, in an article entitled 'The Metaphysics of the Time Process.' (*Mind*, N. S. Vol. IV. No. 14.) I have endeavoured

to consider his acute and courteous objections to my view with that care which they merit, but I have not succeeded in finding in them any reason for changing the position indicated in the preceding sections. I have already discussed one of Mr Schiller's objections[1], and there are some others on which I will now venture to make a few remarks.

Mr Schiller complains that I overlook "the curious inconsistency of denying the metaphysical value of Time, and yet expecting from the Future the discovery of the ultimate synthesis on which one's whole metaphysics depends[2]." It was not, of course, from the advance of time as such, but from the more complete manifestation through time of the timeless reality that I ventured to expect a solution. But it is, no doubt, true that I did express a hope of the discovery of a synthesis which has not yet been discovered, so that its discovery must be an event in time. I fail, however, to see the inconsistency. Time is certainly, on the theory which I have put forward, only an appearance and an illusion. But then, on the same theory, the inconsistency which requires a synthesis is also an illusion. And so is the necessity of *discovering* a synthesis for two aspects of reality which are really eternally moments in a harmonious whole.

Sub specie aeternitatis, the temporal process is not, as such, real, and can produce nothing new. But then, *sub specie aeternitatis*, if there is an ultimate synthesis, it does not require to be produced, for it exists eternally. Nor does the contradiction require to be removed, for, if there is a synthesis, the contradiction never, *sub specie aeternitatis*, existed at all. *Sub specie temporis*, on the other hand, the contradiction has to be removed, and the synthesis discovered. But, *sub specie temporis*, the time process exists, and can produce something new.

The inconsistency of which Mr Schiller accuses me comes only from combining the assertions that a change is required, and that no change is possible, as if they were made from the same stand-point. But, on the theory in question, the first is only true when we look at things from the stand-point of time, and the second when we look at them from the standpoint of the timeless idea. That the possible solution is

---

[1] Chap. III. Section 96.　　[2] *Op. cit.* p. 37.

incomprehensible, I have fully admitted.   But I cannot see that it is inconsistent.

176.   Mr Schiller further says, if I understand him rightly, that it is obviously impossible that Hegel could have accounted for time, since he started with an abstraction which did not include it.   Without altogether adopting Mr Schiller's explanations of the motives of idealist philosophers we may agree with him when he says that their conceptions "were necessarily *abstract, and among the things they abstracted from was the time-aspect of Reality* [1]."   He then continues, " Once abstracted from, the reference to Time could not, of course, be recovered."   And, a little later on, " You must pay the price for a formula that will enable you to make assertions that hold good far beyond the limits of your experience.   And part of the price is that you will in the end be unable to give a rational explanation of those very characteristics, which had been dismissed at the outset as irrelevant to a rational explanation."

I have admitted that Hegel has failed, not indeed to give a deduction of time, but to give one which would be consistent with the rest of his system.   But this is a result which, as it seems to me, can only be arrived at by examining in detail the deduction he does give, and cannot be settled beforehand by the consideration that the abstraction he starts from excludes time.   Such an objection would destroy the whole dialectic.   For Hegel starts with pure Being, precisely because it is the most complete abstraction possible, with the minimum of meaning that any term can have.   And if nothing which was abstracted from could ever be restored, the dialectic process, which consists of nothing else than the performance of this operation, would be completely invalid.

I have endeavoured to show in the earlier chapters that there is nothing unjustified in such an advance from abstract to concrete.   Of course, if we make an abstraction, as we do in geometry, with the express intention of adhering to it uncritically throughout our treatment of the subject, and ignoring any inaccuracy as irrelevant for our present purposes,— then, no doubt, our final conclusions must have the same abstractness as our original premises.   But this is very unlike

[1] *Op. cit.* p. 38.

the position of the dialectic. Here we begin with the most complete abstraction we can find, for the express purpose of seeing how far we can, by criticism of it, be forced to consider it inadequate, and so to substitute for it more concrete notions which remedy its incompleteness. Right or wrong, this can scarcely be disposed of as obviously impossible.

Nor does it seem quite correct to say that Hegel's philosophy was "constructed to give an account of the world irrespective of Time and Change[1]," if, as appears to be the case, "constructed to give" implies a purpose. Hegel's purpose was not to give any particular account of the universe, but to give one which should be self-consistent, and he declared time and change to be only appearances, because he found it impossible to give a consistent account of the universe if he treated time and change as ultimate realities. He may have been wrong, but his decision was the result of argument, and not a preconceived purpose.

177.   Mr Schiller suggests that the whole device of using abstract laws and generalisations at all in knowledge is one which is justified by its success, and which may be discarded, in whole or in part, for another, if another should promise better. " Why should we want to calculate the facts by such universal formulas? The answer to this question brings us to the roots of the matter. We make the fundamental assumption of science, that there are universal and eternal laws, i.e. that the individuality of things together with their spatial and temporal context may be neglected, not because we are convinced of its theoretic validity, but because we are constrained by its practical convenience. *We want to be able to make predictions about the future behaviour of things for the purpose of shaping our own conduct accordingly.* Hence attempts to forecast the future have been the source of half the superstitions of mankind. But no method of divination ever invented could compete in ingenuity and gorgeous simplicity with the assumption of universal laws which hold good without reference to time; and so in the long run it alone could meet the want or practical necessity in question.

"In other words that assumption is a *methodological* device

[1] *Op. cit.* p. 38.

and ultimately reposes on the practical necessity of discovering formulas for calculating events in the rough, without awaiting or observing their occurrence. To assert this methodological character of eternal truths is not, of course, to deny their validity,—for it is evident that unless the nature of the world had lent itself to a very considerable extent to such interpretation, the assumption of 'eternal' laws would have served our purposes as little as those of astrology, chiromancy, necromancy, and catoptromancy. What however must be asserted is that this assumption is *not* an ultimate term in the explanation of the world.

"That does not, of course, matter to Science, which is not concerned with such ultimate explanation, and for which the assumption is at all events ultimate enough. But it *does* matter to philosophy that the ultimate theoretic assumption should have a methodological character[1]."

178.   But, I reply, our habit of abstracting and generalising (and all universal laws are nothing more than this) is not a tool that we can take up or lay down at pleasure, as a carpenter takes up or lays down a particular chisel, which he finds suited or unsuited to the work immediately before him. It is rather the essential condition of all thought—perhaps it would be better to say an essential moment in all thought. All thought consists in processes which may be described as abstractions and generalisations. It is true, of course, that we could have no thought unless the complex and the particular were given to us. But it is no less true that everything which thought does with what is given to it involves abstraction and generalisation.

If we had merely unrelated particulars before us we should not be conscious. And even if we were conscious, unrelated particulars could certainly give us no knowledge. We can have no knowledge without, at the lowest, comparison. And to compare—to perceive a similar element in things otherwise dissimilar, or the reverse—is to abstract and to generalise. Again to find any relation whatever between two particulars is to abstract and to generalise. If we say, for example, that a blow causes a bruise, this is to separate and abstract one

---

[1] *Op. cit.* p. 42.

quality from the large number which are connoted by the word blow, and it is also to generalise, since it is to assert that a blow stands in the same relation to a bruise, as, let us say, friction to heat.

Without abstraction and generalisation, then, we can have no knowledge, and so they are not a methodological device but a necessity of our thought. It is, indeed, not certain beforehand that the laws which are the result of generalisation and abstraction will be, as Mr Schiller says, " eternal," that is, will disregard time. But if the result of the criticism of reality does lead us to laws which do not accept time as an ultimate reality, and if these laws do, as I have admitted they do, plunge us into considerable difficulties, still we cannot, as Mr Schiller seems to wish, reject the process of generalisation and abstraction if, or in as far as, it does not turn out well. For it is our only mode of thought, and the very act of thought which rejected it would embody it, and·be dependent on it.

There remain other points of high interest in Mr Schiller's paper—his conception of metaphysics as ultimately ethical, and his view of what may be hoped for from time, regarded as real and not as merely appearance. But he is here constructive and no longer critical, and it would be beyond the purpose of this note to attempt to follow him.

CHAPTER VI.

179. FROM a practical point of view the chief interest in Hegel's system must centre in the last stages of the Philosophy of Spirit. Even if we hold that the pure thought of the Logic is the logical *prius* of the whole dialectic, and that all Nature and Spirit stand in a purely dependent relation, still our most vital interest must be in that part of the system which touches and interprets the concrete life of Spirit which we ourselves share. And this interest will be yet stronger in those who hold the view, which I have endeavoured to expound in previous chapters, that the logical *prius* of the system is not pure thought but Spirit. For then, in the highest forms of Spirit we shall see reality in its truest and deepest meaning, from which all other aspects of reality—whether in Logic, in Nature, or in the lower forms of Spirit—are but abstractions, and to which they must return as the only escape from the contradiction and inadequacy which is manifested in them. Upon this view the highest form, in ,which Spirit manifests itself, will be the ultimate meaning of all things.

Many students must have experienced some disappointment when, turning to the end of the Philosophy of Spirit, they found that its final stage was simply Philosophy. It is true that any thinker, who has the least sympathy with Hegel, must assign to philosophy a sufficiently important place in the nature of things. Hegel taught that the secrets of the universe opened themselves to us, but only on condition of deep and systematic thought, and the importance of philosophy was undiminished either by scepticism or by appeals to the healthy instincts of the plain man. But there is some difference between taking philosophy as the supreme and completely adequate means, and admitting it to be the supreme end. There is some difference between holding that philosophy is the knowledge of the highest form of reality, and holding that it is itself the highest form of reality.

It seems to me that Hegel has been untrue to the tendencies of his own system in seeking the ultimate reality of Spirit in philosophy alone, and that, on his own premises, he ought to have looked for a more comprehensive explanation. What that should have been, I shall not attempt to determine. I only wish to show that it should have been something more than philosophy.

180. Hegel does not give any very detailed account of philosophy, considered as the highest expression of reality. Most of the space devoted, in the Philosophy of Spirit, to Philosophy is occupied in defending it against the charge of pantheism—in Hegel's use of the word. The following are the passages which appear most significant for our purpose.

571. "These three syllogisms" (i.e. of religion) "constituting the one syllogism of the absolute self-mediation of spirit, are the revelation of that spirit whose life is set out as a cycle of concrete shapes in pictorial thought. From this its separation into parts, with a temporal and external sequence, the unfolding of the mediation contracts itself in the result—where the spirit closes in unity with itself,—not merely to the simplicity of faith and devotional feeling, but even to thought. In the immanent simplicity of thought the unfolding still has its expansion, yet is all the while known as an indivisible coherence of the universal, simple, and eternal spirit in itself. In this form of truth, truth is the object of *philosophy*." ...

572. Philosophy "is the unity of Art and Religion. Whereas the vision-method of Art, external in point of form, is but subjective production and shivers the substantial content into many separate shapes, and whereas Religion, with its separation into parts, opens it out in mental picture, and mediates what is thus opened out; Philosophy not merely keeps them together to make a total, but even unifies them into the

simple spiritual vision, and then in that raises them to self-conscious thought. Such consciousness is thus the intelligible unity (cognised by thought) of art and religion, in which the diverse elements in the content are cognised as necessary, and this necessary as free."

573. "Philosophy thus characterises itself as a cognition of the necessity in the content of the absolute picture-idea, as also of the necessity in the two forms—on the one hand, immediate vision and its poetry, and the objective and external revelation presupposed by representation,—on the other hand, first the subjective retreat inwards, then the subjective movement of faith and its final identification with the presupposed object. This cognition is thus the *recognition* of this content and its form; it is the liberation from the one-sidedness of the forms, elevation of them into the absolute form, which determines itself to content, remains identical with it, and is in that the cognition of that essential and actual necessity. This movement, which philosophy is, finds itself already accomplished, when at the close it seizes its own notion,—i.e. only *looks back* on its knowledge." ...

574. "This notion of philosophy is the self-thinking Idea, the truth aware of itself (Section 236),—the logical system, but with the signification that it is universality approved and certified in concrete content as in its actuality. In this way the science has gone back to its beginning: its result is the logical system but as a spiritual principle: out of the pre-supposing judgment, in which the notion was only implicit, and the beginning an immediate,—and thus out of the *appearance* which it had there—it has risen into its pure principle, and thus also into its proper medium."

181. The word Philosophy, in its ordinary signification, denotes a purely intellectual activity. No doubt, whenever we philosophise we are acting, and we are also feeling either pleasure or pain. But philosophy itself is knowledge, it is neither action nor feeling. And there seems nothing in Hegel's account of it to induce us to change the meaning of the word in this respect. It is true that he speaks of philosophy as the union of art and religion. Both art and religion are more than mere knowledge, since they both present aspects of

volition and of feeling. But, if we look back on his treatment
of art and religion as separate stages, we shall see that he
confines himself almost entirely to the truth which lies in them,
ignoring the other elements. And when, in Section 572, he
points out how philosophy is the unity of these two, it is
merely as expressing the truth more completely than they
do, that he gives it this position. There is nothing said of a
higher or deeper ideal of good, nothing of any increased harmony between our ideal and our surroundings, nothing of any
greater or deeper pleasure. Philosophy is " the intelligible
unity (cognised by thought) of art and religion, in which the
diverse elements in the content are cognised as necessary, and
this necessary as free."

We are thus, it would seem, bound down to the view that
Hegel considered the supreme nature of Spirit to be expressed
as knowledge, and as knowledge only. There are two senses
in which we might take this exaltation of philosophy. We
might suppose it to apply to philosophy as it exists at present,
not covering the whole field of human knowledge, but standing
side by side with the sciences and with the mass of unsystem-
atised knowledge, claiming indeed a supremacy over all other
sources of knowledge, but by no means able to dispense with
their assistance. Or we might suppose that this high position
was reserved for philosophy, when, as might conceivably happen,
it shall have absorbed all knowledge into itself, so that every
fact shall be seen as completely conditioned, and as united
to all the others by the nature of the Absolute Idea. Which
of these meanings Hegel intended to adopt does not seem
to be very clear, but neither appears, on closer examination,
to be acceptable as a complete and satisfactory account of the
deepest nature of Spirit.

182. Let us consider first philosophy as we have it at
present. In this form it can scarcely claim to be worthy of
this supreme place. It may, no doubt, reasonably consider
itself as the *highest* activity of Spirit—at any rate in the department of cognition. But in order to stand at the end of
the development of Spirit it must be more than this. It must
not only be the highest activity of Spirit, but one in which all
the others are swallowed up and transcended. It must have

overcome and removed all the contradictions, all the inadequacies, which belong to the lower forms in which Spirit manifests itself.

Now all the knowledge which philosophy gives us is, from one point of view, abstract, and so imperfect. It teaches us what the fundamental nature of reality is, and what, therefore, everything *must* be. But it does not pretend to show us *how* everything partakes of that nature—to trace out in every detail of the universe that rationality which, on general grounds, it asserts to be in it. It could not, indeed, do this, for, in order to trace the Notion in every detail, it would have first to discover what every detail was. And this it cannot do. For what the facts are in which the Notion manifests itself, we must learn not from philosophy but from experience.

183.   But, it may be said, Hegel did not accept this view. He held that it was possible, from the nature of the pure Idea, to deduce the nature of the facts in which it manifested itself, and on this theory philosophy would cover the whole field of knowledge, and our criticism would fall to the ground.

My object here, however, is to show that Hegel's view of the ultimate nature of Spirit is inconsistent with the general principles established in his Logic, and not that it is inconsistent with the rest of his attempts to apply the Logic. Even, therefore, if Hegel had attempted to deduce particular facts from the Logic, it would be sufficient for my present purpose to point out, as I have endeavoured to do above, that, on his own premises, he had no right to make the attempt. But, as I have also tried to show, he never does attempt to deduce facts from the Logic, but only to interpret and explain them by it[1].

Moreover, whether we are to consider the applications of the Logic as deductions or as explanations, it is perfectly clear that they are limited in their scope. Hegel says, more than once, that certain details are too insignificant and contingent to permit us to trace their speculative meaning. Even in the cases which he works out most fully, there is always a residuum left unexplained. He may have pushed his desire to find speculative meanings in biological details beyond the limits of prudence, but he never attempted to find any significance

---

[1] Chap. ii. Sections 55—57.

in the precise number of zoological species. He may have held that the perfection of the Prussian constitution was philosophically demonstrable, but he made no endeavour to explain, from the nature of the Idea, the exact number of civil servants in the employment of the Crown. And yet these are facts, which can be learned by experience, which are links in chains of causes and effects, and which, like everything else in the universe, the dialectic declares on general grounds must rest on something, which is rational because it is real.

Philosophy then must be contented with an abstract demonstration that things must be rational, without being able in all cases to show how they are rational. Part of our knowledge will thus remain on an empirical basis, and the sphere of philosophy will be doubly limited. Not only will it be limited to knowledge, but to certain departments of knowledge. An activity which leaves so much of the workings of Spirit untouched cannot be accepted as adequately expressing by itself the ultimate nature of Spirit. Indeed, taken by itself, philosophy proclaims its own inadequacy. For it must assert things to be completely rational, and therefore completely explicable, which, all the same, it cannot succeed in completely explaining.

184. It has been asserted that it is natural and right that Hegel's system should end simply with philosophy, since it is simply with philosophy that it begins. Thus Erdmann says: "It is with intelligible sarcasm that Hegel was accustomed to mention those who, when the exposition had reached this point, supposed that now for the first time (as if in a philosophy of philosophy) that which was peculiar and distinctive had been reached. Rather has everything already been treated, and it only remains to complete by a survey of it the circle of the system, so that its presence becomes an Encyclopaedia. If, that is to say, religion fallen into discord with thought (as, for that matter, the Phenomenology of Spirit had already shown) leads to speculative, free thought, while logic had begun with the determination to realise such thought, then the end of the Philosophy of Religion coincides with the beginning of the Logic, and the requirement laid down by Fichte that the system be a circle is fulfilled[1]."

[1] *History of Philosophy*, Section 329, 9.

This, however, scarcely disposes of the difficulty. The object of philosophy is not simply to account for the existence of philosophy. It aims at discovering the ultimate nature of all reality. To start with philosophising, and to end by explaining why we must philosophise, is indeed a circle, but a very limited one, which leaves out of account most of our knowledge and most of our action, unless we are prepared to prove independently that all reality is synthesised in the conscious spirit, and all the reality of the conscious spirit is synthesised in philosophising. Without this proof philosophy would leave vast provinces of experience completely outside its influence—a position which may be modest, but is certainly not Hegelian.

It is true that, on the way to Philosophy as it occurs at the end of the Philosophy of Spirit, Hegel goes through many other branches of human activity and experience. But since the process is a dialectic, the whole meaning of the process must be taken as summed up in the last term. Either then we must make philosophy include all knowledge—to say nothing, for the present, of anything besides knowledge—or else we must admit at once that Hegel is wrong in making philosophy the highest point of Spirit, since at that point we have to find something which adequately expresses all reality, and philosophy, in the ordinary sense of the word, does not even include all cognition of reality.

185. Let us take then the second meaning of philosophy—that in which we conceive it developed till all knowledge forms one harmonious whole, so that no single fact remains contingent and irrational.

This ideal may be conceived in two ways. Philosophy would, in the first place, become equivalent to the whole of knowledge, if pure thought could ever reach the goal, at which it has been sometimes asserted that Hegel's dialectic was aiming, and deduce all reality from its own nature, without the assistance of any immediately given data. If this could ever happen, then, no doubt, philosophy and knowledge would be coincident. The only reality would be pure thought. The nature of that thought would be given us by the dialectic, and so philosophy would be able to explain completely the whole of reality.

But, as we have seen above[1], such a goal is impossible and contradictory. For thought is only a mediating activity, and requires something to mediate. This need not, indeed, be anything alien to it. The whole content of the reality, which thought mediates, may itself be nothing but thought. But whatever the nature of that reality, it must be given to thought in each case from outside, as a *datum*. Supposing nothing but thought existed, still in the fact that it existed, that it was there, we should have an immediate certainty, which could no more be deduced from the nature of thought, than the reality of a hundred thalers could be deduced from the idea of them.

It is thus impossible that any acquaintance with the nature of thought could ever dispense us with the necessity of having some immediate *datum*, which could not be deduced, but must be accepted, and we have seen that there are reasons for believing that Hegel never proposed to philosophy such an impossible and suicidal end. There is, however, another sense in which it is possible to suppose that philosophy may become coincident with the whole of knowledge, and thereby make knowledge one single, symmetrical, and perfectly rational system. And it may be said that when philosophy has thus broadened itself to include all knowledge, it may be taken as expressing adequately the whole nature of spirit, and therefore, on Hegel's system, of all reality. Let us examine more closely what would be the nature of such a perfected knowledge.

186. All knowledge must have immediate *data*, which are not deduced but given. But it does not follow that knowledge must consequently be left imperfect, and with ragged edges. That which indicates the defect of knowledge is not immediacy, but contingency, in the Hegelian sense of the word, that is, the necessity of explanation from outside. Now all data of knowledge as originally given us, by the outer senses or through introspection, are not only immediate but contingent. But the two qualities do not necessarily go together, and we can conceive a state of things, in which knowledge should rest on *data*—or, rather, on a *datum*—which should be immediate, without being contingent.

---

[1] Chap. II. Sections 55—57.

Supposing that the theory of the nature of reality, which Hegel lays down in his Logic, is true, then, if knowledge were perfect, the abstract certainty (Gewissheit) of ·what *must* be would be transformed into complete knowledge (Erkennen) of what *is*. We should then perceive all reality under the only form which, according to Hegel, can be really adequate to it—that is, as a unity of spirits, existing only in their connection with one another. We should see that the whole nature of each individual was expressed in these relations with others. And we should see that that nature, which was what marked him out as an individual, was not to be conceived as something merely particular and exclusive, so that reality consisted of a crowd or aggregate of separate individuals. On the contrary the nature of each individual is to be taken as determined by his place in a whole, which we must conceive on the analogy of an organism,—a unity manifesting itself in multiplicity. The individual has his entire nature in the manifestation of this whole, as the whole, in turn, is nothing else but its manifestation in individuals. Through this unity the parts will mutually determine one another, so that from any one all the rest could, with sufficient insight, be deduced, and so that no change could be made in any without affecting all. This complete interdependence is only approximately realised in the unity which is found in a picture or a living being, but in the Absolute the unity must be conceived as far closer than aesthetic or organic unity, though we can only imagine it by aid of the analogies which these afford us. And in this complete interdependence and mutual determination each individual would find his fullest self-development. For his relations with others express his place in the whole, and it is this place in the whole which expresses his deepest individuality.

If knowledge ever did fill out the sketch that the Hegelian logic gives, it must be in some such form as this that it would do so. For it is, I think, clear, from the category of the Absolute Idea, that reality can only be found in selves, which have their whole existence in finding themselves in harmony with other selves. And this plurality of selves, again, must be conceived, not as a mere aggregate, but as a unity whose intimacy and strength is only inadequately represented by the idea of Organism. For, if not, then the relations would be merely external and secondary, as compared with the reality of the individuals between whom the relations existed. And this would be incompatible with Hegel's declaration that the individuals have their existence for self only in their relation to others.

187. Of course such an ideal of knowledge is indefinitely remote as compared with our present condition. It would require, in the first.place, a knowledge of all the facts in the universe—from which we are now separated by no inconsiderable interval. And, at the same time, it would require a great increase in the depth and keenness of view which we can bring to bear in knowledge, if all that part of reality which we only perceive at present under the lower categories of Being and Essence, is to be brought under the Absolute Idea, and, in place of the inorganic, the merely animal, and the imperfectly spiritual, which now presents itself to us, we are to see the universe as a whole of self-conscious selves, in perfect unity with one another.

But that the ideal should be remote from our present state need not surprise us. For it is the point at which the world-process culminates, and whatever view we may hold as to the ultimate reality of the conception of process, it is clear enough that, from any point of view which admits of the conception of process at all, we must have a long way still to go before we reach a consummation which leaves the universe perfectly rational and perfectly righteous. It would be more suspicious if any ideal not greatly removed from our present state should be held out to us as a complete and adequate satisfaction. It is enough that this ideal is one which, if Hegel's logic be true, must be attainable *sub specie temporis,* because, *sub specie aeternitatis,* it is the only reality. And it is an ideal which is not self-contradictory, for the immediacy of the *data* is retained, although their contingency has vanished.

The immediacy is retained, because we should have, as a given fact, to which reason mounts in the process of discovery, and on which it bases its demonstrations in the process of explanation, that there are such and such selves, and that they are connected in such and such a way. On the other hand, the contingency has vanished. For while everything is determined, nothing is determined merely from outside. The universe presents, indeed, an aspect of multiplicity, but then it is not a mere multiplicity. The universe is a super-organic unity[1], and therefore, when one part of it is determined by another, it is determined by the idea of the whole, which is also in itself, and the determination is not dependent on something alien, but on the essential nature of that which is determined. Hence determination appears as self-development, and necessity, as Hegel points out at the beginning of the Doctrine of the Notion, reveals itself as in reality freedom.

188. Neither this, nor any other possible system of knowledge, could give us any ground of determination for the universe as a whole, since there is nothing outside it, by which it could be determined. This, however, would not render our knowledge defective. If we reached this point the only question which would remain unanswered would be:—Why is the universe as a whole what it is, and not something else? And this question could not be answered. But we must not infer from this the incomplete rationality of the universe. For the truth is that the question ought never to have been asked. It is unmeaning, since it applies a category, which has significance only inside the universe, to the universe as a whole. Of any part we are entitled and bound to ask Why, for by the very fact that it is a part, it cannot be directly self-determined, and must depend on other things[2]. But, when we speak of an all-embracing totality, then, with the possibility of finding a cause, disappears also the necessity for finding one. Independent and uncaused existence is not in itself a contradictory or impossible idea. It *is* contradictory when it is applied to anything in

---

[1] This expression is, I believe, new. I fear that it is very barbarous. But there seems a necessity for some such phrase to denote that supreme unity, which, just because it is perfect unity, is compatible with, and indeed requires, the complete differentiation and individuality of its parts. To call such unity merely organic is dangerous. For in an organism the unity is not complete, nor the parts fully individual (cp. Hegel's treatment of the subject under the category of Life).

[2] The parts of a super-organic whole are, indeed, self-determined, but not directly. Their self-determination comes through their determination by the other parts.

the universe, for whatever is in the universe must be in connection with other things. But this can of course be no reason for suspecting a fallacy when we find ourselves obliged to use the idea in reference to the universe as a whole, which has nothing outside it with which it could stand in connection.

Indeed the suggestion, that it is possible that the universe should have been different from what it is, would, in such a state of knowledge, possess no meaning. For, from the complete interdependence of all the parts, it would follow that if it was different at all, it must be different completely. And a possibility which has no common element with actuality, which would be the case here, is a mere abstraction which is devoid of all value.

This, then, is the highest point to which knowledge, as knowledge, can attain, upon Hegel's principles. Everything is known, and everything is known to be completely rational. And, although our minds cannot help throwing a shadow of contingency and irrationality over the symmetrical structure, by asking, as it is always possible to ask, what determined the whole to be what it is, and why it is not otherwise, yet reflection convinces us that the question is unjustifiable, and indeed unmeaning, and that the inability to answer it can be no reason for doubting the completely satisfactory nature of the result at which we have arrived.

189. But even when knowledge has reached this point, is it an adequate expression of the complete nature of reality? This question, I think, must be answered in the negative. We have, it is true, come to the conclusion,—if we have gone so far with Hegel—that Spirit is the only and the all-sufficient reality. But knowledge does not exhaust the nature of Spirit. The simplest introspection will show us that, besides knowledge, we have also volition, and the feeling of pleasure and pain. These are *prima facie* different from knowledge, and it does not seem possible that they should ever be reduced to it. Knowledge, volition, and feeling remain, in spite of all such attempts, distinct and independent. They are not, indeed, independent, in the sense that any of them can exist without the others. Nor is it impossible that they might be found to be aspects of a unity which embraces and transcends them

all. But they are independent in so far that neither of the others can be reduced to, or transcended by, knowledge.

Let us first consider volition. Volition and knowledge have this common element, that they are activities which strive to bring about a harmony between the conscious self and its surroundings. But in the manner in which they do this they are the direct antitheses of one another. In knowledge the self endeavours to conform itself to its surroundings. In volition, on the other hand, it demands that its surroundings shall conform to itself. Of course the knowing mind is far from being inactive in knowledge—it is only by means of its own activity that it arrives at the objective truth which is its aim. Nor is the self by any means purely active in volition. For it has sometimes only to recognise and approve a harmony already existing, and not to produce one by its action. And sometimes the surroundings react on the self, and develop it or crush it into acquiescence in facts against which it would previously have protested.

But it remains true that in knowledge the aim of the self is to render its own state a correct mirror of the objective reality, and that, in so far as it fails to do this, it condemns its own state as false and mistaken. In volition, on the contrary, its aim is that objective reality shall carry out the demands made by the inner nature of the self. In so far as reality fails to do this, the self condemns it as wrong. Now this is surely a fundamental difference. Starting with the aim, which is common to both, that a harmony is to be established, what greater difference can exist between two ways of carrying out this aim, than that one way demands that the subject shall conform to the object, while the other way demands that the object shall conform to the subject ?

190. We may put this in another way. The aim of knowledge is the true. The aim of volition is the good (in the widest sense of the word, in which it includes all that we desire, since all that is desired at all, is desired *sub specie boni*). Now one of these aims cannot be reduced to the other. There is no direct transition from truth to goodness, nor from goodness to truth. We may of course come to the conclusion, which Hegel has attempted to demonstrate, that the content

of the two ideas is the same, that the deepest truth is the highest good, and the highest good is the deepest truth, that whatever is real is righteous, and whatever is righteous is real. But we can only do this by finding out independently what is true and what is good, and by proving that they coincide.

If we *have* come to this conclusion, and established it to our own satisfaction as a general principle, we are entitled, no doubt, to apply it in particular cases where the identity is not evident. To those, for example, who have satisfied themselves of the existence of a benevolent God, it is perfectly open to argue that we must be immortal, because the absence of immortality would make life a ghastly farce, or, by a converse process, that toothache must be good because God sends it. But if the harmony of the two sides has not been established by the demonstration of the existence of a benevolent and omnipotent power, or of some other ground for the same conclusion, such an argument depends on an unjustifiable assumption.

There is nothing in the mere fact of a thing's existence to make it desired or desirable by us. There is nothing in the mere fact that a thing is desired or desirable by us to make it exist. Two mental activities for which the test of validity is respectively existence and desirability must surely, therefore, be coordinate, without any possibility of reducing the one to a case or application of the other. If indeed we considered volition as merely that which leads to action, it might be considered less fundamental than knowledge, since it would inevitably disappear in a state of perfect harmony. But volition must be taken to include all affirmations of an ideal in relation to existence, including those which lead to no action because they do not find reality to be discrepant with them. And in this case we shall have to consider it as fundamental an activity of Spirit as knowledge is, and one, therefore, which cannot be ignored in favour of knowledge when we are investigating the completely adequate form of Spirit.

191. No doubt the fact that knowledge and volition have the same aim before them—a harmony between the self and its surroundings—and that they effect it in ways which are directly contrary to one another, suggests a possible union of the two. The dialectic method will lead us to enquire whether, besides being species of a wider genus, they are not also abstractions from a deeper unity, which unity would reveal itself as the really adequate form of Spirit. But although this may be a Hegelian solution, it is not Hegel's. Whatever he may have hinted in the Logic—a point to which we shall presently return—in the Philosophy of Spirit he attempts to take knowledge by itself as the ultimate form of Spirit. And such a result must, if volition is really coordinate with knowledge, be erroneous.

192. There is yet a third element in the life of Spirit, besides knowledge and volition. This is feeling proper—pleasure and pain. And this too must rank as a separate element of spiritual activity, independent of knowledge. This does not involve the assertion that we could ever experience a state of mind that was purely pleasure or pain. So far as our experience reaches, on the contrary, we never do feel pleasure or pain, without at the same time recognising the existence of some fact, and finding ourselves to be or not to be in harmony with it. Thus feeling is only found in company with knowledge and volition. But although it is thus inseparable from knowledge, it is independent of it in the sense that it cannot be reduced to it. Knowledge is essentially and inevitably a judgment—an assertion about matter of fact. Now in the feeling of pleasure and pain there is no judgment and no assertion, but there is something else to which no judgment can ever be equivalent.

Hegel's views as to feeling proper are rather obscure. He says much indeed about Gefühl, but this does not mean pleasure and pain. It appears rather to denote all immediate or intuitive belief in a fact, as opposed to a reasoned demonstration of it. The contents of Gefühl and of Philosophy, he says, may be the same, but they differ in form. It is thus clear that he is speaking of a form of knowledge, and not only of pleasure and pain. But whatever he thinks about the latter, it seems certain that they cannot, any more than volition, find a place in philosophy. And in that case Hegel's highest form of Spirit is defective on a second ground.

193. To this line of criticism an objection may possibly be

taken. It is true, it may be said, that philosophy includes neither volition nor feeling. But it implies them both. You cannot have knowledge without finding yourself, from the point of view of volition, in or out of harmony with the objects of pure knowledge, and without feeling pleasure or pain accordingly. This is no doubt true. And we may go further, and say that, on Hegel's principles, we should be entitled to conclude that perfect knowledge must bring perfect acquiescence in the universe, and also perfect happiness. For when our knowledge becomes perfect, we should, as the Logic tells us, find that in all our relations with that which was outside us, we had gained the perfect realisation of our own natures. Determination by another would have become, in the fullest and deepest sense, determination by self. Since, therefore, in all our relations with others, the demands of our own nature found complete fulfilment, we should be in a state of perfect acquiescence with the nature of all things round us. And from this perfect harmony, complete happiness must result.

Hegel would, no doubt, have been justified in saying that in reaching complete knowledge we should, at the same time, have reached to the completeness of all activities of Spirit. But he did say more than this. He said that complete knowledge would be by itself the complete activity of Spirit. He tried, it would seem, to ignore volition, and to ignore pleasure and pain. And a view of Spirit which does this will be fatally one-sided.

194. But we must go further. We have seen that knowledge cannot, by itself, be the full expression of the complete nature of Spirit. But can it, we must now ask, be, as knowledge, even part of that full expression? Can it attain its own goal? Or does it carry about the strongest mark of its own imperfection by postulating an ideal which it can never itself reach?

195. The ideal of knowledge may be said to be the combination of complete unity of the subject and object with complete differentiation between them. In so far as we have knowledge there must be unity of the subject and object. Of the elements into which knowledge can be analysed, one class—the *data* of sensation—come to us from outside, and consequently involve the unity of the subject and the object,

without which it is impossible that anything outside us could produce a sensation inside us. On the other hand the categories are notions of our own minds which are yet essential to objective experience. And these, therefore, involve no less the unity of the subject and the object, since otherwise we should not be justified in ascribing to them, as we do ascribe, objective validity.

Differentiation of the subject and object is no less necessary to knowledge than is their unity. For it is of the essence of knowledge that it shall refer to something not itself, something which is independent of the subjective fancies of the subject, something which exists whether he likes it or not, which exists not only for him, but for others, something in fact which is objective. Without this, knowledge changes into dreams or delusions, and these, however interesting as objects of knowledge, are totally different from knowledge itself. In so far as knowledge becomes perfect, it has to apprehend the object as it really is, and so in its full differentiation from the subject.

All knowledge, in so far as it is complete, requires unity and differentiation. Perfect knowledge will require perfect unity and differentiation. And since the dialectic has taught us that all knowledge, except that highest and most complete knowledge which grasps reality under the Absolute Idea, is contradictory and cannot stand except as a moment in some higher form—we may conclude that all knowledge implies complete unity and differentiation. For the lower knowledge implies the higher, and the complete unity and differentiation are implied by the higher knowledge.

This is confirmed by the final results of the Logic. There we find that the only ultimately satisfactory category is one in which the self finds itself in relation with other selves and in harmony with their nature. To be in harmony with other selves implies that we are in unity with them, while to recognise them as selves implies differentiation.

Knowledge requires, then, this combination of antithetical qualities. Is it possible that this requirement can ever be realised by knowledge itself?

196. The action of knowledge consists in ascribing predicates to an object. All our knowledge of the object we owe

to the predicates which we ascribe to it.   But our object is not
a mere assemblage of predicates.   There is also the unity in
which they cohere, which may be called epistemologically the
abstract object, and logically the abstract subject.

Here,—as in most other places in the universe—we are met
by a paradox.   The withdrawal of the abstract object leaves
nothing but a collection of predicates, and a collection of predicates taken by itself is a mere unreality.   Predicates cannot
exist without a central unity in which they can cohere.   But
when we enquire what is this central unity which gives reality
to the object, we find that its unreality is as certain as the
unreality of the predicates, and perhaps even more obvious.
For if we attempt to make a single statement about this
abstract object—even to say that it exists—we find ourselves
merely adding to the number of predicates.   This cannot help
us to attain our purpose, which was to know what the substratum is in which all the predicates inhere.   We get no
nearer to this by learning that another predicate inheres in it.

Thus the abstract object is an unreality, and yet, if it is
withdrawn, the residuum of the concrete object becomes an
unreality too.   Such a relation is not uncommon in metaphysics.
All reality is concrete.   All concrete ideas can be split up into
abstract elements.   If we split up the concrete idea, which
corresponds to some real thing, into its constituent abstractions,
we shall have a group of ideas which in their unity correspond
to a reality, but when separated are self-contradictory and
unreal.   The position of the abstract object is thus similar to
that of another abstraction which has received more attention
in metaphysics—the abstract subject.

Mr Bradley has given this abstract object the name of the
This, in opposition to the What, which consists of the predicates
which we have found to be applicable to the This.   While knowledge remains imperfect, the This has in it the possibility of an
indefinite number of other qualities, besides the definite number
which have been ascertained and embodied in predicates.
When knowledge becomes perfect—as perfect as it is capable
of becoming—this possibility would disappear, as it seems to
me, though Mr Bradley does not mention this point.   In perfect
knowledge all qualities of the object would be known, and the

coherence of our knowledge as a systematic whole would be the warrant for the completeness of the enumeration. But even here the abstract This would still remain, and prove itself irreducible to anything else. To attempt to know it is like attempting to jump on the shadow of one's own head. For all propositions are the assertion of a partial unity between the subject and the predicate. The This on the other hand is just what distinguishes the subject from its predicates.

197. It is the existence of the This which renders it impossible to regard knowledge as a self-subsistent whole, and makes it necessary to consider it merely as an approximation to the complete activity of spirit for which we search. In the This we have something which is at once within and without knowledge, which it dares not neglect, and yet cannot deal with.

For when we say that the This cannot be known, we do not mean, of course, that we cannot know of its existence. We know of its existence, because we can perceive, by analysis, that it is an essential element of the concrete object. But the very definition which this analysis gives us shows that we can know nothing about it but this—that there is indeed nothing more about it to know, and that even so much cannot be put into words without involving a contradiction. Now to know merely that something exists is to present a problem to knowledge which it must seek to answer. To know that a thing exists, is to know it as immediate and contingent. Knowledge demands that such a thing should be mediated and rationalised. This, as we have seen, cannot be done here. This impossibility is no reproach to the rationality of the universe, for reality is no more mere mediation than it is mere immediacy, and the immediacy of the This combines with the mediation of the What to make up the concrete whole of Spirit. But it *is* a reproach to the adequacy of knowledge as an activity of Spirit that it should persist in demanding what cannot and should not be obtained. Without immediacy, without the central unity of the object, the mediation and the predicates which make up knowledge would vanish as unmeaning. Yet knowledge is compelled by its own nature to try and remove them, and to feel itself baffled and thwarted when it cannot succeed.

Surely an activity with such a contradiction inherent in it can never be a complete expression of the Absolute.

198. In the first place the existence of the This is incompatible with the attainment of the ideal of unity in knowledge. For here we have an element, whose existence in reality we are forced to admit, but which is characterised by the presence of that which is essentially alien to the nature of the knowing consciousness in its activity. In so far as reality contains a This, it cannot be brought into complete unison with the knowing mind, which, as an object, has of course its aspect of immediacy like any other object, but which, as the knowing subject, finds all unresolvable immediacy to be fundamentally opposed to its work of rationalisation. The real cannot be completely expressed in the mind, and the unity of knowledge is therefore defective.

And this brings with it a defective differentiation. For while the This cannot be brought into the unity of knowledge, it is unquestionably a part of reality. And so the failure of knowledge to bring it into unity with itself involves that the part of the object which *is* brought into unity with the subject is only an abstraction from the full object. The individuality of the object thus fails to be represented, and so its full differentiation from the subject fails to be represented also. The result is that we know objects, so to speak, from the outside, whereas, to know them in their full truth, we ought to know them from inside. That every object[1] has a real centre of its own appears from the dialectic. For we have seen that the conclusion from the dialectic is that all reality consists of spirits, which are individuals. And, apart from this, the fact that the object is more or less independent as against us—and without some independence knowledge would be impossible, as has already been pointed out—renders it certain that every object has an individual unity to some extent. Now knowledge

[1] In saying "every object" I do not necessarily mean every chair, every crystal, or even every amoeba. Behind all appearance there is reality. This reality we believe, on the authority of the dialectic, to consist of individuals. But *how many* such centres there may be behind a given mass of appearance we do not know. Every self-conscious spirit is, no doubt, one object and no more. It is with regard to the reality behind what is called inorganic matter and the lower forms of life that the uncertainty arises.

fails to give this unity its rights. The meaning of the object is found in its This, and its This is, to knowledge, something alien. Knowledge sees it to be, in a sense, the centre of the object, but only a dead centre, a mere residuum produced by abstracting all possible predicates, not a living and unifying centre, such as we know that the synthetic unity of apperception is to our own lives, which we have the advantage of seeing from inside. And since it thus views it from a standpoint which is merely external, knowledge can never represent the object so faithfully as to attain its own ideal.

199. And here we see the reason why knowledge can never represent quite accurately that harmony of the universe which knowledge itself proves. We saw above that when knowledge should have reached the greatest perfection of which it is capable there would still remain one question unanswered—Why is the universe what it is and not something else? We may prove the question unmeaning and absurd, but we cannot help asking it. And the possibility of asking it depends on the existence of the This, which knowledge is unable to bring into unity with the knowing subject. The This is essential to the reality of the object, and is that part of the object to which it owes its independence of the subject. And the question naturally arises, Why should not this core of objectivity have been clothed with other qualities than those which it has, and with which the subject finds itself in harmony?

The question arises because the existence of this harmony is dependent on the This. The This alone gives reality to the object. If it vanished, the harmony would not change into a disharmony, but disappear altogether. And the This, as we have seen, must always be for knowledge a something alien and irrational, because it must always be an unresolved immediate. Now a harmony which depends on something alien and irrational must always appear contingent and defective. Why is there a This at all? Why is it just those qualities which give a harmony for us that the favour of the This has raised into reality? To answer these questions would be to mediate the This, and that would destroy it.

200. It may be urged, as against this argument, that we do not stand in such a position of opposition and alienation towards the This in knowledge. For we ourselves are objects of knowledge as well as knowing subjects, and our abstract personality, which is the centre of our knowledge is also the This of an object. Now it might be maintained that the interconnection of the qualities of all different objects, which would be perfect in perfect knowledge, would enable us to show why all reality existed, and why it is what it is, if we could only show it of a single fragment of reality. The difficulty, it might be said, lies in reaching the abstract realness of the real by means of knowledge at all. And if, by means of our own existence as objects we were able to establish a single connection with the objective world, in which the immediate would not mean the alien, it is possible that no other connection would be required. The last remaining opposition of the subject to the object would disappear.

The difficulty, however, cannot be escaped in this way. For the self as the object of knowledge is as much opposed to the self as the subject as any other object could be. We learn its qualities by arguments from data based on the "internal sense," as we learn the qualities of other objects by arguments from data given by the external senses. We are immediately certain of the first, but we are immediately certain of the second. And the central unity of our own nature can no more be known directly in itself, apart from its qualities, than can the central unities of other objects. We become aware of its existence by analysing what is implied in having ourselves for objects, and we become aware of the central unities of other things by analysing what is implied in having them for objects. We have no more direct knowledge of the one than of the other. Of course nothing in our own selves is really alien to us,—not even the element of immediacy which makes their This. But then the existence of knowledge implies, as we have seen, that the reality of other things is not really alien to us, although we know it immediately. It is the defect of knowledge that it fails to represent the immediate except as alien.

201. Here, then, we seem to have the reason why our minds could never, in the most perfect state of knowledge possible, get rid of the abstract idea of the contingency of the whole system. We saw, in the first part of this chapter

that such an idea was unmeaning, since it would be impossible
for any reality to be destroyed or altered, unless the same
happened to all reality, and the possibility of this, which has
no common ground with actuality, is an unmeaning phrase.
And we have now seen another reason why the possibility
is unmeaning. For we have traced it to the persistence of
thought in considering its essential condition as its essential
enemy. The existence of such a miscalled possibility, therefore, tells nothing against the rationality of the universe. But
it does tell against the adequacy of knowledge as an expression
of the universe. By finding a flaw in perfection, where no
flaw exists, it pronounces its own condemnation. If the possibility is unmeaning, knowledge is imperfect in being compelled to regard it as a possibility.

It may seem at first sight absurd to talk of knowledge as
inadequate. If it were imperfect, how could we know it?
What right have we to condemn it as imperfect when the
judge is of necessity the same person as the culprit? This
is, of course, so far true, that if knowledge did not show us
its own ideal, we could never know that it did not realise it.
But there is a great difference between realising an ideal and
indicating it. It is possible, and I have endeavoured to show
that it is actually the case, that knowledge can do the one, and
not the other. When we ask about the abstract conditions
of reality, it is able to demonstrate that harmony must exist,
and that immediacy is compatible with it, and essential to it.
But when it is asked to show in detail *how* the harmony
exists, which it has shown *must* exist, it is unable to do so.
There is here no contradiction in our estimate of knowledge,
but there is a contradiction in knowledge, which prevents
us from regarding it as adequate, and which forces us to
look further in search of the ultimate activity of Spirit.

We saw before that this activity could not consist solely
of knowledge, but we have now reached the further conclusion
that knowledge, as knowledge, could not form even a part of
that activity. For it carries a mark of imperfection about it,
in its inability to completely attain the goal which it cannot
cease to strive for, and in its dependence on that which it
must consider an imperfection. We must therefore look for

the ultimate nature of Spirit in something which transcends and surpasses cognition, including it indeed as a moment, but transforming it and raising it into a higher sphere, where its imperfections vanish.

202. In doing this we are compelled, of course, to reject Hegel's own treatment of the subject, in the Philosophy of Spirit. But we may, I think, find some support for our position in the Logic. For there, as it seems to me, we find the sketch of a more complete and adequate representation of Absolute Reality, than the one which is worked out in the Philosophy of Spirit.

We have in the Logic, immediately before the Absolute Idea, a category called Cognition in general. This is again divided into Cognition proper and Volition. These two categories are treated by Hegel as a thesis and antithesis, and, according to the method pursued in every other part of the Logic, the triad should have been completed by a synthesis, before we pass out of Cognition in general to the final synthesis—the Absolute Idea. No such synthesis, however, is given by Hegel as a separate term. According to his exposition, the Absolute Idea itself forms the synthesis of the opposition of Cognition proper and Volition, as it does also of the larger opposition of Life and Cognition in general.

The significance of this part of the Logic for us lies in the fact that Cognition proper requires to be synthesised with Volition before we can reach the absolute reality. Of course Hegel is not dealing, in the Logic, with the concrete activities of cognition and volition, any more than he is dealing, rather earlier in the Logic, with the concrete activities of mechanism and chemistry. The Logic deals only with the element of pure thought in reality, and when its categories bear the names of concrete relations—this only means that the pure idea, which is the category in question, is the idea which comes most prominently forward in that concrete relation, and which therefore can be usefully and significantly called by its name.

This, however, does not destroy the importance of the Logic for our present purpose. Although the concrete activities are not merely their own logical ideas, they must stand in the same relation *inter se* as the logical ideas do *inter se*. For the process in the Philosophy of Spirit, as in all the applications of the dialectic, while it does not profess to be logical in the sense that all its details can be logically deduced, certainly professes to be logical in the sense that the relation of its stages to one another can be logically explained[1]. Indeed, if it did not do this, it could no longer be called an application of the Logic at all, but would be a mere empirical collection of facts. If then the idea of cognition proper—that is, of knowledge as opposed to volition—is by itself so imperfect and one-sided, that it must be transcended, and must be synthesised with the idea of volition, before the adequate and Absolute Idea can be reached, it would seem to follow that a concrete application of this philosophy is bound to regard cognition as an inadequate expression of the full nature of reality, and to endeavour to find some higher expression which shall unite cognition and volition, preserving that which is true in each, while escaping from their imperfections and one-sidedness.

203. It may be objected that the Cognition proper, which is treated by Hegel as an inadequate category, denotes only that knowledge which is found in ordinary experience and in science, and that the place of knowledge in its highest shape—the shape of philosophy—must be looked for under the Absolute Idea. This view does not appear tenable on closer examination. At the end of Cognition proper, Hegel tells us, the content of cognition is seen to be necessary. This would indicate philosophic knowledge, if "necessary" is taken as referring to the necessity of freedom, which is its normal use in the Doctrine of the Notion. There is certainly a good deal of discussion of philosophic method under the head of the Absolute Idea. But this appears to be introduced, not because this category is the one under which our philosophising comes, but because it is the last category of the philosophy, and it is therefore natural to look back, at this point, on the method which has been pursued.

The most cogent argument, however, against this view is that the Absolute Idea is defined as the union of Cognition

---

[1] Cp. Chap. vii. Sections 207, 210.

proper with Volition. Therefore the Absolute Idea must be an idea richer and fuller than that of Cognition—richer and fuller by the content of the idea of Volition. Now we can have no reason to suppose that philosophic knowledge is the union of ordinary knowledge with volition. For philosophy stands in just the same relation to volition as ordinary knowledge does. We never have knowledge without having volition, but neither can be reduced to the other. The Absolute Idea then contains within itself the idea of Knowledge only as a transcended moment. If there is any difference between them, indeed, we must consider the idea of Volition the higher of the two, since it is Volition which forms the antithesis, and we have seen that, in the Doctrine of the Notion, the antithesis may be expected to be more adequate than the thesis to which it is opposed[1].

I am not attempting to argue from this that we ought to take Hegel as putting anything more concrete than philosophy into the nature of absolute reality. We are especially bound in the case of so systematic a writer as Hegel, to look for the authoritative exposition of his views on any subject in the part of his work which professedly deals with that subject. And in the Philosophy of Spirit it seems clear that Hegel means the highest stage of Spirit to be nothing but philosophy. But, in giving the abstract framework of absolute reality in the Logic, he has given, as we have seen above, a framework for something which, whatever it is, is more than any form of mere cognition. And so, when saying that the conclusion of the Philosophy of Spirit is inconsistent with the general tenor of Hegel's philosophy, we can strengthen our position by adding that it is inconsistent with the final result of the Logic.

204. Let us now turn to the Philosophy of Spirit, and consider the way in which Hegel introduces Philosophy as the culminating point of reality. The three terms which form the triad of Absolute Spirit are Art, Revealed Religion, and Philosophy. Of the relation of these three stages he speaks as follows: "Whereas the vision-method of Art, external in

---

[1] Chap. IV. Sections 109, 110.

point of form, is but subjective production and shivers the substantial content into many separate shapes, and whereas Religion, with its separation into parts, opens it out in mental picture, and mediates what is thus opened out; Philosophy not merely keeps them together to make a total, but even unifies them into the simple spiritual vision, and then in that raises them to self-conscious thought. Such consciousness is thus the intelligible unity (cognised by thought) of art and religion, in which the diverse elements in the content are cognised as necessary, and this necessary as free[1]."

On examining this more closely, doubts present themselves. Is Philosophy really capable of acting as a synthesis between Art and Religion? Should it not rather form part of the antithesis, together with Religion? All the stages in this triad of Absolute Spirit are occupied in endeavouring to find a harmony between the individual spirit—now developed into full consciousness of his own nature—on the one hand, and the rest of the universe on the other hand. Such a harmony is directly and immediately presented in beauty. But the immediacy makes the harmony contingent and defective. Where beauty is present, the harmony exists; where it is not present—a case not unfrequently occurring—the harmony disappears. It is necessary to find some ground of harmony which is universal, and which shall enable us to attribute rationality and righteousness to all things, independently of their immediate and superficial aspect.

This ground, according to Hegel, is afforded us by the doctrines of Revealed Religion, which declares that all things are dependent on and the manifestation of a reality in which we recognise the fulfilment of our ideals of rationality and righteousness. Thus Revealed Religion assures us that all things *must* be in harmony, instead of showing us, as Art does, that some things *are* in harmony.

205. Now Philosophy, it seems to me, can do no more than this. It is true that it does it, in what, from Hegel's point of view, is a higher and better way. It is true that it substitutes a completely reasoned process for one which, in

---

[1] *Enc.* Section 572.

the last resort, rests on authority. It is true that it changes the external harmony, which Revealed Religion offers, into a harmony inherent in the nature of things. It is true that the process, which is known to Revealed Religion as "a cycle of concrete shapes in pictorial thought," and as "a separation into parts, with a temporal and external sequence," is in Philosophy "known as an indivisible coherence of the universal, simple, and eternal spirit in itself[1]." But all this does not avail to bring back the simplicity and directness of Art, which must be brought back in the synthesis. Art shows us that something is as we would have it. Its harmony with our ideals is visible on the surface. But Philosophy, like Religion, leaving the surface of things untouched, points to their inner nature, and proves that, in spite of the superficial discord and evil, the true reality is harmonious and good. To unite these we should require a state of spirit which should present us with a harmony direct and immediate on the one hand, and universal and necessary on the other. Art gives the first and Philosophy the second, but Philosophy can no more unite the two than Art can.

This is clear of philosophy, as we have it now, and so long as it has not absorbed into itself all other knowledge. For it is the knowledge of the general conditions only of reality. As such, it can lay down general laws for all reality. But it is not able to show how they are carried out in detail. It may arrive at the conclusion that all that is real is rational. This will apply, among other things, to toothache or cowardice. Now we are shown by the whole history of religion that optimism based on general grounds may be of great importance to the lives of those who believe it, and philosophy, if it can give us this, will have given us no small gift. But philosophy will not be able to show us how the rationality or the righteousness come in, either in toothache or in cowardice. It can only convince us that they *are* there, though we cannot see them. It is obvious that we have as yet no synthesis with the directness and immediacy of art.

If philosophy should ever, as was suggested in the earlier

---

[1] *Enc.* Section 571.

part of this chapter, develop so as to include all knowledge in one complete harmony, then, no doubt, we should not only know of every fact in the universe that it was rational, but we should also see how it was so. Even here, however, the required synthesis would not be attained. Our knowledge would still be only mediate knowledge, and thus could not be the synthesis for two reasons. Firstly, because, as we have seen, it has to regard the immediate element in reality as to some extent alien. Secondly, because the synthesis must contain in itself, as a transcended moment, the immediate harmony of art, and must therefore be lifted above the distinction of mediate and immediate.

Besides this, a merely intellectual activity could not be the ultimate truth of which art and religion are lower stages. For both of these involve not merely knowledge, but volition, and also feeling. And so the highest stage of spirit would have to include, not only the perception of the rationality of all things, which is offered by philosophy, but also the complete acquiescence which is the goal of successful volition, and the pleasure which is the inevitable result of conscious harmony.

206. The result of all this would appear to be, that, in order to render the highest form of Absolute Spirit capable, as it must be on Hegel's theory, of transcending and summing up all other aspects of reality, we shall have to recast the last steps of the Philosophy of Spirit, so as to bring the result more in accordance with the general outlines laid down at the end of the Logic. Philosophy, together with Revealed Religion, will be the antithesis to Art. And a place will be left vacant for a new synthesis.

It forms no part of the object of this work to enquire what this synthesis may be. My purpose has been only to give some reasons for thinking that Hegel had not found an adequate expression for the absolute reality, and I do not venture to suggest one myself. But we can, within very wide and general limits, say what the nature of such an expression must be. It must be some state of conscious spirit in which the opposition of cognition and volition is overcome—in which we neither judge our ideas by the world, nor the world by our ideas, but are aware that inner and outer are in such close

and necessary harmony that even the thought of possible discord has become impossible.   In its unity not only cognition
and volition, but feeling also, must be blended and united.   In
some way or another it must have overcome the rift in discursive knowledge, and the immediate must for it be no longer
the alien.   It must be as direct as art, as certain and universal
as philosophy.

CHAPTER VII.

207. WE have now to enquire in what manner the results which we have gained by the dialectic process are applicable to real life. I do not propose to discuss the utility of these results as a guide to conduct, but there is another question more closely connected with the dialectic itself. How, if at all, can the pure theory, which is expounded in the Logic, be so used as to assist in the explanation of the various facts presented to us in experience? Hegel divides the world into two parts—Nature and Spirit. What can his philosophy tell us about them?

We have seen in our consideration of the dialectic that there are certain functions, with regard to our knowledge of Nature and Spirit, which pure thought cannot perform, and which there is no reason to think, in spite of the assertions of some critics, that Hegel ever intended it to perform. In the first place, we saw that the concrete world of reality cannot be held to be a mere condescension of the Logic to an outward shape, nor a mere dependent emanation from the self-subsistent perfection of pure thought. For, so far from pure thought being able to create immediate reality, it cannot itself exist unless something immediate is given to it, which it may mediate and relate. And we saw that, so far from Hegel's theory being inconsistent with this truth, it is entirely dependent on it. The force of his deduction of Nature and Spirit from Logic lies in the fact that pure thought is a mere abstraction which, taken by itself, is contradictory. And therefore, since pure thought unquestionably exists somehow, we are led to the conclusion that it cannot exist independently, but must be a moment in that more concrete form of reality, which is expressed imperfectly in Nature and adequately in Spirit.

And we saw, in the second place, that even this deduction can only extend to the general nature of the reality, because it is only that general nature which we can prove to be essential for the existence of pure thought. We know, *a priori*, that the reality must contain an immediate moment, in order that thought may mediate it, that something must be given in order that thought may deal with it. But further than this we cannot go without the aid of empirical observation. No consideration of the nature of pure thought can demonstrate to us the necessity that a particular man should have red hair. To do this we require immediate *data*. And here again we found no reason to suppose that this limitation of pure thought was ignored by Hegel. His attempts to apply his logical results may have gone too far, but he never attempted to deduce the necessity of all the facts he was attempting to rationalise. His object was to point out that through every part of reality there runs a thread of logical connection, so that the different parts stand in intelligible relations to one another, and to Absolute Reality. But he never tried to deduce the necessity of each detail of reality from the nature of pure thought, or even to hold out such a deduction as an ideal. This is evident, both from the number of details which he mentions without even an attempt to explain them, and also from his own direct statement[1].

208. This then is one way in which we can apply the conclusions of the Logic in the solution of more concrete problems. We may trace the manifestations of the dialectic process in the experience round us, and in so far as we do this we shall have rationalised that experience. But, besides this, we may gain some information from the dialectic concerning the ultimate nature of Absolute Being. It will be convenient to consider this latter point first.

No idea which is self-contradictory can be true until it is so transformed that the contradictions have vanished. Now no category in the Logic is free from contradictions except the

---

[1] Cp. Chap. I. Section 27, and the passage from the Philosophy of Spirit there quoted. Also Chap vI. Section 183.

Absolute Idea. Reality can therefore be fully apprehended under no category but this. We shall find it to be true of all reality, that in it is found "der Begriff der Idee, dem die Idee als solche der Gegenstand, dem das Objekt sie ist[1]." From this we can deduce several consequences. All reality must, on this view, be Spirit, and be differentiated. Moreover, it must be Spirit for which its differentiations are, in Hegel's phrase, "transparent," that is, it must find in them nothing alien to itself. It might also be maintained, though the point is too large to be discussed here, that it must consist of finite self-conscious spirits, united into a closely connected whole. And it might not be impossible to determine whether the whole in question was also a self-conscious being, or whether it is a unity of persons without being itself a person. The questions discussed in the last chapter are also examples of the use that may be made, in this connection, of the results of the dialectic.

209. The information thus attained would be enough to justify us in saying that the results of Hegel's philosophy, apart from their theoretic interest, were of the greatest practical importance. It is true that such results as these can but rarely be available as guides to action. We learn by them what is the nature of that ideal, which, *sub specie aeternitatis*, is present in all reality, and which, *sub specie temporis*, is the goal towards which all reality is moving. But such an ideal is, *sub specie aeternitatis*, far too implicit, and, *sub specie temporis*, far too distant, to allow us to use it in deciding on any definite course of action in the present. Nor can it be taken to indicate even the direction in which our present action should move. For one of the great lessons of Hegel's philosophy is that, in any progress, we never move directly forwards, but oscillate from side to side as we advance. And so a step which seems to be almost directly away from our ideal may sometimes be the next step on the only road by which that ideal can be attained.

But those who estimate the practical utility of a theory only by its power of guiding our action, take too confined a view. Action, after all, is always directed to some end. And, whatever view we may take of the supreme end, it cannot be denied that many of our actions are directed, and rightly

[1] *Enc.* Section 236.

directed, to the production of happiness for ourselves and others. Surely, then, a philosophical theory which tended to the production of happiness would have as much claim to be called practically important, as if it had afforded guidance in action.

Now such conclusions as to the ultimate nature of things as we have seen can be reached by Hegel's philosophy have obviously a very intimate connection with the problems which may be classed as religious. Is the universe rational and righteous? Is spirit or matter the fundamental reality? Have our standards of perfection any objective validity? Is our personality an ultimate fact or a transitory episode? All experience and all history show that for many men the answers to these questions are the source of some of the most intense and persistent joys and sorrows known in human life. Nor is there any reason to think that the proportion of such people is diminishing. Any system of philosophy which gives any reasons for deciding such questions, in one way rather than another, will have a practical interest, even if it should fail to provide us with counsel as to the organisation of society, or with explanations in detail of the phenomena of science.

210. We must now turn to the second way in which Hegel endeavours to apply the dialectic to experience. It is to this that he gives the greater prominence. His views on the nature of absolute reality are to be found in the Philosophy of Spirit, and also in the Philosophy of Religion, but they are not given at any length. On many important points we have no further guide than the development of the Absolute Idea in the Logic, and we must judge for ourselves what consequences can be drawn, from that development, as to the concrete whole of which the Absolute Idea is one moment.

A much larger portion of his writings is occupied in tracing, in the succession of events in time, the gradual development of the Absolute Idea. To this purpose are devoted almost the whole of the Philosophies of Nature, Spirit, Religion, Law and History, as well as the History of Philosophy. He does not, as has been already remarked, endeavour to deduce the facts, of which he treats, from the Absolute Idea. Nor does he ever attempt to deduce each stage from the one before it. We pass, for example, from Moralität to Sittlichkeit, from the Persian religion to the Syrian, or from the Greek civilisation to the Roman. But there are, in each case, many details in the second which are not the consequence of anything in the first, and which must be explained empirically by science, or else left unexplained. His object is to show that the central ideas of each stage are such that each follows from its predecessor—either as a reaction from its one-sidedness, or as a reconciliation of its contradictions—and that these ideas express, more and more adequately as the process gets nearer to its end, the Absolute Idea which had been expounded in the Logic.

It is sometimes said that Hegel endeavoured to show that the stages of development, in the various spheres of activity which he considered in his different treatises, corresponded to the various categories of the Logic. This, however, seems an exaggeration. His theories of Nature, Spirit, Religion, and Law are each divided into three main sections, which doubtless correspond, and are meant to correspond, to the three primary divisions of the Logic—Being, Essence, and the Notion. But to trace any definite correspondence between the secondary divisions of these works (to say nothing of divisions still more minute) and the secondary divisions of the Logic, appears impossible. At any rate no such correspondence is mentioned by Hegel. The connection with the Logic seems rather to lie in the similarity of development, by thesis, antithesis, and synthesis, and in the gradually increasing adequacy of the manifestation of the Absolute Idea, as the process gradually develops itself.

Of the Philosophy of History, indeed, we cannot say even as much as this. For it is divided, not into three, but into four main divisions, thus destroying the triadic form and the analogy to the three divisions of the Logic. And although Hegel would probably have found no difficulty, on his own principles, in reducing the second and third divisions to one, it is a fact of some significance that he did not think it worth while to do so. It seems to indicate that he attached less importance, than has sometimes been supposed, to the exact resemblance of the scheme of the concrete processes to the scheme of pure thought in the Logic. In the History of Philosophy, again, many of the subordinate divisions are not triple.

211.   The applications of the dialectic to various aspects of reality have been the part of Hegel's work which has received of late years the most notice and approbation.   This is, no doubt, largely due to a reaction against Hegel's general position. To those who reject that position the whole of the dialectic of pure thought must seem a stupendous blunder—magnificent or ridiculous according to the taste of the critic.   With the dialectic of pure thought would fall also, of course, all general and demonstrated validity of its applications.   But the brilliance and suggestiveness of many of the details of these applications have often been acknowledged by those who reject the system in which they were arranged, and the basis from which it is sought to justify them.

Among the followers of Hegel a different cause has led to the same effect.   The attraction of Hegel's philosophy to many of them appears to lie in the explanations it can give of particular parts of experience rather than in its general theory of the nature of reality.   These explanations—attractive by their æsthetic completeness, or because of the practical consequences that follow from them—are adopted and defended by such writers in an empirical way.   It is maintained that we can see that they do explain the facts, while others do not, and they are believed for this reason, and not because they follow from the dialectic of pure thought.   Hegelian views of religion, of morals, of history, of the state are common enough among us. They appear to be gaining ground in many directions.   Nor can it be said that their advocates are neglectful of the source from which they derive their theories.   They often style themselves Hegelians.   But the dialectic of pure thought tends to fall into the background.   Hegel's explanations of the rationality to be found in particular spheres of existence are accepted by many who ignore or reject his demonstrations that everything which exists *must* be rational.

212.   I wish to put forward a different view—that the really valid part of Hegel's system is his Logic, and not his applications of it.   In the preceding chapters I have given some reasons in support of the view that the general position of the Logic is justifiable.   With regard to its applications, on the other hand, although they doubtless contain much that is

most valuable, their general and systematic validity seems indefensible.

As we have already seen, there is nothing in the nature of Hegel's object here, which should render his success impossible *a priori*. The difficulties which arise are due rather to the greatness of the task, and to the imperfection of our present knowledge. These difficulties we have now to consider.

213. The movement of the Idea, as we learned in the Logic, is by thesis, antithesis, and synthesis, the first two being opposed, and the third reconciling them. If we are able to trace the progressive manifestations of the Idea in facts, these manifestations will arrange themselves in triads of this kind. And Hegel has attempted to show that they do so.

But how are we to determine which stages are theses, which are antitheses, and which again syntheses? This can, I believe, only be done safely, in the case of any one term, by observing its relation to others, which have already been grasped in the system. And, as these again will require determination by their relation to others previously determined, we shall be able to build up a dialectic system only if we have fixed points at one or both ends of the chain to start from. We cannot safely begin in the middle and work backwards and forwards.

There is nothing in the nature of any term which can tell us, if we take it in isolation from others, whether it is a thesis or an antithesis—that is, whether it will require, as the process goes forward, the development of another term opposite and complementary to itself, before a synthesis can be reached, or whether it is itself opposed and complementary to some term that came before it, so that a reconciliation will be the next step to be expected in the process. Theses may be said to be positive, antitheses negative. But no term is either positive or negative *per se*. In a dialectic process we call those terms positive which reaffirm, on a higher level, the position with which the process started, the negative terms being the complementary denials which are necessary as means to gain the higher level. But to apply this test we should have to know beforehand the term with which the process started. Or we may say that the terms are positive which express the reality to which the process is advancing, though they express it inadequately, while the negative terms are those which, in recognising the inadequacy, temporarily sacrifice the resemblance[1]. But this distinction, again, is useless until we know what is the last term of the whole process.

Nor would it be possible to recognise any term, taken in isolation, as a synthesis. Every term in a dialectic process, except the two first, contains within itself some synthesis of opposition, for all that is accomplished is transferred to all succeeding terms. On the other hand, every synthesis in a process, except the last, contains within itself a latent one-sidedness, which will break out in the opposition of the next thesis and antithesis, and require for its reconciliation another synthesis. We can therefore only determine that a term is a synthesis if we see that it does reconcile the two terms immediately in front of it—in other words, if we see it in relation to other terms. And the impossibility of recognising a synthesis as such, if seen by itself, would be far greater in the applications of the Logic than in the Logic itself. For every fact or event has many sides or aspects, in some of which it may appear to be a reconciliation of two opposites, and in others to be one of two opposites which need a reconciliation. (So Hegel, for example, appears to regard Protestantism as the synthesis of the oppositions of Christianity, and as its highest point, while Schelling opposes it as the "religion of Paul" to the "religion of Peter," and looks forward to a "religion of John" which shall unite the two.) Now which of these aspects is the significant one for our purpose at any time cannot be known if the term is looked at in isolation. We can only know that we must take it as a synthesis by seeing that it does unite and reconcile the opposition of the two terms that go before it. That is to say, we can only ascertain its place in the series if we have previously ascertained the places of the adjacent terms.

214. It would seem, then, that we can only hope to arrive at a knowledge of any dialectic process, when we know, at least, either the beginning or the end of the process as a fixed point. For no other points can be fixed, unless those round them have been fixed previously, and unless we get a starting-point in this

[1] Cp. *Enc.* Section 85.

manner, we shall never be able to start at all. Now in the Logic we do know the beginning and end. We know the beginning before we start, and, although we do not know the end before we start, yet, when we have reached it, we know that it must be the last category of the Logic. We know that the category of Being must be the beginning, because it is the simplest of all the categories. And we should defend this proposition, if it were doubted, by showing that all attempts to analyse it into simpler categories fail, while in any other category the idea of Being can be discovered by analysis. Again, we know that the Absolute Idea is the last of the categories because it does not develope any contradiction, which will require a reconciliation in a higher category.

215. We can determine in this way the highest and lowest points of the Logic, because all the steps in the Logic are categories of pure thought, and all those categories are implicit in every act of thought. All we have to do, in order to construct the Logic, is to analyse and make explicit what is thus presented. The subject-matter of the analysis can never be wanting, since it is presented in every act of thought. But when we are trying to discover, in a series of concrete facts, the successive manifestations of the pure Idea, the case is different. For these facts can only be known empirically, and the further off they are in time the more difficult they will be to remember or to predict. We are situated at neither end of the process. Philosophy, religion, history—all the activities whose course Hegel strives to demonstrate—stretch backwards till they are lost in obscurity. Nor are we yet at the end of any of them. Years go on, and new forms of reality present themselves. And this is the first difficulty in the way of our attempts to find the fixed points from which we may start our dialectic. The beginnings of the series are too far back to be remembered. The ends, so far as we can tell, are too far forward to be foreseen.

216. And, even if we did happen to know the stage which was, as a matter of fact, the first or the last of a dialectic process, should we be able to recognise it as such on inspection ? By the hypothesis, its relation to the other terms of the process is not yet known—for we are looking for an independent fixed

point in order that we may begin to relate the terms to one another. And, since this is so, one term can, so far, only differ from the others in expressing the Absolute Idea more or less adequately. This is so far, therefore, only a quantitative difference, and thus, below the lowest stage that we know, and above the highest stage that we know, we can imagine others yet, so that our fixed points are still not found.

If, indeed, each stage in each of the applications of the dialectic clearly corresponded to some one category of the Logic, we might know that the stage which corresponded to the category of Being was the lowest, and that the stage which corresponded to the Absolute Idea was the highest. But this is not the case. As has been mentioned above, the stages in each of Hegel's applications of the Logic are arranged, in some cases, on the same principle as the categories of the Logic, but without any suggestion of such definite correspondence. And so, until the mutual relations of the stages are determined, they can only be distinguished by quantitative differences which can never define the beginning and end of their own series.

We cannot say of any stage, in any one of the applications of the Logic, that it completely fails to embody the Absolute Idea. For then, according to Hegel, it would have lost all semblance of reality, and could not be given in experience. And, if it does embody the Absolute Idea at all, we can always imagine that something may exist which embodies that Idea still less completely, still more abstractly. And so we can never be sure that we have got to the right basis, from which our dialectic process may start. Of course, such quantitative estimates are succeeded by far deeper and more significant relations when once the dialectic process is established. But these will not help us here, where we are seeking the point on which to establish the dialectic process.

217. In the Philosophy of Nature, indeed, the risk which we run in taking space as our starting point is perhaps not great. For, since the process of Nature includes all reality below the level of Spirit, its lowest stage must be that at which reality is on the point of vanishing altogether. And we may take space as representing the absolute minimum of reality without much danger of finding ourselves deceived. But it

will be different in dealing with religion, history, law, or philosophy, where the lowest point of the particular process is still relatively concrete, and leaves room for possible stages below it.

And, except in the Philosophy of Spirit, the same may be said of the highest stage in any process. In none of the applications of the dialectic but this can we hope to meet with a perfect embodiment of the Absolute Idea. For all the other processes deal only with an aspect of reality, and their realisation of the Absolute Idea must be partial, and therefore imperfect. In no religion, in no national spirit, or form of government, in no system of metaphysics[1], can we find a complete realisation of the Absolute Idea. And so we are always in uncertainty lest some new stage should arise in each of these activities, which should embody the Absolute Idea a little less imperfectly than any yet known.

218. Let us consider this in more detail. In the first place, although the Philosophy of Spirit has a well-defined end, and the Philosophy of Nature a fairly certain beginning, yet it is impossible to find a point at which it is certain that the Philosophy of Nature ends, and the Philosophy of Spirit begins. What form can we take as the lowest in which Spirit is present? The series of forms is continuous from those which certainly belong to Spirit to those which certainly belong to Nature. If we call everything Spirit, which has the germs of self-consciousness in it, however latent, then we should have to include the whole of Nature, since on Hegel's principles, the lower always has the higher implicit in it. On the other hand, if we reserved the name of Spirit for the forms in which anything like our own life was explicit, we should have to begin far higher up than Hegel did, and we should have the same difficulty as before in finding the exact place to draw the line.

In the Philosophy of Religion, the points at each end of the

---

[1] In the Philosophy of Spirit, Hegel says that Philosophy is the highest stage of Spirit. But it is clear that Philosophy must here mean more than the existence of a system of metaphysics held by professed metaphysicians as a theory. It must be something which is universally accepted, and which modifies all spiritual life. The highest point which could be reached in such a History of Philosophy as Hegel's would leave much to be done before Spirit had reached its full development.

process seem uncertain. Might not something be found, by further historical investigation, which was lower even than Magic, and which yet contained the germ of religion, and ought to be treated as a form of it? And at the other end of the series a similar doubt occurs. It is clear, from the Philosophy of Spirit, that Hegel regards Christianity, like all other forms of "revealed religion," as in some degree an inadequate representation of the Absolute Idea. How can his system guard against the possibility that a yet more perfect religion may arise, or against the possibility that Christianity may develope into higher forms? Hegel would probably have answered that the Philosophy of Religion has demonstrated Christianity to be the synthesis of all other religions. But if, as we have seen reason to think, the relations of the stages cannot be accurately determined, until one end at least of the series has been independently fixed, we cannot rely on the relation of the stages to determine what stage is to be taken as the highest, beyond which no other is possible[1].

219. In the History of Philosophy we find the same difficulty. Hegel begins his systematic exposition with Thales, excluding all Oriental philosophy. This distinction can scarcely be based on any qualitative difference. The reason that Hegel assigns for it is that self-consciousness was not free in the earlier systems[2]. But in what sense is this to be taken? If implicit freedom is to be taken into account, Hegel himself points out, in the Philosophy of Religion, that the Oriental religions had the germ of freedom in them. But if we are only to consider freedom in so far as it is explicit, then we might find it difficult to justify the inclusion of the earlier Greek philosophies, in which the idea of freedom is still very rudimentary.

The end of the History of Philosophy, as expounded by Hegel, is his own philosophy. Yet since his death several new systems have already arisen. There is no ground to attribute to Hegel any excessive degree of self-confidence. The system in

---

[1] This criticism does not apply to Hegel's demonstration of the nature of Absolute Religion, which is really an attempt to determine the ultimate nature of reality. (Cp. Section 208.) The difficulty arises when he tries to connect his own idea of Absolute Religion with historical Christianity.

[2] *History of Philosophy*, Vol. I. p. 117. (Vol. I. p. 99 of Haldane's translation.)

which anyone believes fully and completely will always appear to him the culminating point of the whole process of philosophy. For it has solved for him all the contradictions which he has perceived in former systems, and the fresh contradictions which are latent in it cannot yet have revealed themselves to him, or he would not have complete confidence in it. Thus it naturally seems to him the one coherent system, and therefore the ultimate system. But the appearance is deceptive, and we cannot regard with confidence any theory of the growth of philosophical systems which leaves no room for fresh systems in the future.

The Philosophy of Law has not quite the same difficulties to meet, since it is rather an analysis of the functions of a state, and of the ethical notions which they involve, than an attempt to describe a historical progression. But it is significant that it ends by demonstrating that the ideal form of government was very like the one under which Hegel was living. There seems no reason to suspect that he was influenced by interested motives. The more probable supposition is that he had come to the conclusion that constitutional monarchy was the best possible form of government for an European nation in 1820. This is a legitimate opinion, but what is not legitimate is the attempt to lay down à priori that it will always be the best possible form. No form of government can completely embody the Absolute Idea, since the idea of government, as we learn in the Philosophy of Spirit, is itself but a subordinate one. And it is very difficult to predict social changes which are still far distant. So Hegel passed to the conclusion that the best which had appeared was the best which could appear. He thus imposed on empirical variety an à priori limit, which was not critical but dogmatic, and liable to be upset at any moment by the course of events.

220. In the Philosophy of History the contingency of the starting point is still plainer. He begins with China, it is clear, only because he did not happen to know anything older. He had indeed a right, by his own definition of history, to exclude tribes of mere savages. But he could have no reason to assert—and he did not assert—that, before the rise of Chinese civilization, there was no succession of nation to nation,

each with its distinct character and distinct work, such as he traces in later times. He did not know that there was such a succession, and he could not take it into account. But this leaves the beginning quite empirical.

And he admits in so many words that history will not stop where his Philosophy of History stops. His scheme does not include the Sclavonic races, nor the European inhabitants of America. But he expressly says that the Sclavonic races may have hereafter a place in the series of national developments, and, still more positively, that the United States will have such a place[1]. All attempt to fix the final point of history, or to put limits to the development which takes place in it, is thus given up.

In view of passages like these, it would seem that there is not much truth in Lotze's reproach, that modern Idealism confined the spiritual development of the Absolute to the shores of the Mediterranean[2]. In the first place Hegel speaks only of this planet, and leaves it quite open to us to suppose that the Absolute Idea might be realised in other developments elsewhere. It is scarcely fair, therefore, to charge such a philosophy with ignoring the discoveries of Copernicus. And, as to what does happen on the earth, Hegel devotes a large—perhaps disproportionately large—part of the Philosophies of Religion and History to China and India, which do not lie very near the Mediterranean. We have seen also that he realised that room must be left for the development of Russia and the United States.

221. It appears, then, that of all the terminal points of the different applications of the dialectic, only two can be independently recognised, so as to give us the fixed points which we find to be necessary in constructing the processes. These are at the beginning of the Philosophy of Nature, and at the end of the Philosophy of Spirit. Now Nature and Spirit, taken together, form the chief and all-embracing process reaching from the most superficial abstraction to the most absolute reality, in which the evolution of society, of religion, and of

[1] *Philosophy of History*, pp. 360, and 83. (pp. 363 and 90 of Sibree's translation.)

[2] *Metaphysic.* Section 217.

philosophy are only episodes. And it may at first sight seem improbable that we should be able to determine, with comparative certainty, the two points most remote from our present experience—the one as the barest of abstractions, the other as absolute and almost unimaginable perfection—while points less remote are far more obscure. But further reflection shows us that it is just because these points are the extremes of all reality that they are comparatively determinable. Of the first we know that it must be that aspect of reality which, of all conceivable ways of looking at reality, is the least true, the least significant, the least adequate to the Absolute Idea. Of the second we know that it must be a conception of reality in which the Absolute Idea is expressed with perfect adequacy. We have thus the power, since the Logic tells us the nature of the Absolute Idea, to anticipate to some degree the nature of the first and last terms in the main process of reality. We may be justified in recognising Space as the one, and in predicting more or less what is to be expected in the other. But in the subordinate processes of History, Law, Religion and Philosophy, the highest and lowest points are not highest and lowest absolutely, but only the highest and lowest degrees of reality which can be expressed in a society, a creed, or a metaphysical system. How low or how high these can be, we can only know empirically, since this depends on the nature of societies, of creeds, and of systems, all of which contain empirical elements[1]. And if it can only be known empirically, it can never be known certainly. We can never be sure that the boundaries we place are not due to casual limitations of our actual knowledge, which may be broken down in the immediate future.

And so there is nothing mysterious or suspicious in the fact that many philosophers would be quite prepared to predict, within certain limits, the nature of Heaven, while they would

---

[1] The subject-matter of metaphysical systems is, no doubt, pure thought. But the circumstances which determine that a particular view shall be held at a particular time and in a particular shape are to a large extent contingent and only to be known empirically. Nor can we determine by pure thought how large an element in the complete perfection of Spirit consists in correct views on general questions of metaphysics—or in other words, what is the relation of the process given in the History of Philosophy to the main process of Spirit.

own their philosophy quite incompetent to give any information about the probable form of local government which will prevail in London one hundred years hence.   For on such a theory as Hegel's we should know that in Heaven the Absolute Idea was completely and adequately manifested.   But of the government of London we should only know that, like all earthly things, it would manifest the Absolute Idea to some extent, but not completely.   And to determine, by the aid of the dialectic, how much and in what form it would manifest it, we should have to begin by determining the position of the municipal organisation of London in 1996 in a chain which stretches from the barest possible abstraction to the fullest possible reality.   This we cannot do.   Philosophers are in much the same position as Mr Kipling's muleteer—

> "We know what heaven and hell may bring,
> But no man knoweth the mind of the king [1]."

For they are on firmer ground in theology than in sociology. And perhaps there is not much to regret in this.

222.   We must now pass on to a second defect in Hegel's application of his Logic to experience.   The difficulty of fixing the first and last points in the dialectic process is not the only obstacle in our way.   Much of Hegel's work, as we have seen, consisted in applying the dialectic process to various special fields—to Religion, to History, to Law, and to Philosophy. Now in doing this, he is in each case dealing with only one aspect of reality, leaving out of account many others.   Can we expect such a fragment of reality, taken by itself, to be an example of the dialectic process?   No side of reality can be really isolated from all the others, and, unless we fall into quite a false abstraction, we must allow for the interaction of every aspect of reality upon every other aspect.   This is a truth which Hegel fully recognises, and on which, indeed, he emphatically insists.   For example, he points out that the constitution possible for a country at any time must depend on its character, and both History and Philosophy are, in his exposition, closely connected with Religion.

But these various dialectical processes are not, according to

---

[1] *The Ballad of the King's Jest.*

Hegel, synchronous. Philosophy, for example, begins for him in Greece, which in historical development is already in the second stage. History, again, begins for him in China, whose religion on the other hand represents an advance on primitive simplicity. If, then, these three processes react on one another, it follows that the spontaneous development of each according to the dialectic will be complicated and obscured by an indefinite number of side influences introduced from other aspects of reality then in different stages. It is true that everything which influences, like that which is influenced, is obeying the same law of the dialectic. But still the result will not exhibit that law. Suppose a hundred pianos were to play the same piece of music, each beginning a few seconds after its neighbour, while the length of these intervals was unequal and regulated by no principle. The effect on the ear, when all the hundred had started, would be one of mere confusion, in spite of the fact that they were all playing the same piece.

223. The same difficulty will not occur in the process of Nature and Spirit. For this relates, not to one side of reality only, but to the whole of it, and there are therefore no influences from outside to be considered. But there is an analogous difficulty, and an equally serious one.

It is a fact, which may perhaps be explained, but which cannot be disputed, that, if we consider the world as a dialectic process, we shall find, when we look at it *sub specie temporis*, that its different parts are, at any moment, very unequally advanced in that process. One part of the world is explicitly Spirit, another part is that implicit form of Spirit which we call Matter. One creature is a jelly-fish, and another is a man. One man is Shakespeare, and another is Blackmore. Now these different parts of the world will react on one another, and, since they are engaged in different parts of the process, and we cannot trace any system in their juxtaposition, the course of the dialectic will be altered in each case, as it was in Religion, History, and Philosophy, by the influence of various other forces, themselves obeying the same law of the dialectic, but producing, by casual and contingent interactions, a result in which it will be impossible to trace the dialectic scheme.

If, for example, we try to follow the working of the dialectic process in the lives of individual men, we find that one of the most prominent facts in the life of each man is his death at a certain time. Whatever importance death may have for his spiritual development, it is obviously all-important to our power of explaining his spiritual development, since with death we lose sight of him. Now it is but seldom that death comes as a consequence or even as a symbol of something significant in a man's spiritual history. It generally comes from some purely material cause—an east wind, a falling tile, or a weak heart. And this is only the most striking of the innumerable cases in which our spiritual nature is conditioned and constrained by outside facts, which may be developing along their own paths, but which, as regards that spiritual nature, must be looked on as purely arbitrary.

And if the dialectic cannot be observed in the individual, owing to these external disturbances, we shall not be more successful in tracing it accurately in the race as a whole. In the first place, material causes—the Black Death, for example,— often produce results on the spiritual development of nations, or of the civilised world. And, secondly, the development of the race must manifest itself in individuals, and if it is hampered in each of them by material conditions, it will not exist at all, free from those conditions. This could only be denied on the supposition that, if we took a sufficient number of cases, the results of the external influences would cancel one another, leaving the inherent development of spirit unchecked. This would, however, be a pure assumption, and not likely, as far as we can judge at present, to be in accordance with the facts. For the influence which material causes have on the development of Spirit has a distinctive character, and its effects are more probably cumulative than mutually destructive.

224. Of course anyone who accepts Hegel's Logic must believe that the nature of the Absolute, taken as a whole, is entirely rational, and that, consequently, all the facts of experience are really manifestations of reason, however irrational and contingent they may appear. But this takes us back to the other practical use of Hegel's philosophy, which we admitted as valid, namely, that it will assure us, on general grounds, that everything *must* be rational, without showing us *how* particular things are rational. It will not alter the fact that if we are trying to explain *how* the various facts of any particular kind are rational, by tracing their dialectical connection with one another, we shall fail in so far as they are influenced by the facts which are not part of that chain, however sure we may be on general grounds that they, like everything else, must be rational.

The only way in which we could get a dialectic process, dealing with actual facts, secure from extraneous influences, would be to trace the connection of the state of the whole universe, taken *sub specie temporis*, at one moment of time, with the state of the whole universe at some subsequent moment. This, of course, could not be done, unless we knew what the state of the whole universe at one particular moment really was, which is obviously impossible, since, to mention only one point, our knowledge is almost entirely confined to this planet.

We have found so far, then, that the attempts to trace the dialectic process, as it manifests itself in Religion, Law, History, or Philosophy, suffered under two defects. In the first place, we could not hope to find the fixed points which were necessary before we could begin to construct the dialectic, and, in the second place, the course of the dialectic process must be continually disturbed by external causes. With regard to the main process of Nature and Spirit, we found that it might be free from the first fault, but not from the second.

225. I need only touch on a third obstacle which presents itself. This consists in the extent and intricacy of the subject-matter which must be known, and unified by science, before we can hope to interpret it by means of the dialectic. The hindrance which this throws in the way of Hegel's purpose has perhaps been overestimated by his opponents. For they have represented him as trying to deduce, and not merely to explain, the facts of experience. And they have exaggerated the extent to which he believed himself to have succeeded in making his system complete[1]. But after allowing for all this, it must be admitted that the task which Hegel did undertake was one which often required more knowledge of facts than he had, or than, perhaps, can be obtained. This difficulty is least promi-

---

[1] Cp. Section 220.

nent in Religion and Philosophy, where the facts to be dealt with are comparatively few and easy of access. It is most prominent in the Philosophy of Nature, which, as we saw, was comparatively fortunate in being able to fix its starting-point with tolerable certainty. The abuse which has been heaped on this work is probably excessive. But it cannot be denied that it has a certain amount of justification.

226. We seem thus reduced to a state of almost complete scepticism as to the value of Hegel's applications of the dialectic, taken as systems. We may continue to regard as true the idea of the evolution, by inherent necessity, of the full meaning of reality, since that follows from the Logic. But Hegel's magnificent attempt to trace the working of that evolution through the whole field of human knowledge must be given up.

Must we give up with it all attempts to apply the conclusions, so hardly won in the Logic, to our present experience, and content ourselves with the information that they can give us as to Absolute Reality seen in its full completeness? It seems to me that we need not do so, and that experience, as we have it now, may be interpreted by means of the dialectic in a manner possibly not less useful, though less ambitious, than that which Hegel himself attempted.

We saw that two of the difficulties in the way of Hegel's scheme were the multiplicity of the details, which are found in any subject-matter as given in experience, and the fact that the different chains of the dialectic process acted irregularly on one another, so that none of them remained symmetrical examples of the dialectic development. Now both these difficulties would be avoided, if, instead of trying to trace the dialectic process in actual events, which are always many-sided, and influenced from outside, we tried to trace such a process in some of the influences at work on these events, taken in abstraction from other influences.

For example, it would probably be impossible to trace a dialectic process in the moral history of any man or nation, except in a few prominent features. For the causes which determine moral development are indefinitely complex, and many of them have themselves no moral significance. A man's moral nature is affected by his own intellectual development, by

THE APPLICATION OF THE DIALECTIC.   253

his relations with other men, and by his relations with material things. All these causes, no doubt, also move in dialectic processes, but they are not processes in unison with the process of his moral nature, and so they prevent it exhibiting an example of the dialectic movement. A man may have committed a sin of which, by the inner development of his own will, he would soon come to repent. But if, through some disease, he loses his memory shortly after committing the sin, his repentance may, to say the least, be indefinitely postponed.

Difficulties like these arise whenever our subject-matter is concrete moral *acts*, which have always other aspects besides that of their moral quality, and which are affected by many circumstances that are not moral acts. Let us now consider what would be the case if we took comparatively abstract moral *qualities*—e.g. Innocence, Sin, Punishment, Repentance, Virtue. Between these there would be a much greater chance of discovering some dialectic connection. By considering abstract qualities we save ourselves, in the first place, from the complexity caused by the indefinite multiplicity of particulars which are to be found in any given piece of experience. For we deal only with those characteristics which we have ourselves selected to deal with. And, in the second place, we escape from the difficulties caused by the intrusion of outside influences. For we are not considering what does happen in any actual case, but what would happen if all but a given set of conditions were excluded, or, to put it in another way, what influence on actual facts a certain force tends to exert when taken by itself. We abstract, in the case given above, from all aspects of actions except their morality, and we abstract from all causes which influence action, except the deliberate moral choice of the agent. In the same way, every moving body is under the influence of an indefinite number of forces. But it is possible to isolate two of them, and to consider how the body would move *if* only those two forces acted upon it. The result, in its abstraction, will not apply exactly to any concrete case, but it may render us important aid in explaining and influencing concrete cases.

The third difficulty which met us in dealing with Hegel's own applications of the dialectic was the impossibility of deter-

mining the relation of the various stages to one another, unless
we knew the beginning or the end of the process beforehand,
which we seldom did. This difficulty does not arise in our
proposed abstract applications of the dialectic, on account of
their comparatively humble aim. There is no attempt here, as
there was before, to construct even a part of the chain of stages
which reaches from beginning to end of the whole temporal
process. We only assert that, when a certain number of abstract
terms are taken in connection with one another, they stand in
certain relations which are an example of the dialectic movement.
Here we are sure of our starting-point, because we have made it
ourselves.

227. The best example of such an application of the
dialectic method, which is to be found in Hegel's own work,
is his theory of Sin, referred to above. It is rather implied
than directly stated, but, if we compare his treatment of the
subject in the Philosophy of Spirit and in the Philosophy of
Religion, it appears that he regards Innocence (Unschuldigkeit)
and Virtue as the thesis and synthesis of a triad, whose antithesis consists of a subordinate triad, of which the terms are
Sin, Punishment, and Repentance.

This process gains, of course, its simplicity, its independence
of external influences, and its fixed starting-point, merely by
abstraction—the only way in which definiteness can ever be
gained in our present state of imperfect knowledge. And
therefore, like every result gained by abstraction, it is more
or less untrue. Its value must depend on its being approximately true sufficiently often, and with sufficient exactitude, to
make it practically useful. This is the case with all abstractions. No one, for example, ever acted exclusively from purely
economic motives, but most people act from them enough to
make it worth while to work out what would happen if everyone always did so. On the other hand it would not be worth
while to work out what would happen if everyone desired to
suffer as much bodily pain as possible, because few people are
greatly influenced by such a desire.

Now the conditions of Hegel's dialectic of virtue do occur in
life sufficiently often and with sufficient exactitude to make the
knowledge we have gained by the abstraction practically valuable.

For whenever men are acting so that their acts have a moral quality—and this is almost always the case—then the moral aspect of a particular action will be one of the most important of the factors which determine whether it shall, under given circumstances, take place or not, and what its results will be, if it does take place. And so the relation which exists between the moral aspects of actions and mental states will afford us, in many instances, materials for explaining those actions and states with sufficient accuracy, although, resting on abstraction, it will never succeed in giving a complete explanation of the facts in any actual case, and in some cases will give us scarcely any help in explaining them.

228. Another relation of abstract terms which can often throw great light on experience is that which is sometimes summed up in the maxim, Die to live. Here the thesis is the possession or assertion of something good in itself, while the antithesis is the abandonment or the denial of that good, on account of some defect or narrowness in the statement of the thesis. The synthesis, again, is the enjoyment of the original good in a deeper and better way, when the defect has been purged out by the discipline of the antithesis. As an abstraction, this relation can never express the whole nature of any event. That which, from one point of view, is positive, may from another be negative, and from a third be a reconciliation of two extremes. But when, as often happens, we are looking at things from one limited point of view, and temporarily ignoring others, the arrangement of our subject-matter upon such a scheme may be very valuable.

229. But, after all, the main practical interest of Hegel's philosophy does not lie in such interpretations, useful and suggestive as they are. It is rather to be found in the abstract certainty which the Logic gives us that all reality is rational and righteous, even when we cannot in the least see *how* it is so, and also in the general determination of the nature of true reality, which we saw above was a legitimate consequence of the Logic[1]. In other words, when we ask of what value philosophy is, apart from the value of truth for its own sake, we

[1] Sections 208, 209.

shall find that it lies more in the domains of religion than in those of science or practice. Its importance is not that it shows us how the facts around us are good, not that it shows us how we can make them better, but that it proves, if it is successful, that they, like all other reality, are, *sub specie aeternitatis*, perfectly good, and, *sub specie temporis*, destined to become perfectly good.

The practical value of the dialectic, then, lies in the demonstration of a general principle, which can be carried into particulars or used as a guide to action, only in a very few cases, and in those with great uncertainty. In saying this we shall seem at first sight to deny that the dialectic has really any practical use at all. But reflection may convince us that the effect of philosophy on religion is quite as practical, and perhaps even more important, than the effect which it might have exercised on science and conduct, if Hegel's applications of the dialectic could have been sustained.

That the effect on religion is one which we are entitled to consider of practical, and not merely of theoretical interest, was pointed out above[1]. For, through religion, philosophy will influence the happiness of those who accept its theories, and nothing can have more immediate practical interest than any cause which increases or diminishes happiness.

230. We may go, I think, even further than this. It is more important, for our general welfare, to be able to apply philosophy to religion, than to science and conduct. We must consider that the general conviction of the rationality and righteousness of the universe must be reached by philosophy, or else not reached at all—at least as a matter of reasoning. Now the application of the dialectic to the particular facts is not indispensable in the same way. It is true that it is essential to life, and to all that makes life worth having, that we should be able to some extent to understand what goes on round us, and should have some rules by which we can guide our conduct. And, no doubt, it would assist us in both these terms if we could succeed in tracing the manifestations of the dialectic process in the facts around us, and in anticipating the facts in which it

---

[1] Section 209.

will be manifested in the future. But still, for these aims, the aid of the dialectic is not essential. The finite sciences can explain the facts of our life, incompletely, indeed, and imperfectly, but still to a great extent, and to an extent which is continually increasing. And we shall find in common sense, and in the general principles of ethics, the possibility of pursuing a coherent and reasonable course of action, even if we do not know the precise position at which we are in the dialectic process towards the perfection which is the goal of our efforts.

Here, then, philosophy would be, from the practical point of view, useful, but not necessary. But its importance with regard to religion is greater. We cannot observe that all reality is rational and righteous as a fact of experience, nor can we make it rational and righteous by any act of ours. If we do believe that it is so, it must either be by some reasoning which falls within the jurisdiction of philosophy, or by the acceptance of some form of what Hegel calls Revealed Religion. Now, without considering whether the acceptance of the latter is justifiable or not, it cannot be denied that the number of people to whom it does not seem justifiable is always considerable, and shows no marked signs of diminishing. And many of those who do accept some form of Revealed Religion, base their belief in large measure on a conviction, reached by philosophical methods, that the rationality and righteousness of the universe are antecedently probable, or, at all events, not antecedently improbable[1].

Our religious views then, if challenged,—and they do not often pass now-a-days without being challenged—rest to a larger and larger extent on philosophical arguments. The practical importance of religious views—one way or the other—to the world's happiness, is likely to increase rather than to diminish. For, as increasing wealth and civilisation set a greater proportion of mankind free from the constant pressure of mere bodily wants, the pressure of spiritual needs becomes more clearly felt, and is increased by every advance which is made in intelligence and culture. The more we succeed in removing such of the evils

---

[1] Cp. Mr Balfour's *Foundations of Belief*, Part II., Chap. 4, and Part IV., Chap. 5, Section v.

and limitations of life as can be removed, the more clearly do those which cannot be removed reveal themselves, and the more imperative becomes the demand for some assurance that these also are transitory, and that all things work together for good. Nor does this tendency of our nature deserve to be called, as it often is called, either selfish or abstract. If we care for virtue, we can scarcely fail to be interested in the ultimate righteousness or iniquity of the universe, as judged by our moral ideals. If we care for the men and women we know, it seems not unnatural that we should sometimes ask ourselves what—if anything—will happen to them when their bodies have ceased to exist.

I maintain, therefore, that we have reached a conclusion which is not really sceptical, even as to the practical value of Hegel's philosophy, when we reject his attempts to trace the manifestations of the dialectic process in the particular facts of our experience. For the more important of the practical effects of philosophy is left untouched—more important, because here philosophy is indispensable if the result is to be attained at all.

231. It may be objected that such a view as this is more than a partial difference from Hegel, and that its abstractness violates the whole spirit of his system. To say that we know of the existence of a rationality and righteousness, which we are yet unable to trace in detail in experience, may appear at first sight to mean a trust in some other-worldly reality. Such a trust would doubtless be completely opposed to the most fundamental principles of Hegel's philosophy. But this objection misrepresents the position. It is not asserted that the rational and righteous reality is something behind and separate from experience. On the contrary, it is and must be perfectly manifested in that experience, which is nothing but its manifestation. But we do not see in detail how it is such a manifestation. Thus it is not the reality which is abstract, but only our knowledge of it. And this is not surprising, since all imperfect knowledge must be abstract, and it is matter of common notoriety that our knowledge is as yet imperfect.

Nor need we much regret such a limitation of the province of philosophy. For if our present knowledge were completely adequate to reality, reality would be most inadequate to our ideals. It is surely at least as satisfactory a belief, if we hold that the highest object of philosophy is to indicate to us the general nature of an ultimate harmony, the full content of which it has not yet entered into our hearts to conceive. All true philosophy must be mystical, not indeed in its methods, but in its final conclusions.

CAMBRIDGE: PRINTED BY J. AND C. F. CLAY, AT THE UNIVERSITY PRESS.